Common Cents

Common Cents

A Retiring Six-Term Congressman Reveals How Congress Really Works — and What We Must Do to Fix It

BY
TIMOTHY J. PENNY
AND
MAJOR GARRETT

LITTLE, BROWN AND COMPANY
BOSTON NEW YORK TORONTO LONDON

To our mothers

First Edition

Library of Congress Cataloging-in-Publication Data
Penny, Timothy J.
Common cents / by Timothy J. Penny and Major Garrett. —
1st ed.
p. cm.
ISBN 0-316-69912-8
1. United States. Congress — Reform. 2. United States — Politics and government — 1993– I. Garrett, Major. II. Title.
JK1061.P45 1995
328.73'07 — dc20 94-37643
CIP

10 9 8 7 6 5 4 3 2 1

MV-NY

Published simultaneously in Canada
by Little, Brown & Company (Canada) Limited

Printed in the United States of America

Contents

Foreword

America has witnessed three convulsive elections in a row, each with an angry electorate lashing out at Washington's inability to provide adequate services at a tolerable price.

In 1990, voters sought to punish congressional incumbents. The outcome claimed only a handful of them, but many incumbents saw once-lofty reelection margins dwindle to pitifully small majorities. In 1992, voters punished George Bush for his perceived indifference to domestic policy. Voters also embraced third-party candidate Ross Perot, giving him 19 percent of the vote — the highest total for a third-party candidate since 1912. At the same time, voters handed control of the White House and Congress to the Democrats. This was the first time one party had controlled both centers of power since 1980.

In 1994, voters uprooted forty years of Democratic control of the House and eight years of Democratic rule in the Senate and replaced them with Republican majorities in both chambers. The last time a Democratic president had to confront such an obstacle was 1946, midway through Harry S Truman's first term and the year of Bill Clinton's birth.

In their own way, each of these elections amounted to a primal scream. Voters were fed up with America's doldrums — real or imagined — and were eager to punish Washington. In its own way, each election represented a yearning for a new method of governance. The pundits have said over and over again that voters are sick and tired of what's become known as "politics as usual."

Let me suggest that the biggest nightmare for America would be an end to politics as usual. Democracy is politics as usual and has been for 219 years. It's the best politics mankind has ever known and is now copied the world over. Politics as usual in this country protects the sacred values of free speech, free worship, free assembly, and freedom from government coercion or intrusion. Politics as usual is a blessing and bounty for this and every other generation wise enough to protect it from encroachments large and small.

Nevertheless, our nation is frustrated with politics and what it has come to regard as an elitist and cavalier ruling class within the marble majesty of the U.S. Capitol. Never has the Congress been held in lower regard. Never have American voters been more critical of legislators' motives, more suspicious of their values, and more incensed by their actions. Today, fewer than one in five Americans trusts the Congress to act in their best interest or spend their tax dollars wisely.

Voters understand democracy is a deliberate process. This nation submits all new ideas to the fires of public debate. The strongest of these ideas are then refined and cooled in the chambers of the federal legislature. Those that emerge add to the structure of laws that unite all of us and echo the sentiments of the Latin inscription on the seal of our great nation: E Pluribus Unum. From many, One.

Voters know this is an imperfect process that sometimes allows prejudice and passion to get the best of us. Voters don't expect perfection from Congress. They simply ask that legislators give their best and put the country's interest first.

Congress tries to meet this standard. But it fails more often than it should. It fails because lawmakers have forgotten that our nation does not derive its strength from politicians, but from our political system. The Founding Fathers designed a system to withstand the random and rapid comings and goings of every legislative player. Ours was never meant to be a system of political permanence, but of dynamism. Congress was never meant to be a sinecure for a crafty political class distracted by the next election, bald power plays, petty partisanship, or pork barrel gorging. Instead, Congress was meant to be a legislative outpost where, from its symbolic perch on Capitol Hill — the highest ground in the city of Washington — lawmakers could focus their gaze on the nation's most distant horizons and chart the best course for the future.

The results from the 1994 election prove voters don't think they got it right in 1990 or 1992. And my guess is they won't be happy with the solution they came up with in 1994 either. That's not because a Republican-controlled Congress is going to be worse than the Democratically controlled one it replaced. (In some important ways — reforming Congress, for example — it probably will be better.) Voters will be unhappy, I suspect, because in one crucial respect Republicans are no different than Democrats. They both want to acquire and protect power.

Republicans have waited nearly fifty years to control Congress and campaigned on a platform called the Contract with America to do it. The contract was drafted by pollsters and made up of promises favored by no fewer than 60 percent of the voters tested. It includes some worthwhile reforms. It also includes several familiar contradictions — increasing defense spending, cutting taxes, and reducing deficits (Do you remember this from the 1980s?). Beneath the sweet popularity of the Republican contract lies a bitter core of political cynicism voters have yet to taste. Most Republicans know they cannot keep all of the contract's promises. Only days after the election, Senate Majority Leader Bob Dole was saying some of the promised tax cuts would have to be phased in and that spending cuts would start small and grow over time. This is the same way Congress has supposedly been cutting spending for years — a little now and more later. Except later never comes.

After serving in Congress for twelve years and studying the habits of Democrats and Republicans alike, I have learned that Congress spends too much time looking out for itself and too little time focusing on America's distant horizons.

To understand why, you must understand the cultures modern lawmakers have brought to Congress. These cultures have gradually — and for many years imperceptibly — gnawed away at the sturdy foundations of republican democracy and trustworthy public service that our Founding Fathers bequeathed to this great country. These are cultures that cause lawmakers — Democrat and Republican — to spend more than the country can afford; abuse power in ways that undermine the national interest; engage in acts of hypocrisy that keep them in office while allowing serious problems to fester; distract themselves, their party, and their country in meaningless partisan squabbles that generate plenty of eye-catching headlines but few durable solutions; and, lastly, abandon in abject fear a policy they know is right simply because pollsters tell them it's unpopular.

This book is about these cultures and what voters can do to change them. After serving in Congress for twelve years I know that no single lawmaker — or even a motivated group of lawmakers — can do as much to change Congress as an informed and motivated electorate. This book is designed to explain how Congress works and how it can be changed for the better. Voters have been sending lots of new members to Congress in the last six years (more than half of the 435-member House of Representatives was elected in 1990 or later). But sending new lawmakers is not enough. Voters must understand what these new politicians face when they get to Washington. Voters must change the rules of survival in Congress. That means rewarding leaders instead of punishing them. It means demonstrating a willingness to sacrifice for future generations, just as our parents sacrificed for us. It means voting and listening and having a bit of patience. Democracy is necessarily slow. Our government is complex and deliberative for a reason: it prevents dictatorship.

Throughout my years in Congress, I have seen the cultures operate behind closed doors. I've seen the damage they do to this republic. And I have decided to leave Congress in the hope that a voice from a former insider can inspire voters to elect legislators who will overhaul the system.

I could never have accomplished this task without the efforts of my coauthor, Major Garrett. As a journalist who has covered Congress for five years, he has observed many of the same cultures I have and shares my desire to demystify Washington for voters who too often cannot understand what Congress does and why it does it.

We wrote this book together. In the process we reached the same conclusions about the necessary remedies. While these are my stories, the analysis of Congress's woes and the prescriptions are ours. Neither of us has given up on Congress. We respect and cherish the American political system and believe Congress can play an important role in American life. We believe the Capitol is the most beautiful building in America and want to do what we can to improve its image and the image of those who serve there. Congress is where America comes to debate its future. We believe Americans will have more faith in that process when lawmakers agree to some commonsense changes.

More than anything, we want Americans to realize they can change their government any time they want. But voters cannot change the system simply by complaining about it. The Constitution places power in the hands of the people. Every other year Americans elect members to serve in the House of Representatives, also known as the people's house. The real tragedy of modern-day politics is that too many Americans have forgotten the first three words of our nation's Constitution: *We the people*. In the final analysis, we the people *are* the government. If we want to change it, we can.

Common Cents

One

How Congress Fails the Founding Fathers

Society in every state is a blessing, but Government, even in its best state, is but a necessary evil; in its worst state, an intolerable one.

—Thomas Paine, *Common Sense*

THE MORNING of August 6, 1993, arrived with the same lethargy that accompanies every summer day in Washington, D.C. A dense, humid film hung in the air. The sun cast no shadows, only blurry blobs of black. The American flags over the Capitol dome clung to their gray metal staffs like soaked beach towels.

This was the final day before Congress's four-week summer recess — a tradition begun in the years before air conditioning but continued for no logical reason . . . except that traditions die hard in Washington.

On this morning, the politicians were groggy, withered with fatigue borne by the previous day's acrimonious debate and narrow passage of President Clinton's budget. For most House members, this was simply a day to await the outcome of the Senate vote on the same budget.

I had another matter on my mind.

It was shortly before 10 A.M., but I had already been in my seat on the House floor for half an hour.

Just moments after the House convened, I announced I would not seek reelection in 1994. At two minutes and twelve seconds, the speech was one of the shortest — perhaps *the* shortest — of my political career. But no speech was tougher to give; never before had words stolen so much air from my lungs or left my throat so parched. I spoke haltingly, almost as if I'd never given a public speech before. I looked down at my hands and, noticing they were trembling like a wounded bird's wings, steadied them by clutching either side of the lectern.

I explained my decision to the few House members on the floor that day:

> Mr. Speaker I come to the floor today to announce that I will not seek reelection to Congress from Minnesota's first district. I've made this decision based on three factors. First, I viewed this as an opportunity year to dramatically reduce the deficit in a bipartisan fashion. We have failed to take advantage of that opportunity. Second, after 10 years in Congress it is evident to me that far too many politicians end up staying far too long. I don't want to be one of those politicians. Thirdly, Minnesota, my family, my friends, and my roots, call me home. And I want my children, my four children, to finish school in Minnesota so that they might grow to love our state as much as I do.

I devoted the rest of my farewell announcement to the disappointment I felt over the just-concluded debate about the federal deficit. I made it clear I felt the effort had fallen short. After dedicating nearly twelve years of my life to lonely and often fruitless efforts to reduce the deficit, I didn't see much hope for future budget cutting.

As I began to leave the chamber, several lawmakers stopped to shake my hand and wish me well. Big Tom Barlow, a freshman Democrat from Kentucky with whom I had worked on budget-cutting measures, gave me a bear hug. Many other colleagues approached me throughout the day. I saw a glint of subdued envy in their eyes. They looked at me as if I were being set free, liberated from a place and a job that they too found more tormenting than rewarding. What I saw in their eyes I heard in the voices of other politicians to whom I spoke on the phone. I knew my conversations with these people would never be the same. I had crossed an invisible threshold in Washington, one that separates those who covet power from those who walk away from it.

My decision to retire caused me to reflect on my first days in Congress eleven years earlier and how I got there in the first place. It's an unlikely story. First elected to Congress in November of 1982, I was young, idealistic, and, admittedly, naive.

OOPS. . . . DID I DO THAT?

On January 3, 1983, at age thirty-one, I walked onto the House floor with my arms full. I had brought my two sons, Jamie, three, and Joey, two, with me for this momentous occasion, the opening day of the 1983 session. It was time to be sworn in as the Democratic congressman from the 1st District of Minnesota. It was big stuff — especially for those of us among the seventy-nine newly elected legislators. For me, it was the culmination of an unbelievable streak of firsts: I was the first in my family of seven to graduate from college, the first Democrat from my home county in fifty years to be elected to the Minnesota Senate, and now, the first

Democrat in ninety years to be elected to serve southern Minnesota in the U.S. House of Representatives.

On the opening day of the session there is only one thing that absolutely, positively must be done. That is to be sworn in, to take the oath of office administered by the Speaker of the House to all 435 members of the House and witnessed by family and friends in the chamber gallery above. It is one of the very few moments when Washington pauses for sentimentality. It's a big moment.

So there I stood for the first time with my 434 colleagues. Like me, many lawmakers had children in tow. Some children were darting up and down the four sloping aisles that converge beneath the Speaker's dais. Others were playing hide-and-seek in the rows of mahogany chairs. My boys were rambunctious too. It was all I could do to keep them within arm's reach while the speaker tried to bring order to the chaos below. Speaker Thomas P. "Tip" O'Neill patiently rapped the stem of his massive wooden gavel to quiet the crowd. Just as the antics began to simmer down, Jamie and Joey began to wriggle free. I looked upstairs and caught the eye of my wife, Barbara, and motioned that I would take the boys off the floor for a minute so they could cool down. With me out of sight, she took the opportunity to leave the gallery to change the diaper of our youngest child, Molly.

It only took a moment for me to calm the boys down and leave them with a friend. As I pushed open the heavy wooden doors to return to the House floor, I noticed something strange. The members were shaking hands with one another and heading up the aisles toward the exits.

Then it dawned on me: I'd missed the swearing in.

"Oh, my God," I thought. "No. I couldn't have been so dumb as to miss this. My own swearing in? The only obligation on my first day in office. . . . And I missed it?"

I looked up at Barbara just as she sat down. By the placid look on her face I knew she didn't know what had just happened. Or didn't happen. It wasn't until late, late that night that I had the heart to tell her I'd missed the "formal" swearing in. For years we were too embarrassed ever to admit this to our friends and family.

I felt so foolish that I couldn't bring myself to participate fully in a second swearing-in ceremony later that afternoon. A handful of freshmen lawmakers sheepishly announced that they'd missed the first opportunity because they were too distracted at their own office parties. As they lined up beneath the dais, O'Neill peered out over the chamber and bellowed, half-teasingly, "Is there anyone else?"

I stood up in the very back of the chamber, almost as if I were just stretching my legs. The chamber was almost empty, and I could hear the other six lawmakers laughing about their tardiness. O'Neill then asked them to raise their right arm. I inched toward the dais and slowly raised my arm toward my shoulder. It was just like those people on the Sure deodorant commercials. The lawmakers down front were "Sure" and held their arms up high. I was "Unsure" and kept my arm clenched to my body.

HOW THE HECK DID I GET HERE?

Humble was my pedigree. My roots ran deeply into the blue-black soil of southern Minnesota, where my father farmed until I was a teen. Our home was in Mansfield Township. All of the towns in my corner of the world are much the same. Small. Cozy. My family's ancestry was Norwegian, and our faith was Lutheran. My neighbors were predominantly of Norwegian or German descent and belonged to Lutheran or Methodist churches. My family and neighbors were well muscled to work the land or the union jobs in nearby factories or packing plants. They were bighearted and tended to those struck by bad weather, bad health, or a bad economy. Stoic. Dependable. Faithful.

I grew up in a century-old farmhouse alongside a dirt road that winter snows would turn to grimy slush and the summer heat would bake to a fine, dark dust. Until I was in high school my father, Jay, farmed my grandfather Penny's 160-acre homestead. (When I was in high school, my grandfather sold the farm, and my dad found a job as a machinist across the border in Iowa. It was a grittier and more anonymous labor, but my father took pride in it and seldom missed a day of work. He instilled in all of his children an unshakable work ethic.)

On the farm, my dad harvested corn and soybeans and raised dairy cows, hogs, chickens, and sheep for good measure. There were enough chores to keep seven children busy after school and on weekends.

I attended elementary school in a one-room schoolhouse one mile down the road. It was white. Not far away stood the general store. White. Nearby a gas station. White. In the snowy winters, a stranger would have a hard time finding any of these buildings. In the summertime, a stranger would have a hard time telling them apart.

In grade school, after finishing my outdoor chores, one of my other duties was to help my mother, Donna, wash the dishes. Mom washed and I rinsed and dried. It was there my mother taught me about politics. I guess you could say I came by my Democratic politics honestly. I inherited them from my mom's side of the family. Mom gave me the inspiration to vote for John F. Kennedy in a mock election in my grade school in 1960.

I also took political instruction from her father, Grandpa Haukoos. He was a gandy dancer for the Rock Island Railroad. Gandy dancing is tough physical labor. Grandpa was part of a crew that tamped and straightened railroad ties along a sixty-mile stretch of track. What mattered most to Grandpa and the rest of us was that the railroad union gave him the first decent wage he'd ever had. It gave him the only medical and retirement benefits he'd ever had. It gave him a stake in the future. He never forgot it. *We* never forgot it. A union job meant a decent living for a hard-working man. Union workers backed Democrats like John Kennedy.

It was way past my bedtime when John Kennedy was declared the thirty-fifth President of the United States. I had my bedside radio turned down so low the announcer's voice was a mere squeak in the darkness. A few months later, on inauguration day, the voice of our new President roared into my soul:

> In the long history of the world, only a few generations have been granted the role of defending freedom in its hour of maximum danger. I do not shrink from this responsibility — I welcome it. I do not believe that any of us would exchange places with any other people or any other generation. The energy, the faith, the devotion which we bring to this endeavor will light our country and all who serve it — and the glow from that fire can truly light the world.
>
> And so, my fellow Americans: ask not what your country can do for you — ask what you can do for your country.

Like many Americans, I am still inspired by these words.

When I graduated from high school in 1969, student radicalism, as it was commonly known at the time, remained an alien concept in rural Minnesota. Believe it or not, I was disciplined for advocating rock 'n' roll music for our senior prom instead of the classical music the school had sanctioned.

I enrolled that fall at Winona State University. My father gave me $5 a week for spending money. I vividly remember his advice as I left home: "You can learn a lot from books, son. But don't forget: What really matters in this world is good, old-fashioned common sense."

My allegiance to the Democratic Party was further strengthened in 1971. That year the federal government passed a truly revolutionary law, known as the Individuals with Disabilities Act. Among other things, it allowed handicapped children to attend public school. Democrats made it happen, and I have been forever grateful.

My youngest brother, Troy, was born on Valentine's Day in 1960. He came into the world with too much fluid near his brain, a condition called hydrocephalus. Doctors inserted a tube that drained the fluid into Troy's stomach. It worked until he was five, when one day, while at a picnic to celebrate my cousin's confirmation, the tube clogged. Fluid began backing up inside Troy's brain. He wept uncontrollably in my arms as I carried him to my uncle's house nearby. He was soon transferred from our local hospital to the University of Minnesota hospital in Minneapolis. Doctors were preparing to put Troy through further surgery to insert a new tube. Something happened while they ran tests, and Troy lapsed into a coma. Troy has been physically and mentally handicapped ever since, his motor skills and mental development almost completely arrested.

Troy was eleven when Congress passed the new disabilities law. Until that day, he had no hope of attending public school. As far as our school system was concerned, Troy didn't exist. The disabilities act recognized his right to an education. Attending school changed Troy's life. He began taking a bus to Wells, a town about twenty miles away. The school created space in the classrooms for Troy's wheelchair. The teachers created space in their hearts for Troy's spirit. Troy starred each year in the Christmas program, where he would belt out a Christmas carol in a halting monotone that could not convey the joy it gave him to be part of the group. Troy's carols became so well known in Wells that when I ran for the state Senate in 1976, I broke the ice with audiences in that community by introducing myself as Troy's brother.

I won the election in 1976.

Two years later, while I was away from home at a legislative conference, my father died. Without warning. That's the way it is with aneurysms, we were told. This one ruptured inside his already ailing heart. He was fifty-one.

When I came to Washington in 1982, just as when I had left for college in 1969, my dad's words were on my mind. I was thirty-one and a true believer in our political system. I thought any problem could be solved with a little common sense. However, it didn't take long to discover that common sense was in short supply in the nation's capitol.

After less than six months, I realized there wasn't very much about Washington that set well with me, given my system of values. For example, I truly cared about the federal deficit and debt, which were both beginning to spin out of control. I campaigned against them and hoped that my voice and those of other freshmen Democrats would persuade senior Democrats to force Reagan to confront the deficit and debt his policies were creating.

It soon became obvious that my party wasn't interested in dealing with the deficit. The party oracles were content to spend whatever Reagan wanted on defense as long as he allowed them to spend whatever they wanted on Social Security, Medicare, Medicaid, and other social programs. This was a deal the Reagan White House gladly accepted. This deal is why today we have an annual deficit of nearly $180 billion and a public debt of almost $5 trillion.

From my first days in Congress, I dedicated myself to bringing down the deficit and debt. Along the way, I alienated the most powerful leaders in my party. To my dismay, I discovered the definition of a Democrat had changed in the 1980s. It wasn't enough any longer to support basic civil rights, labor rights, equal rights, and education rights — positions that gave Democrats much of the moral (if not political) high ground in the 1960s. In the Congress I joined in 1982, we had to be willing to increase spending to impress the Democratic leaders who had built their careers around maintaining and expanding federal programs that the country could no longer afford.

If we tried to spend less, we were shunned. It didn't matter if we cast dozens of other votes with the Democratic leaders. We had to go along with the spending. If we didn't, we were no longer considered part of "the team."

I swiftly found myself off the team.

Barb and I didn't arrive in Washington with a lot in our savings account, and we spent all of what we did have to scrape together a down payment on the house we bought in the Washington suburbs. (We also maintained our modest home in Minnesota and through the years have divided our time between the two residences.) Barb stayed at home with our four children, returning to the workforce after our youngest started school. In those early years, we barely made ends meet on my salary. My salary increased steadily during my tenure, and I made it a policy to refuse any congressional pay raises until after I had been reelected. I gave the extra amounts to charity or returned it to the Treasury.

Like a lot of other young couples, Barb and I have had to worry about our bills and our taxes. And like a lot of Americans, we have often wondered whether the government has grown too big, if it is trying to do too many things. As a loyal Democrat, these thoughts bothered me, but I knew if I was thinking them, other Democrats were too. Reagan's 1980 and 1984 victories proved that. Reagan won on the strength of many low- and middle-income voters who were traditionally considered part of the Democratic base.

As a young legislator, I tried to persuade others in the party that Democrats had to stand for compassion *and* thrift. Few of the elders would listen. So, together with another freshman Democrat, Buddy MacKay of Florida, I organized a group of freshmen Democrats dedicated to lowering federal spending. We newer Democrats were determined to do something to cut the deficit.

TONGUE-LASHING

We finally got our chance in late 1983.

The economy was still in pretty sorry shape, and House Democratic leaders thought they had a way to ease the pain the recession was inflicting. They compiled a $997 million spending bill to pay for job training, vocational education, special education, child nutrition, and community health programs. Naturally, they wanted to add the bill's cost to the deficit.

The Democratic freshmen were aghast. Many freshmen Democrats supported these programs, but we didn't believe they were important enough to warrant adding another $1 billion to the deficit.

Earlier in the year, the House had passed a bill dropping the third year of the three-year 30 percent income tax cut Reagan pushed through Congress in 1981. The White House and the Republican Senate ignored it, but the message remained: A majority of the House thought the deficit was serious enough to warrant delaying a popular tax cut.

Most freshmen Democrats also thought the deficit was serious enough that we shouldn't support an additional $1 billion for domestic programs unless we were willing to pay for them. So we suggested holding a floor vote on that year's reconciliation bill (a measure that includes spending cuts and tax increases) to accompany a vote on the $1 billion spending bill. That would allow Democrats to demonstrate their willingness to pay for programs they believed were worthwhile.

The Democratic leadership disagreed. To put it mildly, they didn't follow our reasoning.

The spending bill was authored by none other than Jim Wright, the Majority Leader from Texas. Wright wanted a Democratic victory in the House on a spending bill important to our party's constituencies, such as the teachers' unions, the elderly, and the AFL-CIO. Wright knew the Republican Senate might not pass the bill and that Reagan would certainly veto it if it ever reached his desk. That didn't matter. This vote wasn't about policy. It was about power. And political games.

It was a big bill for Wright.

It marked the beginning of his legendary clashes with the Reagan White House over domestic and foreign policy. Wright and every Democrat in the leadership wanted the bill passed and insisted that all Democrats, especially the freshmen, fall in line.

This was not a debatable item. The leadership had spoken. All the factions in the party were on board. Every House Democrat received calls and letters from the National Education Association, the AFL-CIO, and other Democratic special interest constituencies. The leaders couldn't imagine that the freshmen wouldn't comply, so they didn't take the time to consult us. We saw this vote as an opportunity to make our mark.

As the day for the vote drew near, many of us notified the top party leaders of our intention to vote no. They couldn't believe what they were hearing.

Just minutes before the vote, a large group of Democratic freshmen requested a meeting with Speaker O'Neill. He summoned our group into his study just off the House floor. Many of us had never seen this office before. Yet there we were, standing nervously beneath a crystal chandelier. The Speaker sat in a large chair behind a ceremonial desk. We could see our timid expressions reflected in the grand and ornate mirror above him.

He looked a bit irritated. His bright blue eyes peered at us from beneath a shock of white hair that had recklessly tumbled over his furrowed brow.

He heaved a "What do you want?" sigh.

When we told him we opposed the Wright bill, O'Neill looked as if we'd just announced that the entire freshman class had decided to quit the party and become Republicans. His forehead reddened as he rose up in his chair. He ran his thick, square fingers through his hair and glowered at us. Frustration and bewilderment fought for supremacy on his flushed and fleshy face.

He said there was no way to link a vote on the two measures, and he refused to delay the vote on the Wright spending bill. O'Neill was trying to shake us off by suggesting that our effort was futile, ill-timed, and off-the-mark. He and other House leaders, Wright in particular, could not imagine how freshmen Democrats could oppose a leadership bill freighted with so much political dynamite for the Reagan White House. Politically, they surmised, there was no other vote to cast but a "yes" vote.

But the freshmen Democrats were thinking a bit differently. Many of us came to Washington determined to demonstrate our credentials as fiscal conservatives. As we sat in O'Neill's office, the bells rang announcing the vote. The meeting had been inconclusive. Now, the vote on the Wright amendment was before the House. And the clock was ticking.

Fifteen minutes later, when the vote concluded, twenty-four freshmen Democrats had opposed the Wright bill. With the help of nearly unanimous Republican opposition, the Wright bill failed. It died at the hands of Democrats . . . of freshmen Democrats. Jim Wright, the Majority Leader of the House, the undisputed political point man in all confrontations with the White House, had lost his first major scrape with Reagan *because twenty-four freshmen Democrats voted against him.* The impudence. The gall. Wright had been beaten by Democrats before, but always senior Democrats and always on matters in which there were deep divisions in the party's position. Never, never, never had he been beaten on a leadership vote by a pack of freshmen whose names and faces he could barely match.

He and other Democratic leaders were furious. This was an affront of immense proportions, and we were about to get a lesson in what happens to frisky freshmen who put their principles on a collision course with the will of the leadership.

The next morning, well before 8 A.M., the Democratic freshmen gathered in Room 138 of the Capitol. Collectively, we felt like the dog who finally caught the car tire. *What do we do now?*

We knew the Democratic leadership was irked and the Reagan White House delighted. Suddenly, we felt very lonely. It began to dawn on us that we'd just helped the Republicans score a big "win" and tarred our party with a big "loss." Sweet success turned bitter. In a hurry.

Many in our group felt we'd better retreat. They argued that we'd made our point; the leadership wouldn't ignore us anymore. With that done, they said it was time to fall into line. At the time, I remember thinking that argument sounded perfectly logical.

Buddy MacKay, now Florida's lieutenant governor, and Jim Slattery of Kansas, said we should not retreat. Instead, they argued, we should stick together and force the leadership to deal with us on our terms. If we won, we'd be in a much better negotiating position in the future *and* we would have kept intact our principle of fighting deficits. Reversing field now, they said, would send the wrong signal: that we wanted to be noticed more than we wanted to be correct.

Most of us, quite frankly, got weak knees. We decided we were willing to change our vote if the leadership promised to bring the reconciliation bill up for a vote in the near future. That position prevailed. As chairman of the freshmen budget task force, I was selected as the emissary to broker a deal with Wright. (As I recall, there weren't any other volunteers.) Wright had a silver tongue or a sharp tongue, depending on his mood. There was no doubt in my mind what mood he was in that morning.

It was the breakfast hour, and Wright's staff told me I could find him in the members' dining room. I walked through the cool and cavernous Capitol corridors feeling as if I were on my way to the principal's office after being late to class (in the 1960s in rural Minnesota, that was still a big deal). My steps grew shorter and more precise as I entered the carpeted lobby that leads to the dining room. With mounting apprehension, I continued until I reached a door that led to a small room off the main dining room. As I peered around the door jamb, my eyes met Wright's.

He was seated with two aides who watched me suspiciously as Wright turned on the Texas charm. A sweet, melodious voice drifted over me as if I were being hypnotized.

"Well, good morning, Tim. Here. Please. Please, sit down. Join us for some breakfast. Are you hungry this morning? Please, make yourself comfortable. Pull up a chair."

Wright had his bearings while I had lost mine. He buttered his bread while I fidgeted, silently groping for the words I would need to start the negotiation.

"So," I began, my voice arid and weightless, "how are you feeling this morning, Mr. Majority Leader?"

Wright looked up from his bowl of cereal and smiled as broadly as he could without exposing any teeth. The smile at once conveyed warmth and wrath, but always slightly more of the former than the latter. It fit his sweet sarcasm perfectly.

"How do I feel this morning? I'll tell you how I feel this morning, Tim. I feel like the football player, the tight end who breaks open into the flat and receives a perfectly thrown pass. He sees a clear path all the way to the end zone and begins to sprint down the field. When he comes within five yards of the end zone, inexplicably, someone from his own bench comes onto the field and tackles him. That's how I feel this morning, Tim."

I sat motionless, waiting for him to turn the blade. It didn't take long.

"Let me put it another way," he said as I groaned inside. "I feel rather like the boxer who is well ahead on points going into the final round of a prize fight. He is within seconds of finishing the fight, and victory is at hand, when someone from his own corner comes into the ring and hits him over the back of the head with a stool, knocking him out. That's how I feel this morning, Tim."

About this time I began to feel the blood rushing to my ears. Cripes, I thought to myself, these metaphors are too much. We denied him a touchdown. We denied him a prize fight. *We knocked him out with a stool!*

I read him loud and clear, but you'd never have known it from my response.

"Gee, I am sorry you feel that way, Mr. Leader."

I composed myself enough to suggest that most of the freshmen were willing to switch their votes if his bill could be brought to a vote again.

Wright frowned and shook his head. He said he didn't know if that could be arranged. He said floor votes are hard to schedule, and since the leadership never dreamed it would lose the first vote, it had no immediate plans to hold a *second* vote on the same bill.

Wright was toying with me. He and other Democratic leaders were counting on the National Education Association and other interest groups to turn up the heat on the freshmen Democrats. There was political action committee (PAC) money at stake, and Wright wanted plenty of pressure applied to the freshmen upstarts. He wasn't about to let us off the hook before the interest groups made us sweat a little.

My one negotiating parry was to suggest the freshmen would support his bill if the reconciliation bill was voted on later. Wright said he would study the idea but offered no commitments.

Later that week, the spending bill came back to the floor, and virtually all of the renegade freshmen Democrats (myself included) switched and supported Wright's bill. MacKay and Slattery, to their credit, stood firm in opposition.

The reconciliation bill came to the floor a few weeks later and the House narrowly defeated it. The Senate never even took it up.

The spending bill died in the Republican Senate. All of that political agony and posturing went for naught. It was the first of many examples I witnessed in which one part of Congress engaged in political theatrics purely to satisfy selected special interests. Meanwhile, the general interest of the country was once again ignored as voters witnessed another display of nonsense in the nation's Capitol.

I've spent twelve years in Congress looking for the most important catalyst for good government that I know of: common sense. I haven't found much. That, I believe, is why voters think so little of our government. One of the most important people in American history understood the power and necessity of common sense.

Thomas Paine was an itinerant British propagandist who wrote a fifty-page pamphlet in January 1776 suggesting the colonists should throw off monarchical rule, assert their independence, and form a government of their own choosing.

The pamphlet was titled *Common Sense.* Paine challenged the colonists to ignore the ornate political arguments still prevalent in America that the colonists and the British could coexist. In the plainest of language, Paine told colonists that the monarchy had to go, and that the colonists had to seize this chance to set their nation on an independent course, one charted by a Constitution guaranteeing liberty inviolate and governed by a legislature committed to the betterment of all.

Paine said it made no sense for a people seeking a life of liberty and independence to take orders from a sovereign whose only qualification was his hereditary claim to the throne. Paine also said it made no sense — and in fact clashed with everything known about the history of man — for an island to rule a continent.

These simple truths, this common sense, resonated with the colonists. The pamphlet sold more than five hundred thousand copies, making it by far the most widely read tract of that or any time in American history (a book today would have to sell more than thirty-five million copies to match Paine's sales).

Common Sense served as the intellectual catalyst to bring the "common man" alongside the Founding Fathers in the war for independence. Without this union, *our union* might never have triumphed. For it was the colonists who held the line at Bunker Hill, who endured the miseries of Valley Forge, and who sealed the colonial victory at Yorktown.

My goal in this book is to inject anew some common sense and plain talk into the nation's political discourse. The times are not nearly as dire as they were when Paine wrote, but the need for a return to common sense is equally profound.

Why?

Because most Americans no longer trust the government to do the right thing. In January of 1994, a national survey conducted by American Talk Issues, a bipartisan group of pollsters, revealed that 75 percent of

Americans trust the government to do "what is right only some of the time or never." The same poll showed that 79 percent of Americans believe that the government "wastes a lot of the money we pay in taxes." Lastly, the poll showed that 77 percent of the public believe that Congress considers the preferences "of the majority of voters only some of the time or never in passing legislation."

I can't tell you how many times in twelve years in Congress I sat awake at night wondering to myself, Why are we doing these things? Why are so many decent and honorable public servants so incapable of acting responsibly on the central issues of our day?

Every time I returned home to the coffee shops and feed stores, the churches and schools, I heard voices as exasperated as my own. My constituents asked the same questions I asked myself. These voices of concern and criticism have grown in number since I came to Congress. They've led me to give a lot of thought to why Congress stumbles more often than it succeeds.

I've concluded it's not so much the people as the system within Congress that's to blame. Oh sure, there are some people here who abuse power (more about them later), but the vast majority of people in Congress desperately want to succeed, desperately want to do the right thing, fervently want to make this nation a better place now and in the future. They come to Washington with a spirit of public service.

But there is a unique Culture of Congress that frustrates their efforts. This culture is something your civics books never told you about. It takes several shapes, many of which are hostile to the high standards our Founding Fathers established for us.

Congress is torn by partisan factionalism, something George Washington warned against in his first and second inaugural addresses. It closes ranks to protect lawmakers whose misdeeds violate the sacred bonds of trust with the voters. Collectively, it spends money it doesn't have and tells voters spending has been cut when it knows this to be untrue.

The Culture of Congress invests vast power in the hands of an elite few lawmakers. It cultivates conformity and punishes originality. It acquires and protects perks that debase the concept of "public service." It confuses cowardice with courage, hypocrisy with virtue.

I've seen this culture operate for twelve years. I've seen the ways it encourages legislators to duck hard decisions. I have seen the way it causes us to invent "crises." I have seen lawmakers propose feeble legislative initiatives designed to provide political cover instead of addressing the problem at hand. I have witnessed the waste of time and energy devoted to petty partisan bickering. I have seen good and able legislators ignore their better judgment for fear of angering a constituency or special interest group.

These observations are not meant to condemn only other lawmakers. Too often, I have fallen short of my own ideals as the Culture of Congress has clouded my vision. It affects all who come here.

I know there is new leadership in Congress but I fear it will fare little better than did the Democrats. The problems that bedevil Congress and American government are systemic and bipartisan. They defy simple solutions or catchy political bromides, both of which Republicans used quite artfully to win control of Congress in the 1994 election. As I look at the new ranks of congressional leaders, it's clear that Republicans will carry out some necessary and long overdue reforms. But I watched virtually all of these new leaders while I was in Congress and I know they will be unable to grapple successfully with the vital problems of our day — the deficit, poverty, crime, health care, and pollution — because they, like the Democrats before them, have shown no inclination to lead voters to tough but necessary sacrifices.

Moreover, I've concluded that you or your next-door neighbor would also have a tough time doing much better. If you were to trade places with a member of Congress, you would find the Culture of Congress a formidable adversary. Attempting to reform Congress single-handedly is a tall order. It means pitting yourself against decades of inertia and bucking powerful leaders who benefit from the status quo. In this environment, complying with most of Washington's nonsensical ways seems not only intellectually rational but politically necessary. My guess is that you would settle into some of the same patterns many lawmakers here do now, such as picking your fights selectively, playing it safe by siding with the majority, and putting your political career at risk as rarely as possible.

In this book I intend to lay bare this Culture of Congress. I'll try to describe where it came from, why it persists, and what you, if so motivated, can do about it.

This book will illustrate the various cultures of Congress through stories about the people and politics I have observed. Bear in mind, lawmakers are human. If you can understand human nature, you can understand Congress.

We will never remove human frailties from our Congress. We can, however, excise some of the cultures within Congress that prey upon the fears, frailties, and faults of all men and women who come to Washington hoping to serve their nation well.

As James Madison said in the *Federalist Papers:* "If men were angels, no government would be necessary. If angels were to govern men, neither external nor internal controls on government would be necessary."

No one is perfect, and I've included many examples of my own failures and foibles. Congress is made up of people who are as virtuous and as frivolous as the voters they are sent to represent. My aim is not to incite but rather to offer insight through anecdotes that reveal the Culture of Congress.

My intention is to highlight the faults of Congress generally, not to vilify anyone personally. I offer a critique of the institution and the forces within it that make otherwise intelligent and honorable people do things that prevent the Congress from serving the nation's interest. Certain lawmakers will find my criticisms unfair. Some may consider them arbitrary. I admit these are stories from my own perspective.

In some ways I'll be confirming your worst fears. In others, I'll reveal problems you hadn't dreamed existed. But it's not my intention to simply stoke the fires of anger. I will have failed if all that's left for you at the end of this book is more anger. More frustration. Anger is an emotion, not a solution.

My dissatisfaction with the modern Congress, however, is not so bitter that I would trade it for any other form of government. I do not despise the Congress and I believe passionately in the virtue of public service. (After all, I've spent eighteen years as a public servant.) For all its flaws, our American system of government remains the citadel for liberty, the symbol of hope for nations making the courageous and trying transition from communism to democracy and republican government.

The modern Congress succeeds more often than its woeful reputation would suggest. I will try to leaven your animus toward Congress with stories about the good things it has done and some of the good people who labor to make the system work as it should.

Throughout the book, I will also offer ways to change a system that displeases so many it was meant to serve.

When you finish this book, I hope you'll have discovered a new desire to participate in politics. It's not nearly as difficult to do as you might imagine. If you want to learn, I'll tell you what you can do to begin your own crusade for change. I'll offer commonsense tips to help you separate candidates who represent real reform from those who represent business as usual. I'll provide simple suggestions to help you become a better-informed and more involved citizen.

If this sounds vaguely like a guide to political empowerment, well, it is. My desire is to challenge all Americans to improve Congress. An empowered electorate can bring change. A frustrated or complacent electorate cannot. I hope to transform anger into electoral action, citizen complacency into civic commitment.

What Washington needs most from the people of this country is something virtually all of you possess: common sense. But Washington won't change unless you demand it.

With his pamphlet *Common Sense,* Thomas Paine showed average colonists that they had a stake in the future of their new country and that they had to choose between a despotic present and a democratic future. While our choice today is not that stark, this nation must begin doing things differently. The Congress must be changed by the people it purports to represent: you.

This book will tell you why Washington lets you down and how your own approach to politics encourages and rewards the nonsense you find so vexing.

It's time to return common sense to Washington. Making sure that happens is what this book is all about.

Two

The Cultures of Congress

We know our duty better than we discharge it.

—John Randolph

I DIDN'T EXPECT things to happen the way they did.

But I should have.

It's just that things had gone so well until the end. My package of $90 billion in spending cuts, one of the largest spending reduction amendments in modern history, had been winning converts from surprising political quarters. Squeamish Republicans and Democrats who had previously shied away from tough budget cuts were warming to the task.

The typical pressures that had foiled lesser efforts in the past had yet to turn the tide against us. The $90 billion package was known around the Capitol as Penny-Kasich. That's because John Kasich, an Ohio Republican, and I led a bipartisan group of thirty-two House members in drafting a deficit-reduction package that at least partly met the voters' desire for deeper spending cuts.

Funny thing, cutting the budget.

All the special interest groups oppose it. When it comes right down to it, so do both parties in Congress. The Bush and Reagan administrations weren't much for it either — but they sure talked a good game.

So there I was, in a very familiar place, peering into the eyes of very familiar lawmakers, trying to do a very unfamiliar thing: seriously cut the budget. No taxes. Just cuts.

It was late November of 1993, and the House was preoccupied with a desperate attempt to pass campaign finance reform legislation and the Brady Bill. Congress was in such a hurry that it worked through the weekend of November 20–21 in a mad dash to get home for Thanksgiving. As the key players toiled to reach a consensus on campaign finance reform (where they succeeded) and on the fine points of the Brady Bill's five-day waiting period on handgun purchases (where they succeeded), many members loitered in the cloakrooms off the House floor to watch college and pro football games.

I spent most of Sunday, November 21 seated in a cramped anteroom on the third floor of the U.S. Capitol seeking permission to bring to the floor a bill to cut $90 billion from the federal budget over the next five years.

$90 billion.

Sounds like a lot of money.

It is. It's about the size of the yearly economic output of Norway, where my ancestors came from.

But in Washington, $90 billion is a trifle. Really. To cut from the federal budget an amount equal to the annual gross domestic product of Norway over five years would mean reducing federal spending by *one penny on the dollar*. In other words, a cut of $90 billion over five years still leaves *99 cents on the dollar to be spent* by the federal government.

In this context, $90 billion looks modest to you and me. You and I might think it means snipping but a few of the hundreds upon thousands of bureaucratic tendrils that comprise the monstrously overgrown federal budget.

But no. To official Washington, each of those tendrils is vital. Vital! On each one hangs a set of very important careers: the lawmakers who created the program, the bureaucrats who spend the money, and the lobbyists who represent those few who benefit from the spending. Cutting a tendril means inflicting pain on lawmakers, bureaucrats, and lobbyists. And in Washington it is *vital* that we not do that!

To be fair, when Congress cuts a program *some* pain is felt. But not often. That's because most cuts are not cuts at all. In Washington, cutting means not spending as much as desired. When, for example, lawmakers want to increase Program A from $100 million to $200 million, but are only able to increase it to $150 million, they have suffered a cut of one-fourth.

As I said, funny thing about cutting the budget.

My list of cuts was virtually painless. Many of the items one chamber of Congress (the House or Senate) had already killed. They remained in the budget because the *other* chamber in Congress had resurrected it. This is one of Washington's many budget games.

Many of the cuts were piddling. They hit programs many of us thought were less important than the larger goal of reducing the nation's triple-digit deficits.

Here are some of the items on our list: $103 million less for the arts and humanities; $560 million less for Congress's budget; $692 million less in federal subsidies for a needless helium reserve in Texas; $6 billion less for projects the Pentagon didn't want and didn't need; and $2 billion less for new federal building construction.

Small things. Timid things were on my list.

What's more, my list had the support of Democrats and Republicans. A task force of thirty-two members of Congress, divided equally among Democrats and Republicans, recommended these cuts. It had seldom been done before. Republicans and Democrats agreed to cut spending (even on things they liked) to build a bigger package. Everyone gave a little. Nobody sought an easy political escape. We stood together. It was, I thought, exactly what the voters said they wanted in the 1992 elections: real spending cuts!

Despite all of this, my list made waves — waves that got bigger as the House moved closer to the vote.

I should have known better. There are forces that flow through Washington with a strength that cannot be denied, like a river rushing into the ocean. My little list had ridden this river for a while. It had skirted some formidable rapids.

But rougher waters lay ahead.

CAPTAIN, MAY I?

There I sat in the cramped anteroom on the third floor of the U.S. Capitol. Just outside, tourists lined the tiled hallways, waiting to enter the visitors' gallery to watch the proceedings in the House of Representatives. I could hear their feet shuffling against the tiles. I could hear the tourists' expectant murmurs rising in the high corridor.

Inside that anteroom, I was seeking permission to bring my $90 billion in spending cuts to the floor. That is the way it works in the House: No bill comes to the floor unless it passes through this anteroom . . . this small room where it's always stuffy and hot, where the chairs always creak, and where you can hear the tourists waiting outside to see *the people's house in action*. This is where the Rules Committee meets. Seeking permission from this committee always reminded me of the child's game Captain, may I? That's because the committee's decisions often seemed as arbitrary as those of the captains I played with as a boy.

This committee is the least democratic institution in the entire Congress. Thirteen people: nine Democrats and four Republicans. They decide *how* a bill will be debated on the floor. They decide if amendments will be allowed and how many. They set the limits of the debate by preventing certain amendments, particularly those they disapprove of, from being debated. It may surprise voters to learn that this committee has the power to change the rules continually to ensure that the power brokers always win. It's an alarming concept, I know. The House is supposed to be the place where the Founding Fathers intended debate to be fair, competitive, and free-wheeling. The new Republican leaders have promised to bring free and open debate back to the House. We'll see if they keep their word and for how long.

How was my list of $90 billion in cuts going to make it to the floor? This committee, in this anteroom, was to decide.

Well, decide is the wrong word. It implies deliberation.

The committee didn't even hear me out. I was to testify on the merit of my bill, my list, my paltry list of $90 billion in cuts from a federal budget that over the next five years would total more than $6.5 trillion. I was to be given a chance to state my case to the full committee. On such occasions, it is customary for *all* members of the Rules Committee to listen.

They did not. At least not the Democrats. With rude and brutal precision, they rose and left for an even smaller cubbyhole just as I began to speak. In that room I am very sure it was impossible for them to hear the footfalls or voices of excited tourists waiting to see the people's House in action. That room is not designed for such things. That room is for listening to marching orders from the party leadership, committee chairmen, and other powerful party insiders.

The Rules Committee tried to complicate greatly if not scotch entirely any chance of my proposal winning. That was not the greatest insult. The greatest insult was watching my fellow Democrats, my colleagues of eleven years, reenter the committee room as I concluded my testimony. They smiled broadly as they took their seats. Rep. Joseph Moakley of Massachusetts, the committee chairman, a burly man, eased into his seat with impeccable grace. He cast his face down upon me, wearing a smile of perfectly ruthless nonchalance.

"That will be all, Mr. Penny. You can go now."

Even though I am not known for parting shots, a zinger luckily came to mind. "I guess I was in the wrong room," I said with disgust.

I rose and made my way to the door, when I caught a glimpse of Rep. Martin Olav Sabo, for whom I had interned when I was first getting started in politics. Martin was in the Minnesota House back then. He was a mentor in those early days. Now he was my foe. He was in that smaller anteroom. As chairman of the Budget Committee, he was among the insiders pitted against me. Content with the "rules" he and the others devised, Martin puffed a fat, round cigar. I don't generally think of Martin this way, but at that moment he looked liked a cigar-smoking backroom politician in an old Thomas Nast cartoon.

I later learned that Speaker Foley kept his word and ordered the Rules Committee to allow a fair vote on the Penny-Kasich package.

The next day, in spite of the insiders' best efforts, the amendment to cut $90 billion lost by only four votes. It was closer than most people thought it was going to be.

The White House and the Democratic leadership had had to pull out all the stops. Again, the big spenders won.

The big spenders' victory brought to light most, if not all, of the flaws of the modern Congress.

The flaws are systemic. The system is comprised, as I've suggested before, of many cultures. These cultures take hold of lawmakers as soon as they arrive in Washington, bending them to their unspoken will. Lawmakers vowing to be an independent voice in Washington soon discover that it is hard to buck the congressional culture, and the powerful lawmakers who enforce its customs.

This was never more true than during the Penny-Kasich fight.

NO RAY OF HOPE

It all started at the White House on August 5, 1993.

The President needed a few more votes to pass his budget. I agreed to help in exchange for an opportunity to offer deeper cuts later in the year. Many other moderate Democrats joined me. We took Clinton at his word when he promised during the days leading up to the cliffhanger vote on his budget that he would support deeper spending cuts and that his plan was the first step and not the final say on deficit reduction.

"There will be one more round of budget cuts," Clinton said on August 5, the day of the House vote.

The Clinton tax bill passed in the House on the vote of freshman Rep. Marjorie Margolies-Mezvinsky of Pennsylvania. Marjorie was the last House Democrat the White House and congressional leaders should have leaned on to vote for Clinton's bill. She had already voted against it two times. She represented a strongly Republican district that despised tax increases. She was a vulnerable freshman who had done the party a great turn by becoming the first Democrat elected from her suburban Philadelphia district since 1916.

When push came to shove on the pivotal vote of the Clinton presidency, the White House and congressional power brokers twisted the arms of freshmen Democrats, while giving free passes to senior Democrats with safe districts and hefty campaign war chests. There were many instances of freshmen cannibalism, but Marjorie's was the worst.

When the House started voting on the Clinton tax bill, the White House still didn't have the votes to win. The bill's fate rested in the hands of three Democrats: Marjorie, Pat Williams of Montana, and Ray Thornton of Arkansas. The President needed two of these three votes. If he got them, his bill would pass 218–217.

I was afraid that congressional leaders would force Marjorie to cast a politically suicidal vote that night, so I kept a sharp eye out for the leadership's allies. As the time wound down, I saw several party leaders approach Marjorie and tried to get to her before they pressured her. One of Speaker Foley's top aides intercepted me and said the leadership wouldn't force Marjorie to cast the decisive vote. I assumed, therefore, that Thornton and Williams were on board. In fact, at that moment I saw Thornton gingerly approach the voting clerk. He held two voting cards — green for "yes" and red for "no." I relaxed, mistakenly believing that Thornton was about to vote yes.

And why not? Thornton represented Clinton's own congressional district and was serving his second stint in Congress. After serving in the House from 1973 to 1979, he had gone home to serve as president of the state's two largest colleges and then returned to Congress in 1990. He was sixty-five and had won his last election with 74 percent of the vote. His political base was safe. Even if he lost the next election — an unlikely occurrence — he had plenty of pension income to fall back on.

Frankly, Thornton should have been there from the very beginning . . . because he said he would be. I had joined Thornton and several other lawmakers on Febuary 11 in a private meeting with Clinton at the White House to discuss the President's economic agenda.

"I'm with you all the way," I remember Thornton telling the President. "I just want you to know, Mr. President, that I am excited about your program and eager to help you succeed."

When the President asked for Thornton's vote, the congressman from his very own district was a no show. What appalled me more than Thornton's cowardice was the leadership's refusal to lean on him. This event symbolized the quivering diffidence of congressional leaders when it comes to pressuring senior members.

While I always doubted the President's commitment to deficit reduction, I was determined to take advantage of the agreement hammered out with Democratic leaders and the White House. I had negotiated the agreement on behalf of House Democrats, many of whom were part of the freshmen class, to set in motion a public debate and floor vote on deeper spending cuts before the fall adjournment. Having cast a tough vote for higher taxes, Marjorie became one of the most reliable and articulate leaders in our effort to enact significant budget cuts. Congresswoman Margolies-Mezvinsky lost her bid for reelection in 1994 and her loss was due in large part to her vote for the Clinton budget. She sacrificed her political career for the President on behalf of the goal of deficit reduction. Yet when it came to helping her and others with support for Penny-Kasich, the President was nowhere to be found.

HANGING TOGETHER

Our group sought support from like-minded lawmakers in both parties. As we toiled, the White House concentrated on other matters, namely passing the North American Free Trade Agreement.

Our package grew out of dozens of meetings in late September and early October between Republicans and Democrats. At first, these gatherings were tense. No one was sure if we could trust one another. Partisanship has become so prevalent in Congress that even people who share the same goal (e.g., deficit reduction) are at first leery of working together.

Many people worried about being double-crossed. Republicans were afraid that a vote on spending cuts would let Democrats off the hook for supporting Clinton's taxes. So they were afraid to lend credibility to an effort that would protect Democrats from anti-tax Republicans in the next election. Democrats were afraid that Republicans would hang them out to dry at the last minute by complaining that the spending cuts — however large they might be — were too small and a sign that even moderate Democrats couldn't give up their addiction to spending.

"It was very awkward at first," said Lynn Schenk, a freshman Democrat from a Republican-leaning district in San Diego. "We Democrats looked around the room and saw the Republicans and, at first, we didn't know why they were there. We were paranoid."

Both sides worried the other would abandon the cause. This was a new experience for nearly everyone involved. For years both parties had waged war over spending issues. The rhetoric had been inflammatory and it had left bad blood on both sides. We were trying to erase all that. Start anew.

John Kasich, the ranking Republican on the House Budget Committee, had joined me in my effort to build a bipartisan coalition. At the start of our deliberations, John and I told everyone in that room (there were thirty-two of us) that our mission was to turn standard procedures upside down, and to do it in a way no one had seen before. Democrats and Republicans were going to work together, suffer equal amounts of political pain, and try to build a serious budget-reduction package.

We told the group that the effort could not survive with competing loyalties. On this issue we checked party labels at the door. We alluded to Benjamin Franklin's words to the Continental Congress upon the signing of the Declaration of Independence: "We must all hang together, or, assuredly, we shall all hang separately."

To add a bit of spine to those stark words, we agreed that once we came up with a package of spending cuts, we would not eliminate any proposed cut unless a majority of Republicans and Democrats agreed.

That prevented members of one party from forcing certain cuts down the throat of the other.

We established two other ground rules that I regretted but that were necessary to keep the coalition together.

First, we agreed to leave Social Security alone. We would propose no changes in the current benefits structure, even though all of us knew that future taxpayers would not be able to pay for all the benefits Social Security was promising.

I had no choice. The first thing John Kasich had said to me when I asked him to join this effort was "Tim, we can't touch Social Security." Republicans had lost several seats in the House and Senate in 1982 and 1986 over the issue of Social Security cuts. Democrats had turned Social Security into a political shop of horrors for Republicans in the 1980s, and John's precondition reminded me that they were still skittish about the issue in the 1990s.

I also had to agree to go lightly on defense cuts. The Clinton budget axed nearly $110 billion from Pentagon budgets over the next five years. Most Republicans and many moderate Democrats thought that was excessive. I could see their point and agreed there was plenty more waste outside the Pentagon that we should tackle first (still, we found an additional $8 billion in defense savings). With only these two exceptions, all other parts of the budget were left "on the table."

Our group had little difficulty finding areas for cuts. We started from a base figure of $10 billion in cuts and just kept adding. Again, we defied conventional wisdom. The more cuts we added to our package, the more committed we became to the effort. As the political pain we inflicted on one another grew, so did our commitment to stand by our plan.

In a sense, we became radicalized.

No idea was too outlandish. As we looked for ways to cut, we discovered ways to consolidate programs under one roof and to turn other projects over to the private sector. We asked the middle class and wealthy to pay more for home health care and clinical lab tests under Medicare. We also asked the wealthy to pay more for Medicare so we could abolish the absurdity of having people earning hundreds of thousands in annual income paying the same Medicare premium as the poor and the near poor. We sought to raise the federal retirement age gradually from fifty-five to sixty-five, thus preventing government workers from collecting a government pension while earning a tidy wage in the private sector (known in Washington as double-dipping). To eliminate waste and duplication and overhead expenses, we decided to consolidate all programs for space exploration, energy, environment, weather research, and general scientific research into one government agency: the Department of Science. We abolished the Interstate Commerce Commission, which Presidents Carter,

Reagan, and Bush had tried to eliminate. We scrapped money for conventional weapons systems the Pentagon didn't want but members of Congress kept stuffing back in the budget. We reduced by $5 billion the budget for U.S. troop deployments to NATO and Southeast Asia.

In every instance, cuts streamlined the government or asked beneficiaries to shoulder the cost of services they were receiving. Nobody got a free pass. We nicked virtually every part of the budget. Everyone in our group had to accept cuts that affected their own district. The process of putting more and more on the table galvanized all of us. When we had finished, our proposal called for more than $90 billion in cuts over five years. The most important feature of our plan was that it dedicated all savings to deficit reduction. We weren't saving money so Congress or the President could spend it elsewhere. This was *pure* deficit reduction, not a budget shell game.

Thirty members of the group supported the plan, fifteen from each party. Amazingly, we suffered only two defections from our original group of thirty-two. We met our goal and proved legions of Beltway skeptics wrong: both parties could work together to cut spending and change government without devastating vital programs.

SOUNDING THE ALARM

We unveiled the plan on October 27. The press practically ignored us. That was the same day Hillary Clinton gave her opening testimony on the Clinton health bill, and the North America Free Trade Agreement was still hanging by a thread with a vote swiftly approaching. The press didn't have time to worry about budget cuts. Besides, most reporters didn't believe our effort would go anywhere.

While we labored in obscurity to promote our plan, debate over NAFTA consumed all of Washington.

The White House was on red alert trying to pass the trade pact while big labor was battering Democrats with threats of lethal political retaliation if they voted for it. Careers all over Washington — from those of the President and members of Congress to high-paid lobbyists — seemed to hang in the balance.

This proved useful and harmful at the same time.

Our biggest opponents, the White House and the special interests, were too busy fighting one another to see what we were doing. At least for the time being, that meant they couldn't mount any opposition. On the other hand, press fascination with the unfolding NAFTA's drama left us with virtually no coverage.

That's right. The press could not find time to cover the efforts of a bipartisan group of House members who were trying to cut the deficit by

$90 billion over the next five years. That's because many in the press — in addition to being distracted by other stories — did not take our effort seriously. They assumed we would lose in a lopsided floor vote.

As the fight over NAFTA wound down, however, more reporters began to cover the Penny-Kasich effort. Official Washington did not like what it saw.

Penny-Kasich was heresy. It was a blatant affront to the way Washington works. Official Washington, personified by the White House, congressional leaders, and the special interests, was determined to kill our drive for spending restraint.

Hillary Clinton told Bill Richardson, a member of the Democratic leadership, after a White House meeting, "I want Penny-Kasich dead in two days."

That process began the morning of November 15, two days before the House passed NAFTA. Top Democratic leaders gathered in a meeting room on Capitol Hill to see where the votes were. It was then the leadership learned that Penny-Kasich might win. Democratic Whips (those who count votes for the leadership) reported that many Democrats seemed to like the plan and that rank-and-file members were looking for some budget cuts with teeth.

The next day, November 16, the Democratic leadership called all the special interest groups to Capitol Hill. Who were they?

The usual suspects: The American Association of Retired Persons; the Children's Defense Fund; the National Education Association; and the Center for Budget and Policy Priorities. All of them dedicated, and fiercely so, to protecting and increasing government spending. They got their marching orders: Gather as much opposition as you can.

And Hurry!

There was no time to waste. They had to start pummeling lawmakers with phone calls and faxes. This was no grassroots movement. This was reveille: a wake-up call to the special interests. The message was clear: if these cuts pass, your piece of the federal pie could be next.

Within two days, the special interests began hypnotizing House members with baroque distortions about Penny-Kasich's "dire" consequences.

Teachers' unions were told it slashed education budgets, but it didn't. The elderly were told it gouged their programs, but it didn't. Environmentalists were told it eviscerated the EPA's budget, but it didn't. Mayors and governors were told it meant deep cuts for priority road, water, and other construction projects, but it didn't.

As the special interest faxes poured in, congressional leaders and administration officials fanned out over the Capitol to warn of Penny-Kasich's hidden dangers.

Budget Director Leon Panetta said the defense cuts would deal a serious blow to morale in the military. Bah! Clinton had already cut defense by $110 billion, and our cuts touched only overseas security groups such as NATO and weapons systems the Pentagon brass had been trying to kill for years.

Deputy Budget Director Alice Rivlin said the Penny-Kasich cuts, which totaled only $8 billion in 1994, could shove the economy into a recession. Whom was she kidding? The federal government spent $1.5 trillion in 1994, and the U.S. economy churned out more than $6 trillion in goods and services that year. That means the Penny-Kasich cuts would have reduced federal spending by less than 1 percent. Certainly not enough of a drain on a growing economy to cause a recession.

Donna Shalala, the head of the Department of Health and Human Services, had her aides round up several Washington reporters for an "exclusive" interview about Penny-Kasich. She said it would inflict needless pain on the sick and elderly by meddling with Medicare subsidies and payments for other health services. Ludicrous. All we asked was that Medicare recipients pay a 20 percent co-payment on home health and clinical lab services they were currently getting for free. This change applied only to patients with incomes above 150 percent of the poverty limit.

Then Clinton weighed in. At two separate press conferences on Friday and Saturday, he said Penny-Kasich's $37 billion in Medicare cuts would scuttle prospects for health care reform in 1994. Meanwhile, Bruce C. Vladeck, the nonpolitical Medicare Administrator, testified before Congress that the $124 billion in Medicare cuts Clinton was proposing in his own health reform bill would not put Medicare beneficiaries at risk. Vladek said the Clinton cuts would reduce the expected growth in Medicare payments only from three times the rate of inflation to twice the rate of inflation. Obviously, compared to Clinton's cuts, our Medicare cuts were mild.

Why all the deception?

The answer's easy: Clinton could not afford to see Penny-Kasich pass. If it had won in the House, it would have drawn immense media attention and gone to the Senate with real momentum behind it. Sen. Bob Kerrey, Nebraska Democrat, and Sen. Hank Brown, Colorado Republican, were waiting for it and had already organized a similar bipartisan group in the Senate. Kerrey had cast the tie-breaking vote for Clinton's budget in August and, just like me, wanted more spending cuts in exchange.

If the bill had ever reached his desk, Clinton would have been forced to veto it, and that would have exposed him as a hypocrite on deeper spending cuts. It would have revealed that his rhetoric about challenging Congress to think anew and for both parties to work together was, well, just that — rhetoric.

No. Clinton had to stop Penny-Kasich before the public really knew what it was and what it meant. The President didn't have much time.

The vote was scheduled for November 20. A Saturday.

I received a visit from Panetta and senior White House aide George Stephanopoulos on November 18. I had five freshmen Democrats in my office to show the White House what it meant to these new members to see Penny-Kasich succeed. All of them had cast a tough vote in support of Clinton's budget. Now they were looking for some support from the White House.

Panetta and Stephanopoulos came to the meeting at my request. I started the discussion this way: "It's too late for us to change or water down the package. But, remember, the White House is in the driver's seat. Before this legislation reaches the President's desk, we are willing to hold some of the Medicare savings in reserve for the President to use for health care reform."

We urged the White House not to go overboard trying to kill the plan, but instead to say it agreed with the thrust of Penny-Kasich but disagreed with the specifics.

Panetta and Stephanopoulos didn't bite. Stephanopoulos said the White House would "modulate" its criticism. I thought that was a good sign. It implied that the White House would be "toning down" its criticism.

Instead, the White House amplified it.

By sunset, their seek-and-destroy mission was in full swing. The faxes and phone calls were pouring into Hill offices. Cabinet secretaries were phoning Democrats. So was the President. So was Gore. On Friday morning Hillary Clinton attended a breakfast for freshmen Democrats and decried the budget cuts. Every public relations asset of the federal government was aimed at us.

Nonetheless, the leadership still feared it would lose.

So they postponed the vote until Monday, November 22. That gave them time to hit even harder.

Did they ever!

BUDGETARY BLACKMAIL

On Saturday I witnessed the most blatant act of political intimidation I had seen in eleven years in Congress.

The leaders of the House Appropriations Committee, the power center that doles out all the federal dough, sent letters to dozens of lawmakers saying a vote for Penny-Kasich would jeopardize projects in their home district.

In other words, the powerful lawmakers who control the federal purse strings were telling other lawmakers that a vote for our deficit-reduction package would result in a punitive cut to a program in their district.

Dozens of these letters went out, many to freshmen members who were infuriated by these brass knuckle tactics.

Guess what?

These letters were signed by the Democrats who ran these committees *and* by the highest ranking committee Republicans. I guess the only way to kill a bipartisan effort to cut spending is to apply bipartisan thumbscrews.

Rep. Jay Dickey, an Arkansas Republican and freshman, was so astonished and appalled by these tactics that he denounced them on the House floor. Dickey said no power broker was going to intimidate him from trying to reduce the deficit.

> I got one of the letters that specified that two of my projects would be in jeopardy if I voted for this Penny-Kasich bill.
>
> I got upset, but now I am thankful that I got it, and I wanted to share with you all as to why I felt this way.
>
> I am a freshman, of course, and I have my concerns about how I am representing my people. But what that letter does is it implies that the most important thing that I have for me is reelection and that I should guide what I do and how I vote based on whether or not I am reelected. Well, I am going back in my mind, when we had the tax bill, what the people of the Fourth District wanted when they said cut spending first. It did not make any difference what was said, how it was said, it was cut spending first.
>
> My reelection is up to the people of the Fourth District. What I have got to do is obey what they say. I cannot listen to the chairmen of this committee or that committee coming around and saying, "We do not do things that way. We do things this way. You will never get reelected if you do not do that." I am for cutting spending first. The people of the Fourth District and I are not going to change, and I do not care who threatens me with anything other than my own integrity.

While many members shared Dickey's outrage, few others spoke out. Dickey did so with the vigor and passion only a freshman can muster upon confronting the various cultures of Congress. Dickey told me later, "I rushed to the floor because I was afraid if I let it [the threat] sit, it would sink in. I knew it was a snake, and the right thing to do was call it a snake."

While some freshmen were understandably horrified, one of my longtime allies on budget matters, Rep. Dave McCurdy of Oklahoma, took the threatening letters in stride. He got one letter from honchos on the Energy and Water subcommittee. It distributes more than $22 billion annually for mining, water, and energy projects (plenty of which fall into the pork barrel category). Someone on the committee dug around and discovered that McCurdy had once written a letter asking the committee to consider funding a project to control chloride buildup in the Red River, which runs through Oklahoma and Texas.

McCurdy had forgotten the project — until he got the letter, which read in part as follows: "I know you would want to be made aware that the Penny-Kasich amendment would jeopardize many projects of the Corps of Engineers, including *Red River Basin Chloride Control.*"

All the letters were written like that. Beneath the description of the project was this catchall paragraph: "We hope you will join our effort to defeat Penny-Kasich."

McCurdy decided two could play that game. He wanted to send the appropriators a message. He fired off a letter of his own to Tom Bevill, the committee chairman who had signed the letter: "The implication of your letter . . . is abundantly clear. In the same spirit, I have noted that the Armed Services Subcommittee on Military Installations and Facilities, *which I chair,* [spent] . . . $5,070,000 for a project for which you have expressed support."

McCurdy made it clear. Retaliate against me, and I might retaliate against you. The very next day Bevill responded, waving the white flag. "I feel you might have misunderstood my motive for writing you. . . . I have always used a project's merit as the determining factor. Any other inference which might have been drawn from my letter is incorrect." His response to McCurdy notwithstanding, Bevill knew that most lawmakers would have viewed his letter as a threat.

In the days leading up to the vote, John and I were scampering all over the Hill, checking with members to see if they were still with us. We got on the phone and tried to set the record straight about all the loony special interest lies. Every time we refuted one distortion we would find another.

Sabo did his part for the pro-spending cause by compiling a nine-page harangue that, among other things, charged that raising deductibles for lab tests for middle class seniors amounted to a "tax on the sick." He conveniently ignored the fact that any senior citizen below 150 percent of the poverty line was exempt from the fee.

Despite the barrage of falsehoods and exaggerations, we kept ourselves in the ball game. Every time the leadership peeled off some votes, we'd find new converts. This ebb and flow lasted all weekend.

To our surprise and delight, many of the intimidating letters from the appropriators seemed to backfire. Many members sided with us just to teach the power brokers a lesson.

The turning point came when powerful Democrats who oversee the defense budget started warning lawmakers that Penny-Kasich would damage the Pentagon. On the day of the vote, Rep. John Murtha, chairman of the committee that distributes all defense spending, began accosting lawmakers on the defense committees and lecturing them about the "dangers" of Penny-Kasich.

Murtha, known as "Big Jack," is a tall, muscular man in his mid-sixties. A former marine, Murtha reenlisted in his mid-thirties to fight in Vietnam. Murtha oversees all spending for the Pentagon. That's more than $250 billion. Because defense spending reaches every congressional district, Murtha can do plenty of favors or withhold plenty of favors. He uses that leverage to the hilt.

He was an unbeatable foe. In the final hours leading up to the vote, Murtha persuaded several conservative Democrats to vote against our plan. Murtha convinced them that Penny-Kasich would devastate the military. It wasn't reality. We didn't propose cuts that deep.

The truth didn't matter. Enough conservative Democrats believed him. Those were votes that could have made the difference.

The final vote was 219–213. We lost by six votes. A switch of four votes was all we needed to win.

All thirteen senior Republicans on the Appropriations Committee voted against us. Some of them had co-authored the "hit list" letters. Yet all of them had voted against Clinton's budget in August, claiming it taxed too much and cut too little. Their votes, too, would have made the difference.

Their votes proved, once again, that when it comes to cutting the budget, John Randolph had it right: "Most members understand their duty better than they discharge it."

PRESSURE COOKER

Some freshmen lawmakers, though, showed that they understood and discharged their duty with courage. Lynn Schenk was one of them.

Schenk, of heavily Republican San Diego, is a pro-business Democrat with extensive experience in environmental law. She's also a tenacious advocate for women's rights. Schenk campaigned to open the exclusively male San Diego Downtown Club and co-founded the Women's Bank of San Diego and a legal service for poor women.

Schenk won a close race to represent the wealthiest (and most Republican) neighborhoods in this conservative coastal paradise. The most politically active constituents in her district are wealthy businessmen and lawyers who peer out over the Pacific Ocean through picture windows in their homes perched on top of lush, sloping hills. These are people who despise taxes and big government and, truth be told, don't care much for Democrats. There are some Democrats clustered in downtown San Diego. They are the voice of the core party interests: big labor, senior citizens, and environmental lobbies. Still there are more Republicans than

Democrats, and the wealthiest and most politically active residents live in La Jolla.

Dissatisfaction with Bush ran so high that San Diego sent Schenk to Congress. She campaigned for lower federal spending and targeted tax breaks for business to spur the local economy and said higher taxes on the wealthy would be a last resort . . . a necessary evil if spending cuts failed to lower the deficit.

When she went home to meet with constituents before the vote on Clinton's bill, she met the very people whose taxes were going to be raised.

"I would stand there looking at a roomful of wealthy La Jolla residents and think to myself, What can I tell them? 'Your taxes are going up. Please vote for me again?' "

When it came time to vote for the Clinton tax bill, Schenk and other Democratic freshmen joined my effort to demand deeper spending cuts. The President refused to add more budget cuts to his tax bill, but his senior advisers agreed to allow another vote on deeper cuts later in 1993. That decision provoked the Penny-Kasich battle.

Democratic leaders put excruciating pressure on Schenk and other freshmen Democrats to pass the Clinton bill. In meeting after meeting, they were told this was a test of their Democratic credentials — that a "no" vote could kill the President's biggest domestic program and lead the country to conclude Democrats were toothless, spineless, and gutless. Everything was at stake, they were told. The economy. The country. The presidency. The Party.

Democratic leaders spared senior Democrats these florid tales of doom. In some cases, they cut deals to win votes. In others, they let the senior (and politically safe) Democrats off the hook. But there was no compromising with the freshmen.

Reluctantly, Schenk and other freshmen supported the President's tax bill.

"I took enormous flak," Schenk said. "The mail and calls were decidedly against the bill. The Republicans immediately started running advertisements calling it the Clinton-Schenk tax bill."

Schenk decided it was worth it to trade support for the President for a shot at making deeper cuts later.

"Ultimately, I couldn't vote no and bring the process to an end," she explained. "It only would have led to more agony. And I concluded there would have been less improvement, not more, if we had killed that budget and tried to write another one."

While the tax vote took guts, the tougher vote proved to be her support for the spending cuts in Penny-Kasich.

The San Diego *Union-Tribune*'s conservative editorial page initially supported Penny-Kasich. Even though Schenk played a big part in brokering the deal for a vote on deeper spending cuts, the *Union-Tribune* never gave her credit. It even refused to print a letter to the editor I wrote with Kasich about Schenk's positive contribution to the effort. Consequently, Schenk got no credit for pursuing more spending cuts but was still catching flak for raising taxes.

Then Schenk learned the bitterest lesson on Capitol Hill. Higher taxes irk constituents. Spending cuts enrage them. That's why you see a steady parade of tax increases from Washington and no serious spending cuts. Constituents hate to see their benefits or subsidies cut. Hate it.

Throughout debate on the Clinton tax bill Schenk's constituents peppered her office with faxes, phone calls, and letters with the same message: Cut spending first.

"It was like a mindless mantra," she said.

When the Penny-Kasich plan neared a House vote, all of Schenk's Democratic constituents turned on her, even those who had urged her to support the Clinton tax bill and oppose NAFTA, as she had done.

The guardians of the status quo fired off angry letters suggesting Schenk was betraying them for supporting spending cuts. Most of the cuts didn't even touch these groups. They staged "sympathy strikes" on behalf of other groups who would lose government funding. The local postal workers union told Schenk she was "assaulting" them.

Schenk had just cast the most important labor vote of the year on NAFTA and within days her labor allies had turned against her.

Within Congress, top leaders on the Energy and Commerce Committee, of which Schenk was a member, were lobbying aggressively against Penny-Kasich. Chairman John Dingell and fellow Californian Henry Waxman met frequently with Schenk and in so many words let her know they wanted Penny-Kasich killed. While they never threatened Schenk, it's not hard to see that these meetings, which occurred almost weekly, were designed to weaken her commitment to deeper cuts.

Schenk resisted these external and internal pressures, but then something changed back home.

When San Diegans discovered that General Atomics Corp., a local fusion research company, stood to lose a federal subsidy under Penny-Kasich, the rock-solid support for spending cuts melted to mush. Schenk even began to hear from wealthy constituents who didn't want the spigot turned off for General Atomics because it might provoke other cuts elsewhere. Remember, these were the same people demanding that Schenk "cut spending first."

Then the *Union-Tribune* reversed itself and editorialized against Penny-Kasich, arguing that cuts affecting San Diego were unwise and punitive during a time when defense cuts were wreaking havoc throughout California.

So, if Schenk were to vote for Penny-Kasich, she would anger the following people and institutions in Washington and San Diego: the chairman of her committee (Dingell); the most powerful Californian in her delegation (Waxman); all of her loyal Democratic activist friends (big labor, seniors, teachers, environmentalists); General Atomics Corp. (a major employer in her district); and the largest and most powerful newspaper in her district (the *Union-Tribune*).

She voted for the cuts anyway.

Of all the freshmen Democrats who supported Penny-Kasich, Schenk had the most to lose. Many of the bill's cuts did not affect such visible programs in other districts as much as the GA Technologies cut affected hers. Believe me, there are several examples of lawmakers who withdrew their support for Penny-Kasich simply because one of the cuts hit too close to home.

Schenk puts it this way: "There is not a value here [in Washington] to cut spending. It's not a dominant value. If you look at the leadership, they come from a different era and have a different notion about what government should be doing. But I look at my granddaughter [she gestures toward a picture on her desk] and say to myself, She's about to go to college and take out loans. On top of that, we're strapping her with other debts. The federal debt. She doesn't have a choice. And she didn't ask for the debt, nor was she consulted. Those of us who came here concerned about the deficit, our views have crystallized and intensified. But we ask ourselves, How do we make it happen?"

Through her courageous votes in 1993, Lynn Schenk was trying to show us the way.

Congresswoman Schenk also lost her battle for re-election in 1994, and she was attacked mercilessly in her campaign for supporting the Clinton budget.

The Republicans who defeated congresswomen Margolies-Mezvinsky and Schenk offered no credible solutions to the nation's future deficit problems. All they offered was feel-good tax cuts, increases in defense spending, and vague promises to cut spending. Consequently, these new members of Congress may do less to reduce the deficit than did congresswomen Margolies-Mezvinsky and Schenk.

The Penny-Kasich effort exposed all the distasteful cultures of the modern Congress: the Culture of Spending, which runs up huge deficits; the Culture of Power, which leads those with power to intimidate those without; the Culture of Fear, which prevents lawmakers from inciting special interest groups they believe hold the key to their reelection; the Culture of Isolation, which creates an inside-the-Beltway mentality at odds with the real world; the Culture of Hypocrisy, which allows members to rail against the deficit while voting against spending cuts; and the Culture of Partisanship, which at first nearly scuttled our group's effort due to Republican and Democratic distrust built up during a decade of partisan posturing.

In the following chapters, I'll discuss the cultures of Congress. I'm convinced that in order for voters to know how to bring change to Washington, they must first understand the way Washington works.

In the modern Congress, power is about money — how much to collect, how much to distribute, or how much to redirect through regulations. The most powerful figures in Congress control committees that make decisions about vast sums of money. That is why much of this book is devoted to the struggles over money I've witnessed and the shamefully large deficits they've produced.

This year the government — your government — will pay $245 billion in interest on a national debt of $5 trillion. What does that mean? Well, when the government runs a deficit, it has to borrow to make up the difference between expenses and revenues. The national debt is the sum of every deficit in American history. The national debt is like a big loan the government — your government — makes to itself. The interest payments cover the cost of servicing the Big Loan.

To pay off the nation's accumulated debt would require $16,000 from every American man, woman, and child. This year, we will spend almost as much just to cover *interest payments* ($245 billion) as we will to finance national defense ($270 billion). We will spend more on these interest payments alone than we will spend on education, job training, social services, law enforcement, science and technology, agriculture, foreign aid, environmental protection, and veterans programs combined.

In a very real sense, interest payments represent money that is wasted. This year's $245 billion interest payment bought nothing of value. Nothing. Worse, the government — your government — has to borrow money for the interest payment from private lenders. When the government borrows, it reduces the amount of money available to other borrowers. Other borrowers — like you or the company you work for. In the past twenty years, rising deficits have forced the government to confiscate more and more of the private sector's available savings. Twenty years ago the government — your government — consumed only 15 percent of all private-sector savings. In 1991 that figure reached 71 percent.

So, deficits mean the government spends billions on interest payments that purchase nothing. They also mean that it's harder for you and the company you work for to secure loans you need or want.

That's why deficits matter.

That's the economics of deficits.

The politics of deficits is a bit more complicated.

In an August 1994 *Wall Street Journal* poll, 61 percent of the voters said they favored cutting government entitlement programs to reduce the deficit. But 66 percent of the voters said they opposed cuts in programs such as Social Security, Medicare (health care for the elderly), Medicaid (health care for the poor), and farm subsidies. The respondents apparently didn't realize that Social Security, Medicare, Medicaid, and farm subsidies *are* entitlement programs.

Politicians are not ignorant. They've seen these numbers before and know very well what they mean. Except for extraordinary circumstances, when a politician tries to cut Social Security, Medicare, Medicaid, or farm subsidies, the voters scream as if they've stepped on a carpet tack in the middle of the night.

For now, politicians would rather keep the deficits *and* their jobs in Washington. That's why all the cultures in Congress conspire to protect the status quo and the deficit spending that results.

The Republicans' ballyhooed Contract with America is a perfect example. Beyond its laudable reform platform, there is nothing but budgetary cotton candy. No accountant in America can reduce the deficit with lower taxes, higher defense spending, and a hands-off approach to Social Security. And that's exactly what the Republicans have promised. They promise a few minor reforms of welfare, Medicaid, and Medicare, but those are unlikely to produce the necessary savings. The contract, in other words, was a tool to get elected with, not a tool to govern with.

Deficit spending causes the distinction to disappear between those things we cherish and those things we simply enjoy. When a nation stops making choices, it silences the essential debate over what it values. All things are not equal. Some are more important than others. Are vaccines more important than subsidies for the arts? Are war ships more important than crop subsidies? Are pensions more important than spacecraft? These questions all have answers.

But deficit spending allows us to dodge the answers.

It's easier for politicians to set these questions aside. They fear if they lay these hard questions before you, you may reject them in favor of a candidate who says you can have it all.

But you can't — we can't — have everything. Someday our irresponsible behavior will exact a heavy price. You and I may not see this day, but our children will.

You've all seen the bumper sticker "We're spending our grandchildren's inheritance." In a very real sense, that's what deficit spending means.

It's that simple.

It's Common Cents.

There's another insidious side to deficit spending. Persistent deficits convey to the electorate that public officials are acting irresponsibly. Deficits are an act of dishonesty. As such, they erode faith in government.

It's instructive to recall there was a time when Congress was held in high esteem. The 1950s was such a time. I do not consider it a coincidence that one of the landmark laws of that period was the interstate highway act, which was financed with higher gasoline taxes. Public officials had the foresight to establish a national priority — a new highway system — and the courage to pay for it. That kind of honest governance builds a stronger nation and a stronger democracy.

Abraham Lincoln once said, "With public trust anything is possible, without it nothing is possible."

Again, it's that simple.

It's Common Cents.

Three

The Culture of Spending

I, however, place the economy among the first and most important of Republican virtues, and public debt as the greatest of the dangers to be feared. And to preserve their independence, we must not let our rulers load us with perpetual debt. We must make our election between economy and liberty, or profusion and servitude. If we can prevent the government from wasting the labors of the people, under the pretense of taking care of them, they must become happy. The same prudence which in private life would forbid our paying our own money for unexplained projects forbids it in the dispensation of the public monies.

—Thomas Jefferson

THIS REPUBLIC is entering its 219th year and remains the most admired and copied form of government ever known. For 192 of those 219 years, this government shared something that no longer exists: an ethic of frugality.

OUT OF CONTROL

In 1969, as I was turning eighteen, the federal government posted the last budget surplus of my lifetime. It wasn't much. Only $3.2 billion. But it was a milestone. At the time, federal debt held by the public equaled $278 billion.

Twenty-six years ago the percentage of mandatory federal spending was 33 percent. In other words, thirty-three cents of every tax dollar in 1969 was devoured by programs Congress did not annually control.

You may be asking yourself, How can spending be beyond Congress's control? Doesn't the Constitution say that Congress controls all government spending?

Yes.

But many social programs started during the New Deal and the Great

Society were put on automatic pilot. These programs include Social Security, Medicare, Medicaid, Food Stamps, farm subsidies, college student loans, veterans benefits, and Supplemental Security Income (which provides aid to the poor elderly, the blind, and the disabled).

Most of these programs deliver benefits on an entitlement basis. If you're old enough to receive Social Security, you collect a check. If you're poor enough to qualify for Medicaid, you get a check to pay your health bills. If you're old enough for Medicare, you get a check to pay your health bills. If you're poor enough to collect Food Stamps, you receive food coupons. If you've qualified for a federal pension, you get a check. If you plant certain crops, you are eligible for a subsidy.

In almost every case, the amount of government spending is determined by the number of people who qualify plus the rate of inflation. If more people qualify or if the inflation rate rises, the government automatically spends more.

In the twenty-six years since 1969, the percentage of mandatory spending has risen to 56 percent. The increase in mandatory spending and a twenty-six-year string of federal deficits is not coincidental.

In 1994, the annual federal deficit exceeded $200 billion. The gross federal debt exceeded $4.6 trillion.

Before I go any further, let me try to give you some idea of how to measure amounts such as $1 million, $1 billion, and $1 trillion.

Look at your wristwatch or a clock on the wall. Study the second hand. Watch it for exactly one minute. Imagine counting out one dollar for each second. By my reckoning, it takes about one second to say the words *one dollar*. Well, it would take 11.5 days to count $1 million. It would take 31.7 years to count $1 billion. The deficit in 1994 was $234 billion. It would take you 7,417 years to count that much money. The federal debt in 1994 will exceed $4.6 trillion. It would take you 145,820 years to count that much money.

Remember, each year of deficit spending increases the federal debt. The deficit is the annual difference between tax dollars collected and government spending. The debt is the grand total of each year's deficit. During the Reagan-Bush years the debt climbed from $994 billion to $4.4 trillion. By the end of Clinton's first term, the debt is projected to grow to $5.6 trillion.

It's true that today's deficits and debts, in relative terms, are not as large as some we've had in the past. But in the past, the deficits and debts were accumulated to finance a war, address an economic catastrophe, or pay for a quantum leap in the nation's borders. The government absorbed staggering debt to pay for the Louisiana Purchase, the Civil War, World War I, the Great Depression, and World War II.

After each of these debt binges, the leaders of both parties and the

President committed the nation to retiring the debts and abolishing the deficits as soon as possible. In every instance the nation did just that.

When we say today that we lack the political will to balance our budgets and begin paying down our debts, we reveal our own cowardice and demean the frugal legacy of our forebears. We ignore a glorious and courageous past, a time when common sense dictated, leaders demanded, and voters understood the need to sacrifice for future generations.

Finally, we confess to our children and grandchildren that we will leave them less so we can have more.

So far, the steady increase in mandatory spending has brought America the twin crises of deficits and debts. The deficit and debt are the result of the willful abandonment of our forebears' legacy of frugality.

Another point about the Culture of Spending: When you hear the media or a politician describe budget "cuts," you must understand that this does not mean what you think it does. A cut isn't really a cut.

Let me explain.

You make a cut in your household budget when you reduce the number of movies the family sees every month from three to one. You make a cut in your family budget when you buy three Christmas presents for each child instead of five. You make a cut when you drop cable television, forgo long-distance calls, put off the purchase of a new appliance, or cancel a magazine subscription.

A cut in Washington is something altogether different. It's not really a cut at all. It's simply a smaller increase than someone in power has requested.

Here's why. Every budget starts from this basic premise: *Every government program will be continued, and each program will grow by at least the rate of inflation.*

That's what Washington policymakers call a budget baseline. Every year the work of budgeting begins with this baseline. That means every program in the budget gets at least an inflation adjustment — *regardless of its merit.*

Baseline. What a deceptive word. It conjures images of something flat, something linear. It almost sounds like *baseboard,* that straight, rigid, and inflexible strip of wood we nail just above the tile or carpet. What an image! A baseline budget sounds like something near the floor, something near the very bottom.

Nothing could be farther from the truth.

In Washington, a baseline rises continuously. It does so gradually, inexorably, like a kite with limitless string riding a steady wind. Congress lets out the string and special interests provide the breeze. And your tax dollar, like the kite, flies farther and farther away. (Republicans have vowed to abolish this practice as they rewrite the nation's budget laws. This would be a great improvement, and I hope once this step is taken no future Congress — regardless of party — ever reverses it.)

As I said, much of the blame lies with the rise in mandatory spending. Under baseline budgeting, every program automatically receives more each year to cover demographic growth and inflation. Cuts are almost never made to the mandatory programs such as Social Security, Medicare, Medicaid, student loans, veterans benefits, Food Stamps, or farm subsidies.

Strictly speaking, none of these programs are mandatory. Congress could pare them back, but is afraid voters will punish them. This fear is rational; in recent years, the public grew inflamed when Congress tried to "cut" Medicare and Medicaid. These weren't cuts at all. Because the number of people eligible for these programs and the inflation rate was rising so fast, Congress tried only to limit their exploding growth.

Those who receive these "mandatory" benefits believe they are entitled to them as if by constitutional decree. In other words, these programs are mandatory only in a political sense. Nothing prohibits Congress from reducing these benefits . . . except well-founded political fear.

In 1969 we spent $5.7 billion for Medicare. In 1979 we spent $26.5 billion. In 1989 we spent $85 billion. We are projected to spend $156 billion this year (FY 1995).

Other programs in the "automatic pilot" category have grown enormously. We spent $7 billion on veterans benefits in 1969 and are projected to spend $39 billion this year (FY 1995). We spent $27 billion on Social Security benefits in 1969 and are projected to spend $337 billion this year (FY 1995).

I am not suggesting eliminating these programs, but Congress must restrain their costs. I'm not going to offer a specific proposal here to accomplish this goal. However, limiting annual cost-of-living adjustments for Social Security and reducing Medicare subsidies for the wealthy must be part of the answer. My main purpose in this section is simply to demonstrate how much of our federal budget is out of control. The average lawmaker is powerless to stop the growth of these programs. A consensus must be built around the idea of reducing entitlement benefits so we can protect future generations from economically ruinous debt. All Americans — and especially those who receive entitlement benefits from these "mandatory" programs — must first agree to accept smaller benefits before Congress can begin a serious debate over how to proceed.

Unless President Clinton (or any future President) and the congressional leadership decide to confront the rising cost of these automatic pilot programs jointly, the deficit will grow. It won't matter how much taxes are raised. It won't matter how much defense spending is reduced. It won't matter if we eliminate every penny of foreign aid (we will spend $18 billion on foreign aid in 1995, or 0.012 percent of our entire budget).

None of this will matter unless the nation decides it can do without some of the Social Security, Medicare, veterans, or other entitlement benefits they receive.

Common sense tells us that the size of the sacrifice shrinks as the size of the program affected increases. That means if everyone sacrifices, the reduction in benefits is manageable.

THE POWER OF THE PURSE

Well, then, what spending does Congress annually control?

Congress directly controls something called discretionary spending. It amounts to about one-third of the $1.5 trillion budget for 1995. This is the part of the budget the Appropriations committees in the House and Senate review annually.

These committees command huge memberships. The Senate Appropriations Committee is the largest of any in that body. Twenty-nine senators — sixteen Democrats and thirteen Republicans. That means nearly one-third of the body is tied directly to the Culture of Spending.

In the House, the Appropriations Committee is the second-largest committee. (Guess what's the largest? The Public Works Committee. It doles out billions for highway construction and other capital projects. There is no greater source of pork barrel spending.) Thirty-seven Democrats and twenty-three Republicans sit on the Appropriations Committee, meaning that 14 percent of the House is tied directly to the Culture of Spending.

Appropriations Committee members in both chambers protect one another and their spending domain with loyalty and ferocity reminiscent of the Knights of the Round Table. They must. If one piece of pork barrel spending is lost, all others become more vulnerable. That's part of the logic — or illogic — of the Culture of Spending.

Many members of Congress vie for a seat on the Appropriations Committee because each year it decides how one-third of the budget — nearly $500 billion — is spent. Once there, a cohesive bond is established with other committee members, and all work together to ward off outsiders who try to cut or eliminate spending the committee supports. With enough seniority lawmakers rise to chair a subcommittee. That means they oversee a segment of the budget, that is, all the spending for such departments as agriculture, education, housing, transportation, veterans, human services, and justice.

Seniority plays a big part in the Culture of Spending. In fact, members of the Appropriations Committee retire at a lesser rate and are seldom defeated for reelection. Seventy-six percent of those on the Appropriations Committee have been in Congress more than ten years. That's the highest of any of the policy-making committees in the House.

The Rules Committee, which sets the rules of debate and is a tool of the House leadership and committee chairmen, is the committee with the most seniority. Eighty-five percent of its members have been in office for more than ten years.

Of those who left the Appropriations Committee in 1992, more than half were caught up in the bank scandal. Nine of the nineteen members to leave the committee in 1992 had more than 125 overdrawn checks (five had more than two hundred). Six of these members retired, two were defeated in primaries, and one lost in the general election. Of the nineteen members to leave the committee, eighteen had served in the House for at least ten years (twelve had served more than fourteen years). The last two men to chair the full Appropriations Committee did so until they were eighty-two and eighty-four, respectively (Jamie Whitten of Mississippi and William Natcher of Kentucky). Natcher died in 1994 and was succeeded by David Obey of Wisconsin. At age fifty-five, Obey is now serving in his twenty-sixth year in Congress.

Although discretionary spending should be easier to control than entitlement spending, it is not. Cuts in any part of the budget are a rare occurrence on Capitol Hill. The powerful Appropriations Committee members reward friends and punish enemies.

Other committees hold sway over spending and protect higher spending with equal vigor. In Congress there is only one Appropriations Committee, but there are seventeen authorizing committees with ninety-one subcommittees. These committees craft the government's programs and recommend the amount Congress should spend on each of them. After these decisions are made, the Appropriations Committee tries to give each program the amount of money the authorizing committees have requested. Often, the authorizing committees request more money than the Appropriations Committee can spend.

The former chairman of the Education and Labor Committee, Rep. Augustus Hawkins, California Democrat, summed up the system this way: "We will authorize [approve] whatever programs we think are necessary, and we'll let the budgeteers determine how to pay for it."

The bottom line here is that each House authorizing committee and all of its subcommittees want to spend more money every year. Full committees and subcommittees fear a loss of power if they economize. After all, the mission of these committees is to create more government programs. Each new program enhances a committee's power. And reducing or eliminating a program diminishes a committee's power.

For these and other reasons, plenty of lawmakers — Democrat and Republican — have fallen in love with what Founding Father John Randolph called "that most delicious of all privileges — spending other people's money."

John F. Cogan, a scholar with the Hoover Institution, described this process in a splendid 1992 analysis of congressional spending entitled "Federal Budget Deficits; What's Wrong With the Congressional Budget Process." About congressional committees and their propensity to spend more each year, Cogan said,

> When many congressional committees have the authority to spend general fund revenue, each committee is less inclined to restrain its spending because the political blame for increased taxes or deficit spending is shared by all committees. In fact, the opposite of restraint occurs. Pressured by interest groups to maintain their share of total spending, each committee becomes an advocate for the programs under its jurisdiction.

Cogan explained that, beginning in 1789, Congress originally confined all spending decisions to one committee, the Ways and Means Committee in the House, and the Finance Committee in the Senate. From 1790 until the Revolutionary War debt was retired in 1835, Congress produced balanced budgets. With the exception of deficits attributable to the recession of 1840–43, that pattern continued until after the Civil War. In the mid-1880s, Congress decentralized the budget process by transferring spending authority to several different committees.

As these changes were being debated, Samuel Randall, a former House Speaker, warned against putting the power to spend in so many hands:

> If you undertake to divide all these appropriations and have many committees where there ought to be but one, you will enter upon a path of extravagance you cannot foresee the length of or the depth of until we find the Treasury of the country bankrupt.

Federal spending from 1885, the year of decentralization, until 1893 rose by 50 percent. By the year 1900, federal spending had grown by more than 100 percent. And by 1916, congressional spending grew another 45 percent.

There are even more committees with spending authority today. It's no wonder there is so much institutional pressure to spend — regardless of the size of the nation's annual deficits and the federal debt.

BUDGET THEATRICS

Whenever a President or lawmakers try to cut spending or cancel a wasteful program, a bipartisan political militia springs up to defend it.

But there is a grace and subtlety to Congress's spending ways. Because the Congress represents the sum total of desires from all parts of the country, different players move in different spending circles. Rare is the lawmaker who is for every piece of federal pork. Most quietly support some pork barrel spending but are wise enough to noisily oppose questionable spending projects that would bring no benefits to their district or state. These premeditated tantrums leave the voters with a vague impression that their representative or senator *isn't like all the rest; our lawmaker is for cuts*.

Unfortunately, most lawmakers are not for cuts. If they were, common sense tells you that deficits would have disappeared long ago. Once they arrive in Washington, most lawmakers embed themselves quickly in the spending culture. In a way, they have little choice. Constituents, interest groups, and leaders in their own party (Democrat and Republican) reward them for spending and punish them for trying to cut programs. And punishment can be severe. Lawmakers who go overboard in trying to cut wasteful spending often find it more difficult to win approval for spending they favor. Powerful lawmakers who control the nation's purse strings routinely resort to quiet threats and intimidation to bully obstinate budget cutters.

And the cast of characters changes all the time. Lawmakers who squirrel away millions on one pork barrel project will, within months, aggressively challenge another project they find objectionable. Several recent books about Congress leave readers with the impression that, on matters of spending, the institution can be cleanly divided, almost like a vaudevillian melodrama, into "good" and "bad" characters.

The vaudevillian allusion is relevant only inasmuch as there certainly are forces of good and evil on each question of pork barrel spending. But in Congress, the good and bad characters change places constantly.

The defenders of wasteful spending one day will be its most severe critics another day, and vice versa. The only iron rule in this melodrama is that the number of "good" characters (i.e., those for cuts) will almost always be outnumbered by the "bad" characters (i.e., those for more spending). The secret is that most of the "bad" characters remain offstage. When a spirited debate over pork barrel spending occurs on the floor of the House or Senate, several "good" and "bad" characters are plainly visible. But when the vote occurs, dozens of additional "bad" characters arrive on the scene — like extras brought in for a bit part in a play or movie — to carry the day.

These theatrics leave the public understandably confused.

The idea of describing the spending patterns of Congress in a sociological or tribal context was first introduced in 1990 by James L. Payne, a government scholar. He published an article in *The Public Interest* magazine entitled "The Congressional Brainwashing Machine." In it Payne explains that virtually everything Congress does encourages lawmakers to spend more public money. All of the cultural signals, both overt and covert, point lawmakers toward the public trough. Payne's concept of placing spending patterns in a tribal or sociological context supports my point that much of what Congress does is governed by shared customs, rituals, and an unspoken code of conduct that most voters can only faintly sense or observe.

Payne's article reveals, among other things, that congressional hearings make no room for opponents of higher spending. After studying fourteen hearings before the House and Senate, Payne found that of 1,060 witnesses who appeared, 1,014 favored spending increases. That boils down to a ratio of 145 people testifying on behalf of spending for every one person testifying against it. Of those bowing at the altar of public profligacy, 63 percent were appendages of the government (federal administrators, 47 percent; members of Congress, 6 percent; state and local government officials, 10 percent). Another 33 percent were drawn from the ever-expanding ranks of special interest groups that seek federal remedies for a variety of real and contrived social woes. (A crucial early test of how serious Republicans are about cutting spending will be visible in the kind of witnesses they call to such spending hearings. If witnesses who attack government spending are heard, it's a sign a new day may have dawned.)

Payne attempts to shatter the prevalent suspicion that special interests steer the Culture of Spending on Capitol Hill. Payne suggests instead that, as it stands now, forces within government (federal, state, and local) chart many of the publicly debated spending decisions within Congress.

Payne summarizes:

> The public supposes, because democratic theory says it should be so, that congressional views on spending are mainly affected by opinions and pressures from outside of government — from the folks "back home" or from interest groups "out there." This is not the case. Overwhelmingly, Congress' views on spending programs are shaped by governmental officials themselves.

APPALACHIAN REGIONAL PORK

Payne's analysis is largely true. My experience in Congress has revealed it over and over. The agencies created to administer programs, even those whose missions have either been completed or rendered obsolete by technology or societal advancement cannot fathom a reduction in government allocations.

That's why taxpayers still foot the bill for the Appalachian Regional Commission, an anti-poverty program tossed in as an afterthought into Lyndon Johnson's Great Society program in 1965.

The Appalachian Regional Commission is now nothing more than a public works project called by another name. Nearly half of its funds in recent years have been devoted to road construction instead of poverty programs. The commission is the vehicle for several powerful lawmakers — among them Reps. Jamie Whitten of Mississippi and Tom Bevill of Alabama and Sen. Robert Byrd of West Virginia, Democrats all — to deliver untold millions in pork to their districts and states.

Except for Bill Clinton, every President since Richard Nixon has tried to kill or cut the commission. Every year it has not only survived, it has thrived.

In the 1992 budget, for example, the Bush administration sought $100 million for the commission ($70 million less than the 1991 congressional allotment, but another example of Bush's timidity when it came to cutting spending). Congress increased that to $190 million. Of that total, $97 million is required by law to be spent in three states: West Virginia ($58 million), Alabama ($23 million), and Mississippi ($16 million). The remaining $93 million is parceled out to ten other states, leaving an average of $9 million per state.

It gets worse. In Clinton's first budget, this agent of change requested $189 million for the commission. That amount was almost the amount spent in the previous year and 89 percent higher than Bush's 1992 budget request! But that wasn't good enough. The Congress approved $249 million, or a 250 percent increase over what Bush requested in 1992 and a 32 percent increase over what Clinton sought! Of that $249 million, $93.3 million, or 37 percent, is required by law to be spent in the same three states: West Virginia ($50 million), Alabama ($13.5 million), and Mississippi ($4.6 million). Again, top leaders got their piece of the action.

I mention Mississippi only because the Appalachian Mountains end near the Tennessee-Alabama border — more than 120 miles from Mississippi!

One of the embedded truths in the Culture of Spending is that spending perpetuates itself. Once a program is enshrined in the federal budget it's nearly impossible to remove it. It doesn't matter if the program is no longer useful. It doesn't matter if there are a hundred other programs in which the money could be better spent. It doesn't matter if there are new programs that might be worth money but can't be created for lack of available funds. None of this matters.

The Culture of Spending resists encroachments on all fronts. Perpetuating the past is more important than preparing for the future. Priorities take a backseat to perpetuity.

MISSING THE TARGET

Nothing better illustrates this phenomenon than a debate that took place in September of 1993 over federal subsidies for recreational gun clubs.

Federal subsidies for what?

That's right. Since 1903, the federal government has subsidized something called the Civilian Marksmanship Program. Like many federal programs, it once served a defensible purpose. And like many federal programs, it persists even though its original mission has been fulfilled.

Congress created the program after discovering in the Spanish-American War that many of the volunteer Rough Riders couldn't adequately fire a rifle.

After the war, the army discovered it didn't have enough skilled riflemen to train the raw recruits. This was doubly vexing as the army was wasting time and money training teachers and recruits. Congress decided to subsidize gun clubs across the country to teach young men how to handle a rifle. It provided used rifles and free ammunition. In 1903, the program was probably justified because it met a temporary national security need.

I know it comes as no surprise to you that the army no longer needs skilled riflemen. High-tech machine guns have replaced rifles, and the army no longer needs or wants a steady stream of rifle-ready recruits.

But Congress does.

Congress has propped up the rifle subsidies every year since 1903. There have been three memorable attempts to abolish the subsidy: one in 1924, one in 1975, and one in 1993. Each failed, even though each set of opponents raised the very same question: Why is the federal government subsidizing recreational shooting? In all three instances, opponents said the program no longer served its military purpose and that all the subsidies amounted to was a free ride for gun owners of all ages to acquire firearms and ammunition for rifle competitions and recreational shooting.

Such arguments are not very persuasive in Washington. You need an official-sounding report to state the obvious. Without it, you lack credibility.

In 1990, Rep. Les Aspin, then the chairman of the Armed Services Committee and Clinton's first Defense Secretary, asked the General Accounting Office to see if there was any military justification for the marksmanship program.

At the time, Congress was spending more than $4 million a year on the program. The Bush budget was calling for $5 million for the next four years, or $20 million to dole out free guns and ammunition for youngsters and adults who belong to gun clubs.

A third of the budget — some $1.4 million — paid for annual shooting competitions at Camp Perry, Ohio. Who competed? Essentially, a few thousand gun club members. By and large, the same people came to the competition year after year. The GAO said about 2 percent of the program's eligible members attended. In other words, one-third of the budget was serving about 2 percent of those eligible.

What about the military role? Did the marksmanship program help the military?

A 1989 report by the House Armed Services Committee showed that only two hundred participants in the marksmanship program joined the military each year. The report said the 1990 budget of $4.7 million meant that Congress was spending $23,000 per military recruit. Furthermore, the GAO report concluded the goals of the marksmanship program — providing skilled instructors and rifle-ready recruits — were incompatible with the needs of a modern army: "Its two mobilization goals appear to have no direct linkage to Army mobilization and training requirements and plans. Army mobilization and wartime training have changed, but the [program's] mobilization objectives have remained essentially as they were conceived during the early part of the century."

This all looked pretty preposterous to freshman Democrat Carolyn Maloney of New York. She tried to find a way to abolish the program and settled on stripping the funding from the annual Pentagon spending bill.

She told the House,

> Without any compelling military purpose, this program amounts to nothing more than a federal subsidy of a sportsman's hobby. If this program is justified, why do we not have government subsidized fishing trips? Or golf fees? Or wind-surfing programs? Why not season tickets to the New York Giants?
>
> This program is a relic from a former time. Preserving it would only prove to the American people that this Congress is out of date and out of touch. It is time for Congress to bite the bullet and end the program.

Those who wanted to preserve the marksmanship program knew they were in dangerous budgetary crosshairs. Everyone was looking for quick and easy budget cuts in 1993, especially after swallowing Clinton's tax bill. Disposing of this military dud would make for great press releases back home and suggest, if only slightly, that Congress could for once end a program that had long since run its course.

The defenders of the marksmanship program needed to mount a strong defense to survive. They couldn't call on the Pentagon, because it didn't want the program. They couldn't call on the National Rifle Association, at least not publicly, because anti-gun fever was running high in Congress. The NRA gained the most from the marksmanship program and was key to its survival. The federal subsidy helped NRA members receive free ammunition and used rifles at gun clubs across the country. The NRA's clout had kept the subsidy alive for years, but invoking the NRA's name in 1993 would have cost more votes than it would have won.

To whom did the members of Congress who were protecting the marksmanship subsidies turn in their time of need?

The Boy Scouts of America.

That's right. Several lawmakers argued that the marksmanship program helped hundreds of thousands of Boy Scouts learn how to shoot a rifle. That was, in fact, true. The GAO report said that in 1989 the government gave the Boy Scouts 8.7 million rounds of ammunition, which was used to expose some 365,000 Boy Scouts to rifle training. To cut the subsidy, these members of Congress said, was an attack on the Boy Scouts of America!

Rep. Paul Gillmor, a Republican from Ohio, led the defense. He had to. The national marksmanship matches that the government subsidized were at Camp Perry, which is in his northwest Ohio district. Gillmor is an example of a lawmaker who contributes good ideas to the budget debate but has a difficult time letting go of something close to home. In 1992, Gillmor led the effort to freeze the expenses for all House committees at 1991 levels, a sane fiscal move if ever there was one. But on the marksmanship program, all Gillmor could see was the loss of a very popular four-week shooting match at Camp Perry.

He was the first to invoke the Boy Scout defense:

> How many people are served? There are 51 state associations, 1,500 clubs, 126,000 affiliated club members and that does not count the more than 400,000 Boy Scouts who benefit from [these] programs.

Another supporter, Bill Brewster, a Democrat from Oklahoma, said the marksmanship program was indispensable in helping young people learn to shoot:

> [It] reaches almost one-half million Boy Scouts and youths at a cost of only $2.5 million. If these Scouts were the only people reached by the programs it would be at a cost of only $5 per participant. However, many more youths other than Boy Scouts benefit from this program, creating an even lower cost per participant. [It] is a good program that teaches self-esteem, discipline, character and weapons safety.

Brewster is a moderate Democrat and one of only twenty-two Democrats smart enough to vote against Clinton's deficit-raising stimulus bill in 1993. (I regret that I didn't join him on that vote.) Brewster is not a spendthrift, and he has been willing to cast tough votes. But his argument on the marksmanship program was off target. By arguing in favor of the Boy Scouts, Brewster was confirming what the critics were saying: the marksmanship did nothing to augment military readiness but was merely a place where young people learned to shoot. Nothing wrong with that, but why does the federal government have to subsidize it?

Besides, I thought it was a bit offensive to use the Boy Scouts to defend this program. After all, who wants to vote against the Boy Scouts? I tried to set the record straight:

> I am a Cub Scout coordinator. All of my children have participated in the Scouting program. Prior to today, I have never heard the argument that this Department of Defense program was central to the success of Scouting. I am here today to tell you that there are gun clubs all over America that would be happy to provide this gun training service to America's youth without a taxpayer's subsidy.

As the debate wore on, another classic rationale for wasteful spending reared its ugly head. The argument goes like this: "You've voted for things I think are wasteful so I'm going to vote for something you think is wasteful."

Rep. Randy Cunningham, a California Republican, summed it up perfectly by attacking Maloney for voting for full funding of the National Endowment for the Arts earlier in the year. "A total boondoggle," Cunningham said of the NEA. "[She] voted not to cut it all and would not even cut it 5 percent. Now she wants to save, through smoke and mirrors, $5 million. Give me a break."

Now, Maloney represents New York City, the liberal but famously wealthy East Side of Manhattan. Her constituents favor funding for the arts and bigger mass transit subsidies, and are, well, suspicious of higher income taxes.

NEA subsidies are far more expensive than the marksmanship program, it's true ($170 million compared to $5 million in 1994). It's this tortured kind of logic that leads members from one part of the country to criticize spending that benefits another part of the country while at the same time defending spending in their area from the encroachments of others.

Nobody on the East Side of Manhattan cares whether the civilian marksmanship program lives or dies. But plenty of them care about NEA grants, which subsidize plays, art exhibits, and musical performances throughout New York.

Cunningham hails from San Diego and was the first fighter ace in the Vietnam War. After the war, Cunningham taught future fliers at the Miramar Naval Air Station. He values military programs and saw attempts to kill the marksmanship program as a gratuitous slap at the military culture by a New York Democrat. It goes without saying that neither Cunningham nor many of his overwhelmingly Republican constituents care much for the NEA.

This fit the pattern of the entire debate. Rural lawmakers who represent people who own and shoot firearms for sport generally favored the marksmanship program. Urban lawmakers who don't represent many people who shoot firearms for sport tended to favor killing the subsidy. I worked hard to persuade a few rural lawmakers to side with Maloney.

In the end, the vote was 242–190 against killing the civilian marksmanship program. So, for at least one more year, Congress forced the Pentagon to spend $5 million to subsidize rifle training it no longer wants and no longer needs. What's worse, in 1994 congressional barons denied Maloney a vote on the same issue . . . once again protecting this senseless subsidy.

As Robert Torricelli, a New Jersey Democrat, said on the House floor: "Now is the time to declare success. We are ready for the Spanish-American War and we can eliminate this program with real safety."

Well, maybe next time.

STEAMROLLED

Still other spending decisions are made behind closed doors. Nothing incites the bipartisan knights of the spending table more than an attack on a program one of their own has secretly inserted into the budget.

The best example of this phenomenon can be found in the dreary coal country of eastern Pennsylvania.

Scranton, Pennsylvania, is home to several things the government does not want but has to buy anyway. One of them is anthracite coal, the hardest of all known coal varieties and a staple at the turn of the century for home heating and other industrial purposes. But softer coal that produced more heat and was easier to burn — known as bituminous coal — began replacing anthracite in the 1920s. As the nation's preference for coal changed, the population in Scranton and the surrounding anthracite counties fell by a third from the 1930s to 1990s. To make up for the lost revenue, a group of powerful Washington insiders has kept this part of Pennsylvania afloat with pork barrel projects.

As a result, the biggest domestic consumer of anthracite coal is the Pentagon. It's not because it wants to be, but because it has to be. Congress requires the Pentagon to buy three hundred thousand tons of anthracite coal every year, even though the military doesn't want it. The coal is shipped to U.S. bases in Europe, where other sources of coal are plentiful and cleaner-burning natural gas is an even more appealing alternative. The anthracite program costs the Pentagon at least $63 million annually.

It all started when Daniel Flood, the vice chairman of the Appropriations subcommittee on defense, persuaded President John F. Kennedy to protect the dying industry by forcing the Pentagon to buy anthracite from Pennsylvania's Pocono Mountains and ship it three thousand miles to heat U.S. military bases in West Germany. Congress passed the law in 1963. In 1972, European nations began switching from coal to oil and natural gas, which caused less pollution. In response, Congress passed a law prohibiting the Pentagon from converting its West German military bases to oil or natural gas.

It wasn't long before Germans began complaining about pollution and offered to supply steam heat. The Pentagon quickly signed up for this cheap and clean energy. Congress blocked that move and forced the Pentagon to keep buying, shipping, and burning anthracite coal. To deal with pollution, it ordered the Pentagon to install anti-pollution devices.

Flood, who represented neighboring Wilkes-Barre and was elected in 1944, protected the anthracite program fiercely until a thirteen-count indictment alleging bribery, perjury, and influence peddling forced him to resign in 1980.

After Flood's departure, another lawmaker stepped in. His name is Joe McDade, a Republican from Scranton. The son of an anthracite coal miner and a miner himself as a boy, McDade has fought hard to keep the coal contract and the three thousand jobs it sustains.

But he hasn't been alone. He's had help from Rep. John Murtha, a Democrat who hails from Johnstown, Pennsylvania. Murtha, by far the most powerful member of Pennsylvania's twenty-three-member delegation, is also a big-time player in the House. He chairs the same Appropriations subcommittee that Flood served on as vice chairman. Tall and strong, mysterious yet plainspoken, Murtha is a former marine who jealously guards defense spending and keeps a hawk eye out for Pennsylvania projects, both military and civilian. While we have differed frequently, I must admit that Murtha has always treated me fairly and his grasp of defense issues is well respected in Congress.

Together, McDade and Murtha keep Flood's flood of Pentagon money coming to eastern Pennsylvania with that wasteful anthracite contract. In 1984, they encouraged Congress to order the Pentagon to buy a strategic stockpile of one year's supply of coal in addition to its yearly consumption. After a year, the Pentagon evaded that edict, but in 1985 Congress ordered the Pentagon to burn the excess anthracite at some thirty-seven U.S. military bases. The Pentagon estimated at the time that it would cost $1.4 billion to convert the bases' heating plants to accommodate anthracite coal.

In 1986, an independent study by the National Defense Council Foundation projected that the anthracite program — including purchasing, shipping, and storing the coal — would cost the Pentagon $5 billion by 1993.

McDade and Murtha have numerous allies in protecting the anthracite program, among them lawmakers who represent railroad unions that haul the coal to U.S. ports and maritime unions that ship it to Europe.

But the anthracite program is only one of McDade and Murtha's spending sprees. The two also joined forces to nurture, create, and protect one of the least justifiable and wasteful government projects ever devised.

It's called Steamtown USA. It started in 1984 as a public-private venture in Scranton. The city bought a collection of trains from a Vermont train collector in hopes of refurbishing them and building a tourist attraction centered on train rides through the Pocono Mountains. The city raised more than $8 million in public and private funds, but the trains proved too costly to refurbish and operate, and the tracks on which they were to ride proved equally costly to build and maintain. In two years, the city realized that Steamtown was out of steam. A failure. An expensive mistake.

Then McDade came to the rescue. He inserted a spending request that the National Park Service acquire Steamtown and spend $35 million to get it back on track. McDade slipped this language at the last minute into a voluminous bill that contained all spending and taxing measures for the entire 1987 fiscal year. There were no hearings on Steamtown.

In fact, no one at the National Park Service, which was supposed to run Steamtown USA, had ever been consulted. Before the bill was passed, the Senate reduced McDade's request to $20 million, but the dollar figure was inconsequential in the grand scheme of things. McDade got what he wanted: federal supervision and responsibility for Steamtown.

Suddenly, and without warning, the U.S. taxpayer was on the hook for tens of millions of dollars in indefensible pork barrel spending.

Over the next five years, McDade funneled $40 million to Steamtown. Each penny arrived without any congressional oversight. Theoretically, all congressional spending is subject to the approval of a policy committee separate from the powerful Appropriations Committee. These policy committees review all relevant requests and decide which programs Congress considers worthwhile. This is supposed to prevent the McDades of Congress from secretly foisting something like Steamtown on the taxpayers. But McDade dodged that process for five years by simply adding Steamtown funds to the spending bill for the National Park Service. As a member of the exclusive Appropriations Committee, he's got that kind of power.

Meanwhile, press reports revealed that Independence Park in Philadelphia, the site of the signing of the Declaration of Independence, had been closed by the National Park Service due to lack of funds.

Think about it: The Graaf House in Philadelphia, the three-story bricklayer's home where Thomas Jefferson wrote the Declaration of Independence, and Old City Hall, where the Supreme Court first convened, stood padlocked to tourists while Steamtown stood open . . . *with no tourists.*

Two years ago, I joined several lawmakers in an attempt to eliminate all Steamtown subsidies. At the time, McDade was seeking a permanent yearly allocation of $6.5 million to cover Steamtown's overhead costs. Rep. Mike Andrews, Texas Democrat, offered an amendment to reduce Steamtown's annual subsidies by $3.1 million.

Why, we thought, should the government pay for this boondoggle? It was abundantly clear that Steamtown would never make money, never become a popular tourist destination, and never celebrate anything having to do with railroads other than the "railroading" of the American taxpayer. As I told the House,

> My four kids loved the story of The Little Engine That Could. But Steamtown USA is no bedtime story, it's a nightmare for the American taxpayers. The National Park Service did not originally request this project. It's time to take the steam out of Steamtown. Over the last several years, as a result of pork barrel politics at its worst, American taxpayers have forked over $66 million to finance this venture. It's an embarrassment that this Steamtown train ever left the station. It is a shame that this project has been kept on track. Steamtown is not a national priority. It is a national disgrace. It ought to be derailed.

Predictably, our amendment provoked the knights of the spending table. Various members of the Appropriations Committee, Democrat and Republican, rallied to McDade's defense.

As I mentioned, seniority makes a difference on the appropriations committees. It's the ultimate source of power. When a member rises to a senior position on a subcommittee, he or she has the authority to spend as he or she sees fit.

That's what McDade did. He pushed Steamtown USA through because he was the highest ranking Republican on the committee that oversaw the National Park Service. There was something else at play. McDade told the *Scranton Times* in 1991: "Fortunately, Senator Robert Byrd is a personal friend of mine. We've worked close to 30 years together."

Mr. Byrd, it should be noted, is the chairman of the Senate Appropriations Committee. He gave up his position as Majority Leader of the Senate in 1988 to wield maximum control over federal spending. In his first three years as chairman, Byrd funneled $1 billion in pork barrel spending to West Virginia.

At any rate, we knew the attempt to derail Steamtown was an attack on the most powerful spenders on the Hill. But we did our best, rallying speaker after speaker to the House floor in hopes that the national news media might shed some light on Steamtown's waste or that a few nationally syndicated talk shows might make it a mini-crusade. Other examples of pork barrel spending — like the attempt to spend $500,000 for a Lawrence Welk Museum in Strasburg, North Dakota — had been defeated after *Reader's Digest* and other media outlets helped blow the whistle. But in the case of Steamtown, it didn't happen.

After the speeches ended, a vote was called on the next installment for Steamtown.

As members filed into the chamber that steamy July afternoon, McDade and Murtha worked the doors. That means they stood at the two main entrances and lobbied lawmakers before they cast their votes. As Democrats filed past Murtha, he told each one of them, "Do this for Joe. He's been good to us."

Another prominent Democrat, Rep. Charlie Wilson of Texas, worked another door. He urged fellow Texans to rescue McDade. "Joe's been helpful on our projects. Let's be helpful to him," he said.

McDade's a cheerful, roly-poly sort with an Irish wit, white hair, and a ready handshake, who is popular in both parties and beloved by Republicans. Their commitment to McDade has helped maintain his political clout while fighting a two-pronged criminal indictment. Republicans let McDade remain as the highest-ranking Republican on the Appropriations Committee even after he was indicted in May 1992 for allegedly accepting illegal campaign contributions and $100,000 in illegal gratuities and bribes from six defense contractors and other lobbyists.

(Republicans forced McDade to step down before he was to assume control of the Appropriations Committee in the 104th Congress. They did not want to explain the spectacle of having a lawmaker indicted for bribery overseeing one-third of the federal budget.)

Sadly, both Democrats and Republicans stood with McDade. The amendment to kill Steamtown failed 229–192 (eighteen lawmakers did not vote).

Now, spending like this infuriates everyone in America *except those who receive it.*

Just look at McDade. Even though he's under indictment, he was renominated in the Republican primary and won *the Democratic primary with 1,518 write-in votes!* Ed Mitchell, a Democrat who gave McDade the toughest race of his thirty-year House career, back in 1976, had this to say about McDade: "He does a good job. He brings home the bacon."

Indeed, he does. And Scranton loves him for it. In 1992, the city built McDade Park with an Anthracite Museum and the McDade Technology Center at the University of Scranton.

Nothing better illustrates the Culture of Spending than a monument to wasteful government spending (the Pentagon Anthracite contract) bestowed upon a lawmaker who isn't dead, but who is under indictment.

In Scranton, there simply is no lobby to cut government spending.

TOP SECRET

There are literally hundreds of examples of pork barrel spending in every budget, and I'm not going to bore you with this predictable story line:

powerful lawmaker brings home bacon, wins accolades from constituents, and is scorned by budget-conscious outsiders.

This is the riveting story about one of the most secretive and ruthless grabs for taxpayer money in modern history. Appropriately, it involves the Central Intelligence Agency, which prides itself on its secrecy and ruthlessness.

In the summer of 1991, a stunning story emerged in Washington that half of the entire CIA complex (situated in Langley, Virginia) was going to be moved to Charles Town, West Virginia. A new facility was to be built there at a cost of at least $1.3 billion, and up to six thousand low-level CIA employees would be uprooted from the Langley campus and shipped out to West Virginia.

The $1.3 billion price tag made it the most expensive government building project in U.S. history. And the idea of splitting CIA operations into two and erecting a second intelligence complex more than sixty miles away struck many as just plain daffy.

But to those shrewd insiders, the deal made perfect sense. It was a political gift to Robert Byrd, the powerful senator from West Virginia. He engineered the move in secret meetings with CIA director William Webster. President Bush, a former head of the CIA, silently signed off on the deal for reasons that remain a mystery to this day.

Byrd's motives were as starkly visible as the Appalachian Mountain Range that subdivides his comparatively impoverished state. Byrd wanted the new CIA complex for its construction dollars and the spin-off economic gain up to six thousand new employees would bring the region.

This reasoning is part of the myopia of the Culture of Spending. Lawmakers too often see only the benefits, not the costs of their actions. Byrd saw a glorious opportunity to latch on to some CIA funds and felt confident he could acquire them secretly.

Keep in mind the tenor of the times. By the summer of 1991, the Cold War was over and many responsible people were asking what, exactly, the CIA's new mission was going to be and how much money would be needed to fulfill it. Talk of shrinking the agency ran rampant, and not just among its legendary critics.

Before this, in the summer of 1990, the CIA told Congress it was going to study a site to relocate. In the fall of 1990, at Byrd's urging, funds were inserted in the Pentagon spending bill to pay for outside consultants to recommend sites for the new CIA complex.

The consultants did not find what Byrd hoped they might. In their first report, consultants did not mention Charles Town, West Virginia. The consultants listed two hundred potential sites. Of those two hundred, they then recommended sixty-five sites that would best fit the CIA's needs. From that list, ten were proposed as the most competitive. Charles Town,

West Virginia, was not on any of the lists. Needless to say, Senator Byrd took corrective action.

The consultants' report arrived in February of 1991. Suddenly, the CIA shifted gears. Until that time, the CIA had been looking for a place to move lock, stock, and, barrel. Now it asked its consultants to reexamine the criteria and see what would happen if they looked at areas suitable for a complex to house half the CIA campus.

Between February 1991 and June 1991, a second report was drafted. This time the consultants recommended Charles Town, West Virginia, as one of four possible sites. Not surprisingly, the other three suggested sites appeared in the consultants' top ten list from February. The only change was the addition of Charles Town.

That wasn't the worst of it. The day the CIA move to Charles Town was announced, it took the House Intelligence Committee completely by surprise. No one, not even its chairman, Dave McCurdy, Democrat of Oklahoma, knew the move was even in the works.

With amazing stealth, Byrd had won the acquiescence of CIA Director Webster and President Bush. He had even managed to secure approval for the most expensive government building project in history without having it reviewed by the Office of Management and Budget or the General Services Administration (agencies that normally have the final say on construction and property acquisition).

It looked as if Byrd had covered all the angles, that the CIA move to West Virginia was a fait accompli. He persuaded all the necessary Senate honchos to fall in line after telling them Webster and Bush were on board.

There was one thing Byrd did not anticipate and, ultimately, could not defeat. His bald power play enraged members of the House Intelligence Committee, and particularly its chairman, Dave McCurdy. He was joined by Rep. Frank Wolf, a Virginia Republican who represented many of the CIA employees who feared Byrd's power play would cost them their jobs.

McCurdy broke with tradition and held open Intelligence Committee hearings on the CIA move. Open hearings for the Intelligence Committee were virtually without precedent. The committee is among the most secretive in Washington; the very nature of its jurisdiction makes it so. Members and staff are sworn to secrecy, and breaches are serious business.

McCurdy saw, correctly, that the only way to checkmate Byrd's move was to expose his power play to the public, and, in effect, put the CIA and Webster through the wringer.

That's exactly what happened at a public hearing on July 30, 1991. Virtually every member of the committee grilled Webster and his senior advisers on the move. But before they got their chance, McCurdy reprimanded the CIA for being Byrd's handmaiden:

> What this committee cannot accept is a site selection decision that has not been examined by this body nor was part of the administration's budget request. An expenditure of public funds in the amount of $1.3 billion, one of the largest Federal construction projects in history, deserves much more scrutiny than has been provided so far. By law a covert action warrants notification to Congress and receives much more oversight than has been provided in this case.

One of the most aggressive questioners and opponents of the CIA move was Rep. Bud Shuster, the ranking Republican on the Intelligence Committee. He called the episode "reprehensible" and suggested that those involved with choosing new facilities at the CIA should switch jobs with those in charge of covert operations,

> . . . because they have run quite a successful covert operation here in keeping virtually everybody but a few people from West Virginia in the other body (the Senate, i.e. Byrd) in the dark about this; and the people in operations should be put over in facilities because their covert operations, we usually read about in the newspapers.

Shuster was, in this case, a classic example of the "good" and "bad" character in the ongoing spending melodrama of Congress. Here he played the role of a "good" guy to the hilt, excoriating Webster and his underlings and taking well-aimed shots at Byrd's hubris. He looked like a true friend to the taxpayer. And in this case he was. But Shuster was identified in a 1993 *U.S. News and World Report* article as one of the barons of pork barrel spending. He's legendary for delivering highway projects — some needed and others superfluous — to Pennsylvania through his position as the ranking member of the Public Works Committee, which doles out such spending.

Throughout the hearing, House members referred to Byrd's maneuver variously as a "handshake and nod behind closed doors" and as a "backroom" deal.

Webster defended the move limply.

Then, when Shuster asked about briefing charts the CIA reviewed in support of the Charles Town move, Webster told them they were secret documents and Congress could not see them. Ever.

Shuster persisted:

> SHUSTER: Is there anything in those charts that you would not want us to see?
>
> WEBSTER: Nothing in those charts that I would not want you to see.
>
> SHUSTER: Why can't we have them?
>
> WEBSTER: As I said, there is a traditional position by the government — by the executive branch — that internal decision memoranda are not

regularly made available. That has been the . . . that has been historically so.

SHUSTER: It certainly makes them suspect, given the circumstances that shroud this whole covert operation.

As the hearings wore on, House members from both parties bore down on Webster and his senior staff. Webster was forced to repeatedly deny what seemed to have happened: that Byrd, who requested the money to pay for the consultant, asked the CIA to change its criteria after Charles Town, West Virginia, failed to make the grade.

By the end of the hearing, Webster was whipped. He said nothing had been locked in and that it was possible the CIA move could be looked at a second time. McCurdy had succeeded in bringing Byrd's ploy out into the open.

Before the matter was settled, however, Byrd made a direct appeal for McCurdy's complicity. He summoned the young, handsome Democrat to his spacious and opulent Capitol Hill office on the first floor.

Byrd positively loves the Senate, especially the imperial trappings of being chairman of the Appropriations Committee. His office is among the largest in all the Capitol and is decorated with immense chandeliers, richly upholstered couches and chairs, thick-pile carpeting, and elegant paintings. Less an office than a Victorian drawing room, Byrd's lair reflects his infatuation with the trappings of power and his imperial sense of self-importance.

He greeted McCurdy as he entered and presented him with a bound copy of the second volume of the history of the Senate. He wrote both volumes and knows the Senate history better than any senator or any historian. He often gives lengthy history lessons on the Senate floor, lecturing without notes on the rise of democratic governments from the days of the Ancient Greeks.

Byrd began to work on McCurdy almost immediately. At first he tried to persuade him with flattery. When that failed, Byrd tried to persuade him on the merits of the move. When that failed, Byrd made elliptical inquiries about future spending needs in Oklahoma (an indirect way of suggesting a trade-off might be possible, though it was never said in so many words). When McCurdy still didn't budge, Byrd made elliptical references to spending requests in Oklahoma that were pending (an indirect suggestion that retribution was possible, though it was never so stated). When McCurdy still didn't budge, Byrd folded his cards. He bid good-bye with all the civility of a Southern gentleman, which Byrd unquestionably is.

By the time McCurdy reached his own office on the other side of the Capitol, his staff told him that the Appropriations Committee had ordered a full review of all spending programs in Oklahoma and particularly those in McCurdy's district. The Southern gentleman had lost the CIA fight, but he wasn't going to go quietly. (McCurdy lost his bid for the U.S. Senate in 1994, and Democrats will miss his fiscal conservatism. Byrd, however, won another lopsided election. And even though he won't control the Appropriations Committee in the 104th Congress, he will still have plenty of power and access to pork.)

The reason Byrd's gambit failed is that it was simply too brazen. Byrd went too far. Perhaps he assumed there were no limits to the Culture of Spending, that power was limited only by the most powerful lawmaker's imagination.

But he was wrong. There are limits. They are, however, nowhere near where they ought to be. What must be remembered, however, is the Byrd episode didn't arise without precedent. Dozens of power plays nearly as bad have succeeded and will continue to succeed in Congress. Byrd happened to cross an invisible line, one that may shift in the future and allow such abuses unless Congress reexamines the way it spends the public's money. To do that, the voters will first have to reexamine their approach to collecting money from the federal government.

Former Speaker of the House Tip O'Neill immortalized the saying "All Politics Is Local." Well, as far as most members of Congress are concerned, all spending *should be* local. Local interests come first. Not national interests. Local interests.

And every locality loves government spending. Rock-ribbed Republican districts love it just as much as bleeding-heart liberal districts. There is no constituency for cuts in this country! Only constituencies for spending.

Until voters decide to punish lawmakers for "bringing home the bacon," instead of building parks and museums in their honor, the Culture of Spending will continue to flourish.

OUTFOXING THE SPENDERS

While I admire some of the laws passed since 1982 under the guidance of the President and congressional leaders (NAFTA in 1993, tax reform in 1986, and the Social Security bailout in 1983 come to mind), I'm most fond of the ad hoc, against-all-odds efforts waged by lesser-known lawmakers that have killed wasteful programs and saved billions in tax dollars.

These stories are not nearly so well known as the big achievements or failures of the modern Congress. They are worth telling, however, because they show how dedicated lawmakers rose above the enervating cultures of Congress. These stories also provide a road map current and future reformers can follow as they attempt to rid the government of still more waste.

Nothing so undermines public trust in government as much as evidence of willful waste and neglect. Government will regain the people's trust when it proves itself willing to identify waste and able to rid the system of it.

These are the stories about young reformers and how they changed our government for the better. In every instance, the reformers confronted all of Washington's power brokers: congressional leaders, committee chairmen, government bureaucracies, and well-financed lobbyists. In addition to these visible foes, the reformers had to confront the hidden enemy of inertia.

The following stories show how the reformers overcame these formidable obstacles. Although each story is different, there are some important similarities in each successful reform: the program targeted was truly wasteful; the efforts were bipartisan; and votes were won with dogged one-on-one persuasion rather than top-down coercion.

The reformers' courage, principles, and perseverance show how Congress can and should work. I hope new members of Congress will study their strategy, adopt their integrity, and replicate their results.

SMASHING THE ATOM SMASHER

Congress killed the Superconducting Super Collider (SSC) in the fall of 1993, saving the taxpayers at least $9 billion. If it had been up to the senior members of Congress, the SSC would have survived. Moderate Republicans and Democrats with middling seniority teamed up with the freshman class of 1992 to cancel construction of a fifty-four-mile circular underground atom smasher in the Texas prairie south of Fort Worth. Scientists hoped to discover the essence of matter and, thus, reveal the origins of the universe by smashing subatomic particles into one another at the speed of light.

This is not an unworthy goal. There may be room for such projects once the government brings its budget into better balance. Even with a balanced budget, however, it would be impossible to justify the runaway costs and scandalous waste of the SSC.

When Congress approved the original funding for the SSC in 1982, the Department of Energy said it would cost $4.4 billion. In 1991 the energy department told Congress the SSC would cost $8.2 billion. This figure was suspect. That same year the DOE's Independent Cost Estimating staff calculated the SSC's cost at $11.8 billion, but the department denied congressional requests to meet privately with the cost-estimating staff. None of these estimates included the $1 billion annual cost to operate the SSC.

The first crucial vote to kill the SSC occurred in 1991. Jim Slattery, Kansas Democrat, led the effort, which lost decisively on a vote of 251–165.

In 1992 Slattery was joined by Sherwood Boehlert, New York Republican, and dozens of other lawmakers who were outraged by the SSC's needless cost overruns. (I was also an early opponent of the SSC.) A General Accounting Office report showed the project was 51 percent over budget for routine construction activities. Audits also revealed that tax dollars had paid for inexcusable perks for SSC contractors: a $35,000 Christmas party; $51,000 for catered lunches, coffee, and cut flowers; and $56,000 to buy and water office plants.

By this time it was also clear that the DOE would not obtain the projected $1.7 billion in foreign investment for the SSC. That meant the federal government's costs were likely to rise even further than the most pessimistic DOE estimates. Lastly, government audits calculated the cost of each SSC research job at $320,000.

Even with these facts, those of us who opposed the SSC found opponents in virtually every corner of the Capitol . . . and at the other end of Pennsylvania Avenue.

President Bush strongly supported the SSC and the roughly seven thousand jobs it was projected to generate. The project also had powerful backers in the Senate, namely Texas Democrat Lloyd Bentsen and Louisiana Democrat J. Bennett Johnston. Bentsen shared Bush's parochial interest in the SSC's job-creating potential. Johnston, who chaired the Energy and Water Committee, which provided all funding for the SSC, admired its job-creating potential in his home state. The powerful magnets scientists needed for accelerating the subatomic particles were manufactured in Louisiana. Moreover, the SSC was funded through the Energy and Water bill, which contained billions in pork barrel spending that many lawmakers had a stake in protecting. Any serious attempt to kill the SSC meant jeopardizing pork barrel spending for literally hundreds of lawmakers.

Under normal circumstances, these factors would have made the SSC impervious to an assault by junior lawmakers.

The tenacity of the SSC opponents and the pressure to reduce at least *some* federal spending, however, led to the SSC's first defeat in 1992. The House voted 231–181 to eliminate all SSC funding, save for $34 million necessary to close the facility. The Senate, however, voted to keep the SSC open. When negotiators from the House and Senate met to resolve their differences, the House caved in to Senate demands to keep the SSC open. Why did the House negotiators cave in? Because they were members of the Energy and Water Appropriations Committee. This committee funded the SSC in the first place. The House negotiators did not share Slattery and Boehlert's disdain for the SSC and gladly granted a stay of the SSC's execution.

Undaunted, SSC opponents tried again in 1993. This time their amendment to kill the SSC passed 280–150. Eighty-one of 114 freshmen voted against the SSC, further proof that newer members are best able to resist the Culture of Spending.

Clinton supported the SSC but with a fraction of the vigor that Bush mustered. Bentsen was no longer in the Senate, and he had a harder time lobbying for the SSC from his perch as Treasury Secretary.

Nevertheless, the Senate followed the advice of Johnston of Louisiana and again voted to keep the SSC operating. When House and Senate negotiators met to decide the SSC's fate, the House members once again ignored the will of the House and restored full project funding.

After getting his way, Johnston told reporters: "The emotional tide of the moment should not direct this committee and its responsibility to science. To walk away from this project after $2 billion has been spent would be something this country just cannot do."

Slattery knew how hard it was to win the lopsided victory against the SSC and was certain an "emotional tide" had nothing to do with it. "It was not an emotional outburst," he said. "It was the result of some damned hard work that was done member to member over a three-year period. This year, some new members have come in here and have taken their campaign pledges to cut spending seriously."

The House negotiators' decision to protect the SSC put Slattery and Boehlert in a bind. The only way to stop SSC funding was to kill the entire Energy and Water bill, a $22 billion behemoth with funding for more than one thousand water projects in virtually every congressional district in the nation. This is one of the hidden aspects of Congress that makes deficit reduction so difficult. Even after defeating congressional leaders, committee chairmen, government agencies, and well-paid lobbyists, budget cutters at times have to persuade lawmakers to kill an entire bill just to eliminate one egregious piece of pork. In most cases this is an impossible task.

Slattery and Boehlert did it though. The House voted 282–143 to send the full Energy and Water bill back to committee without funding for the SSC. On this crucial vote, only one of the eighty-one freshmen who originally voted to kill the SSC reversed his or her position. The House's rejection of the entire $22 billion Energy and Water bill stunned Johnston and the House negotiators who had helped him preserve the SSC. Unable to flout the will of the House any longer, the negotiators agreed to kill the SSC. They did exact a bit of revenge, however. The bill that passed included $640 million to close down the SSC project, hundreds of millions more than was necessary.

A BOMB OF A BOMBER

Originally, the B-2 Stealth Bomber was designed to penetrate Soviet radar and deliver massive explosives to any target behind the Iron Curtain. The B-2's payload capacity (which exceeded that of its forerunner, the B-52) and its advanced radar-evading technology were designed to deter conventional warfare. The B-2 Bomber was, according to Pentagon officials, designed to complement the United States' power and sophisticated intercontinental ballistic arsenal. The B-2 was supposed to be the bomber for the next fifty years of the Cold War.

President Reagan proposed building 132 of the bombers late in his second term. The planes cost between $600 billion and $800 billion per copy — by far the most expensive military airplane manufactured in American history. The plane was a top-secret Pentagon project, and the mystery with which the Pentagon shrouded its production left many members of Congress unaware of its enormous cost and the dubious effectiveness of its radar-evading or "stealth" technology.

That was until Republican John Kasich of Ohio and Democrat Ron Dellums of California trained their sights on the Stealth Bomber and blew it out of the budgetary sky.

It all started at an informal dinner in 1989 at the Capitol Hill townhouse of Tom Downey, a New York Democrat. Kasich and Dellums were there, as were many other House "gym rats" — lawmakers who spent their spare time lifting weights and playing basketball in the House gym. Most of the lawmakers had just left an Armed Services Committee hearing, where several witnesses had questioned the B-2's military effectiveness and its mounting production costs. In a nutshell, the witnesses had said the B-2 probably could not completely evade Soviet radar; without guaranteed "stealth" protection against Soviet radar, the B-2 amounted to little more than a billion-dollar bomber with a space-age fuselage. (Remember the bat-wing design?)

As the lawmakers lounged around in Downey's backyard, Kasich suggested it would be tough to kill the B-2 but, in his opinion, it ought to go. Dellums looked up immediately and, somewhat shocked, asked, "Why can't we kill it?"

From that point forward, Kasich and Dellums led the effort to stop production of the B-2. Congress had already paid for sixteen planes — one full squadron — so Kasich and Dellums concentrated on preventing Congress from approving funds for the other 116 bombers President Bush wanted to build.

It would have been hard to find a more peculiar political tag team than Kasich and Dellums. Kasich is a conservative Republican and the son of a letter carrier. He believes in limited government, self-reliance, low taxes, and a strong defense. Dellums is a former anti-war activist and social worker who believes in paying for more generous social programs with higher taxes and lower defense spending. Before the B-2 fight, the two lawmakers had never been political allies.

In the B-2, both found reason to cooperate. Kasich believed the B-2 would never achieve its military promise and, as such, was a grotesque waste of taxpayer money. He wanted to use the savings to reduce the deficit. Dellums saw the B-2 in exactly the same light as Kasich. But he wanted to use the savings to pay for more social programs. Neither lawmaker worried about each other's "downstream" agenda. All they cared about was grounding the B-2.

"People thought I was crazy, just out of my mind," Kasich said. "It just was not the thing to do if you were a Republican. You just didn't get involved in cutting a major defense contract, and you especially didn't get together with Ron Dellums."

Most members of Congress supported the B-2 — if for no other reason than it provided thousands of jobs to defense contractors all over the country. Also, most lawmakers believed there was no way to stop it. Once Congress agreed to build sixteen planes, most lawmakers assumed the typical weapons system inertia would take over. There was ample evidence to support the "inertia" theory. Since World War II there had never been a successful effort in Congress to kill a defense contract — regardless of its size — that the White House and Pentagon supported.

Since the B-2 was the most expensive aircraft ever produced by the U.S. military, it had the full weight of Dwight Eisenhower's "Military Industrial Complex" behind it. All of the nation's defense contractors supported the B-2. So did the Bush White House, including Defense Secretary Dick Cheney (a former colleague of Kasich in the House Republican caucus) and National Security Adviser Brent Scowcroft. The B-2 also had strong congressional backing from most California members of Congress because much of the work on the B-2 was done in southern California. House Armed Services Chairman Les Aspin, who served briefly as Clinton's Defense Secretary, also backed the B-2.

For a while, the only visible B-2 opponents were Kasich and Dellums. When the two announced their plans to eliminate all funding for the B-2 in the 1990 budget, only three reporters showed up for their press conference (all of them represented the lawmakers' local newspapers).

Kasich and Dellums then began a one-on-one crusade to persuade other lawmakers that the B-2 was a budget-busting boondoggle. They showed them testimony about the B-2's engine problems, its inability to pass its own "stealth" tests, the problems test pilots were having flying it, and the sickening cost overruns. Kasich and Dellums showed other lawmakers how much other programs would have to be cut or how much in new taxes would have to be raised to pay for all 132 bombers.

"We had nothing to offer," Kasich said, contrasting his lack of power with the favors defense contractors, White House officials, and Pentagon brass could do for lawmakers. "I told each member, 'All I can give you is a cold cup of coffee in the cafeteria. That's all.'"

Kasich and Dellums's first stab at the B-2 came in 1989 when the Armed Services Committee defeated an amendment to eliminate all B-2 funding from the 1990 defense budget. The vote was 36–16. The committee provided funds for two more stealth bombers and the parts for five future bombers. At this point, there remained a Cold War rationale for the B-2, even though early reviews suggested it could not perform the missions its designers first envisioned.

By mid-1990, however, it was clear Eastern Europe was crumbling and the Cold War was waning if not entirely over. Suddenly, the climate changed on Capitol Hill and lawmakers who once ignored Kasich and Dellums's entreaties were more interested. Even the Bush administration changed its tune. Instead of asking for 132 bombers, the administration asked for 75. Its 1991 budget called for funds to buy two B-2 bombers and enough spare parts for six additional bombers.

Shortly thereafter, Aspin announced his opposition to the B-2. It turned the entire Armed Services Committee against the bomber and made its demise virtually certain.

"The key was that we finally convinced Aspin," Kasich said. "I don't know if we convinced him the plane was worthless or that we had enough votes to beat him."

Soon thereafter, the Armed Services Committee approved a bill that limited funding to fifteen B-2 bombers and provided no funds for spare parts for future aircraft. Eventually, the 1991 budget provided money for continued stealth research but eliminated funding for all but the current fleet of fifteen bombers.

This story ends at a phone booth on a busy street near Sarasota, Florida. It was the middle of 1992, and the Bush administration was looking for a way to get a few more B-2s out of Congress.

Kasich was at a gym near Sarasota lifting weights when he was informed that Secretary of Defense Dick Cheney was on the phone. Kasich decided the subject was too touchy to discuss in the gym lobby and went outside to the nearest pay phone. He couldn't find a phone booth, so he called Cheney back from a pay phone alongside a busy street. As cars whizzed by the congressman, he connected with Cheney.

CHENEY: What are you doing in Florida?

KASICH: I'm down here pumping iron. It's the only way I can beat you, Dick.

CHENEY: I've got to have a wing. I need twenty [B-2 bombers]. Can you deal with twenty?

KASICH: I can't make a deal without Dellums. I'll check.

Congress and the administration eventually agreed on twenty B-2 bombers.

Without Kasich and Dellums's efforts, there's no telling how many B-2 bombers Congress would have bought. It's safe to say billions of dollars were saved because two lawmakers from diverse backgrounds set aside partisanship in the interest of the American taxpayer.

Four

The Culture of Hypocrisy

He who permits himself to tell a lie once, finds it much easier to do it a second and third time, till at length it becomes habitual; he tells lies without attending to it and truth without the world's believing him. This falsehood of the tongue leads to that of the heart, and in time depraves all its good dispositions.

—Thomas Jefferson

FEW PEOPLE use the word *liar* or *hypocrite* in Washington. It's not considered polite. Yet most voters accept that, on occasion, politicians will stretch the truth.

Instinctively, Americans know that it is impossible to expect the same level of honesty from a politician as they would from a priest or a bishop or a rabbi. But voters also know that dishonesty has been raised to an art form in the nation's capital. Modern politics in Washington is obsessed with the language of hypocrisy. It permeates the way we talk about budgets and taxes, education and health care, welfare and crime. Today's rhetoric is designed to delude voters into believing one thing has been done, while something entirely different has occurred.

Every elected official in Washington knows the following to be true: The federal government is almost powerless in stopping violent crime (only 1 percent of all crimes are federal crimes); the Social Security "trust fund" is being pillaged every day to reduce the size of the "real" federal deficit (and without a balanced budget, no Social Security funds are safe); all budget estimates are speculative and routinely off the mark (which is why the 1990 budget deal failed to deliver its promise of $500 billion in deficit reduction).

Yet few legislators will tell you these simple but hard truths. In pursuit of reelection, they tell you what you want to hear, not what you need to hear.

But voters are also worthy of blame in this transaction of deception. Voters routinely punish lawmakers who try to do unpopular things, who challenge them to face unpleasant truths about the budget, crime, Social Security, or tax policy. Similarly, voters reward politicians for giving them what they want — more spending for popular programs — even if it means wounding the nation in the long run by creating more debt.

Consequently, a Culture of Hypocrisy thrives in Washington.

Incumbents of both parties use it and reinforce it.

WHAT? ME WORRY?

My first encounter with the Culture of Hypocrisy occurred when I attended my first State of the Union Address. It was January 25, 1983, and I was still getting settled into my new job. I walked over to the Capitol a bit early to soak up some of the atmosphere of this most regal Washington ritual. I was awestruck and humbled by the grandeur of the Capitol and the furnishings that pay homage to the heroes and heroics of our great country: the marble and bronze statues of Washington and Jefferson, Adams and Madison, Jackson and Lincoln; and the vast and lustrous paintings capturing the greatest moments in our history.

On my way to the House chamber, I passed by the twenty-by-thirty-foot Howard Chandler Christy painting depicting the signing of the Constitution. This glorious work commands all wall space above the east stairwell on the House side of the Capitol, mere feet from the main door to the House chamber.

I was thrilled by the sight of George Washington as he stood on a small, two-tiered rectangular platform in Independence Hall, waiting for the framers to sign the declaration. Even though he shares the room with giants — Ben Franklin, Alexander Hamilton, and James Madison — Washington appears transfixed by something in the distance. He peers over the heads of the assembled delegates, supremely confident. It's as if he can see what the future holds for this new nation and is already relishing it.

Looking back on it now, it occurs to me that every President tries to present that look of confidence whenever addressing the Congress. A President attempts to set his sights beyond the paneled walls of the House, over the heads of the assembled lawmakers, and into a future he hopes will be brighter than the present. His intention is to challenge an entire nation to follow where he intends to lead.

Certainly that's what President Reagan tried to do on that January night.

I took my seat alongside Democratic Congresswoman Lindy Boggs, a woman of immense grace and political skills, who represented New Orleans. She assumed the seat of her husband, Hale Boggs, after he died in a 1972 plane crash. Lindy's husband had been a courageous reformer, a

Southerner who supported the civil rights laws of 1965 and 1968. These unpopular, but correct, positions nearly cost him his seat in 1968.

As a new member of Congress, I was eager to reform the system as well. My goal was to increase my party's interest in controlling deficit spending. Reagan's deficits appalled me; they had grown from $110 billion in 1982 to more than $200 billion in the next fiscal year. I was glad to be in the presence of a Democrat who knew what it meant to challenge the status quo.

As I listened, President Reagan told the American people that the deep recession was ending and that recovery was near. All that stood in our way, he said, was taming the rising federal deficit:

> The Federal budget is both a symptom and a cause for our economic problems. Unless we reduce the dangerous growth rate in government spending, we could face the prospect of sluggish economic growth into the indefinite future. Failure to cope with this problem now could mean as much as a trillion dollars more in national debt in the next four years alone.

How true, I remember thinking.

Then he described a budget that didn't add up. First, he proposed domestic-spending cuts that many Republicans opposed. Then he said vast increases in defense spending and sharp reductions in taxes played no part in increasing the deficit. When he did that, I saw lawmakers in both parties rolling their eyes. Some in disbelief. Others in disgust.

It's too bad the voters couldn't have seen that on their television screens.

The State of the Union ritual in the television era warps political theater in ways few other events can. When a President arrives at the House dais, framed by the American flag, positioned between the Vice President and Speaker of the House, he stands at the epicenter of American politics. All laws affecting spending and taxing — the staples of government — begin on the House floor.

On the night of the State of the Union speech or any address to Congress, the President basks in the applause of the assembled lawmakers. The theatrics give the impression that the President stands astride the Congress while it sits in obedient repose, willing and eager to transform his proposals into law.

Occasionally, this happens. Presidents have brought momentous issues before Congress and seen them turned swiftly into law. Two years earlier, Reagan had delivered a powerful and moving speech in support of his tax cuts, defense buildup, and modest domestic cuts. Congress had complied.

Now, official Washington wanted to see how Reagan would respond to the deficit his 1981 budget victories unleashed.

As I continued to watch Reagan read from his TelePrompTer, looking as confident and powerful as ever, I knew immediately that he was deceiving the American people. His budget did not match his rhetoric. He knew it. His party knew it. Everyone in Washington knew it. As I sat there, it occurred to me that not only was I a thousand miles from home, but that Reagan's budget was a thousand miles from reality. I came face to face with the Culture of Hypocrisy.

By the end of Reagan's first year in office, everyone in the White House knew — or at least had been warned — that Reaganomics would unleash deficits larger than America had seen since World War II. In fact, the Reagan deficits were the largest ever amassed by the federal government in peacetime.

Throughout his presidency, Reagan blamed Congress for failing to reduce the deficit while adamantly refusing to raise taxes or cut defense spending. His budget director, David Stockman, knew from the start that the only way to cut taxes by 30 percent and vastly increase defense spending without ruining the national balance sheet was by radically cutting spending. Reagan refused to propose the tough spending cuts, largely because a vast array of Republicans in his cabinet and in Congress would not touch their favorite spending programs.

As I look back now on Reagan's tenure, every year of which was scarred by triple-digit deficits (averaging about $200 billion per year during his eight years in office), I can only say that the closing words of Reagan's 1983 State of the Union speech said more than I ever could about the Culture of Hypocrisy and the beguiling sway it holds over this nation still:

> The challenge for us in government is to be worthy of them — to make government a help not a hindrance to our people in the challenging but promising days ahead. If we do that, if we care what our children and our children's children will say of us, if we want them one day to be thankful for what we did here in these temples of freedom, we will work together to make America better for our having been here — not just in this year, or in this decade, but in the next century and beyond.

As I heard those words, moving as they were, I knew by looking at the president's budget that he was not looking out for "our children's children."

There's something you may not know or understand about Reagan and his budgets. Not only did he never produce a balanced budget, but he never even proposed one.

What's more, Congress never, ever spent more than Reagan requested. Never.

Every time he and his Republican acolytes decried congressional spending binges, they knew Congress spent no more than the White House had requested.

Reagan's was a grand act of hypocrisy. There are innumerable discreet ones. The following are some of the most blatant examples.

REMEMBER THE ALAMO

One of the best places to start is with the Republican congressmen and senators from Texas. Throughout the 1980s they contrived elaborate slogans to suggest they opposed deficits when, in reality, they did nothing to reduce federal spending.

Most Texas Republicans say they are against wasteful government spending. They favor a balanced budget amendment. They want a line-item veto. They hate big government. They are fiscal conservatives through and through.

Except when the federal government comes to Texas. That, my friends, is a different story. When the federal government wants to spend money in Texas, the Texas Republicans just cannot get enough. Their partisan attacks on spending end at the Texas border.

Throughout the 1980s, Texas Republicans, with few exceptions, refused to cut spending for the following items:

- All defense programs. Many weapons systems and parts are built in Texas.
- The Space Station Freedom. It is projected to cost at least $30 billion by the year 2000.
- The Superconducting Super Collider. This is a highbrow science experiment to discover the origins of matter by smashing atoms together inside a fifty-four-mile circular tube buried underground near Dallas. (The original cost of $4.4 billion swelled to $11 billion before Congress killed it two years ago.)

By the way, these same Republicans refused to vote for any tax increases, and with few exceptions opposed all attempts to restrain entitlement spending.

They said one thing (that they opposed deficits) while their actions made deficit reduction impossible!

Trust me, I didn't spend much of my time monitoring Texans' budget votes. I rarely gave it much thought until late in the evening of June 10, 1992. As the House debated a constitutional amendment to balance the federal budget, Craig Washington, a Texas Democrat, rose to speak.

Debate had dragged on for nearly nine hours by the time Washington hit the floor. Virtually everything that could be said for or against a balanced budget amendment had been said. Ad nauseam. I didn't expect any new ideas this late in the day. And I certainly didn't expect the broadside Washington fired at his state and its representatives.

As he approached the microphone, at least two other Texans, Democrat Charles Stenholm and Republican Joe Barton, were on the floor. Both were avid supporters of the balanced budget amendment. Stenholm had made far more tough votes to reduce the deficit than Barton ever had, but on this night, Washington didn't give many Texans a break. Lawmakers from other parts of the nation dislike the way Texans champion the balanced budget amendment while simultaneously grabbing for every federal program they can reach. Ordinarily, Texans never attack fellow Texans for this hypocrisy.

But Washington was a rare lawmaker. Intemperate and combative. Independent and passionate. He once got into a fistfight in the Texas Legislature and almost came to blows in 1990 in the House when he rose to defend Massachusetts Democrat Barney Frank after Republican Henry Hyde of Illinois made a flip remark about his homosexuality.

There were no fights the night Washington talked about the balanced budget amendment. But, believe me, his were fighting words in Texas. Washington stunned fellow lawmakers by saying publicly what many of them have long said privately about Texas legislators:

> One hundred and fifty-six years ago on a cold gray morning in 1836 a small band of courageous men demonstrated they had what it took to balance the budget and it wasn't a constitutional amendment, it was courage. Col. William B. Travis drew a line in the sand . . . he put courage on one side and fear on the other side. We members of Congress from Texas are heirs to that legacy of courage. Courage is what it takes to balance the budget. Texas is not part of the solution here, it's part of the problem and let me tell you why.
>
> The Superconducting Super Collider is in Texas. It costs the American people $12 billion. The Space Station will cost somewhere between $30 billion and $100 billion. Where does it go? It goes to Texas; the V-22 tilt rotor aircraft, $500 million after [Defense Secretary Dick] Cheney has already tried to eliminate it and said we did not need it.
>
> The B-2 bomber is not built in Texas, but many of the parts come from there; $7.2 billion going to Texas. Government established target programs for agricultural subsidies — $3.25 billion going to Texas over the next five years; honey, wool and mohair subsidies, $1.22 million that my colleagues from Texas asked for.
>
> We do not have the courage to say no. We can balance the budget if we stop getting all these pork barrel programs going to our states, so let us have Texas say no and stop coming and hounding our friends in the Congress for all these programs to take back to Texas.
>
> Twenty-one people from Texas have the courage to sign a [balanced budget] resolution, but they do not have the courage to stand up and say no to their constituents. We do not need more programs for Texas. They beg for naval stations; they beg to keep the air force bases open; they beg to keep the Army bases open; they beg for highway money; they beg for metropolitan transportation money going to Texas. But they don't want to

> balance the budget with that, they want to balance the budget with money from some other state. They don't know how to say no. Let me say this in closing. If the people from Texas had no more courage 156 years ago than 21 of my colleagues from Texas have today, you'd never heard of the Alamo.

As Washington walked from the floor, one thunderstruck lawmaker let out a congratulatory "Whoop." Several others joined me in sustained applause. Finally, a Texan had spoken the truth!

Sadly, Washington is no longer a member of Congress. The state's oil interests and other businesspeople in his Houston district backed another Democrat in the 1994 primary, and Washington lost. As with any election, there were a number of factors involved, but Washington made himself a target by bucking the age-old compact between all Texas congressmen and senators: If it's in Texas, you vote for it. Washington's refusal to vote for projects he deems wasteful imperiled his political future. Doing what he believed was right earned him no reward from his colleagues or the voters. It's a sad but all too common occurrence in modern American politics. Following his defeat, Washington stopped participating in House votes. At one point, he missed more than thirty consecutive roll call votes. That prompted reporters to ask whether Washington's pay should be docked in compliance with House rules that bar members from willfully ignoring their responsibility to cast roll call votes. Speaker Foley refused to dock Washington's pay. It's regrettable that Washington allowed this episode to tarnish his otherwise valuable service to the House.

Soon after Washington spoke, conservative Texas Republican Sam Johnson, from Dallas, added his two cents worth. He holds the seat once held by former congressman Steve Bartlett who is now mayor of Dallas. Bartlett joined my quixotic attempts to cut government waste. Johnson isn't as independent as Bartlett. He tends to toe the GOP line and salute all Texas projects. As a person, Johnson is a man of courage and valor. He served in Vietnam as an air force fighter pilot and was a prisoner of war for seven years. He served his country bravely and my only regret is that, so far, Johnson has yet to summon the same courage when it comes to the budget:

> I tell my colleagues, this spending is like a horse running wild on an unfenced prairie. Americans don't want, don't need, and don't deserve big government debt. Congress is to blame for this mess. This body has the power to balance the budget on its own. But in the world of partisan politics and special interest groups, Congress refuses to even try. Plain and simple this amendment outlaws deficit spending. That means we'll have to cut the pork and make the hard decisions we should have been making all along.

During his three years in Congress, Johnson has supported Space Station Freedom and the Superconducting Super Collider, voted for defense spending the Pentagon didn't even want, voted against all tax increases, and still supported a balanced budget amendment.

There is still more hypocrisy, which also occurred in the context of the balanced budget amendment debate.

UNBALANCED ATTACK

In an ironic twist, the balanced budget amendment took place in the aftermath of the House bank debacle. The House was due to vote on the balanced budget amendment in early June — less than three months after releasing the names of all members who overdrew their accounts at the House bank.

The balanced budget amendment is not the answer to all of our budget problems. But it's the best place to start. Congress has proven its unwillingness to cut spending, and a constitutional amendment that requires a balanced budget is, sadly, the only remaining way to encourage this behavior. I do not believe a majority in Congress would defy a balanced budget amendment. The amendment would force lawmakers and the constituents they represent to face the tough decisions required to balance the federal budget. Under these conditions, no one could ignore the need for deep spending cuts and, quite possibly, higher taxes. Congress should have the courage to confront these choices without a constitutional amendment. But it doesn't. That's why we need it.

Supporters of the balanced budget amendment to the Constitution felt certain that voter outrage over thousands of overdrawn checks would shame Congress into action on the deficit. The bank scandal, they hoped, would provide enough public support to overcome what they knew would be an onslaught from special interest groups.

Their early soundings confirmed that hunch. Two weeks before a vote on the measure, supporters had commitments from more than three hundred House members. Two-thirds of the members in the House and Senate must approve all constitutional amendments. Balanced budget supporters needed 289 votes in the House. It appeared they had a cushion of 11 votes.

Backers of the balanced budget amendment knew there would be slippage but felt confident that they could win. Of the more than 300 votes they thought they had, 278 House members had co-sponsored the amendment. Supporters of the amendment thought those 278 votes were solid. All they had to do was hold 11 more.

Just then opponents of the balanced budget amendment, led by speaker Foley and then-Budget Committee Chairman Panetta, launched a full-blown campaign to defeat the measure. They organized the senior citizens groups and big labor to pressure Democratic co-sponsors and Democratic fence-sitters to vote against the measure.

Panetta worked tirelessly. He buttonholed members in the hallways. He plopped down next to them during floor votes. He called members. He was a one-man roving lobbyist against the amendment. To supplement his private efforts, Panetta issued a report declaring that Congress would have to approve $560 billion in spending cuts and tax increases over the next five years to balance the budget by 1997 (the current deficit projection for 1997 is $186 billion).

It was a grim picture. Panetta hoped it would scare members into backing away from the balanced budget amendment. He said most members would never support these kinds of cuts or taxes. In essence, he was calling their bluff.

"I can't stop hypocrisy," Panetta said. "But I hope at least I can expose it. If you're serious about doing a constitutional amendment, then you have to be serious about making these kind of choices." (While we differed on this issue, we agreed that a vote on specific cuts should be held at the same time.)

Meanwhile, the seniors and big labor peppered congressional offices with faxes and phone calls denouncing the amendment. In the two weeks before the vote, the AFL-CIO paid for radio commercials in eighteen states, designed to pressure wavering members to vote no. The commercials ran during the "drive time" hours for maximum voter exposure. They called the balanced budget amendment a "hoax" and warned that it would require deep cuts in Social Security, veterans benefits, and would "destroy" three million jobs a year and force increases in state taxes by shifting responsibility to the states. This was typical special interest hyperbole.

The next most powerful labor union, the American Federation of State, County and Municipal Employees (known as AFSCME), sent lobbyists to meet with members face to face. AFSCME represents part of the permanent government, hundreds of thousands of bureaucrats in state and local government. The seemingly unstoppable increase in the size of government means that AFSCME's membership keeps growing while membership in the industrial unions — represented by the AFL-CIO — keeps declining. The AFL-CIO is still the most powerful union in Washington, but AFSCME is a close second. Together, the two are a terrifying force, and most Democrats would do anything not to incite their wrath.

For good measure, five influential special interest groups sent a joint letter to members opposing the amendment.

"We really thought we had the votes, and we did," said Rep. Charles Stenholm, a centrist Democrat from Texas and sponsor of the balanced budget amendment, who has been a mentor for me and dozens of other Democrats interested in cutting federal spending. "The AARP was out there and labor. I would say they were number one and number two. That's the leadership's tool, and it's a very significant tool."

To make sure their efforts were not all stick and no carrot, top leadership officials also suggested, in a roundabout way, that they might reward Democratic co-sponsors who voted no with better committee assignments in 1993.

The stakes could not have been higher.

The Senate was readying its balanced budget amendment and, in a rare display of House-Senate cooperation, members of both chambers met before the House vote to draft an identical amendment. If both chambers passed the amendment, there would be no need to go to a conference committee, where powerful opponents of the amendment could water it down.

Senate supporters were confident that if the more liberal House approved the amendment, it would pass in the Senate and be sent to the states for ratification. If thirty-three states ratified the amendment, it would become a part of the Constitution.

"Two weeks out, we were counting as many as three hundred potential votes," said Stenholm. "Two or three days out we were counting two hundred ninety."

Then momentum began to shift. Silently, Stenholm's vote count began to slip. He had a small group of vote counters, of which I was one, double-checking the status of all the "yes" votes. For every one of Stenholm's vote counters, the leadership had one or two more lawmakers lobbying the other way.

"In that last day or two, we began to sense that some of our co-sponsors were being picked off," Stenholm said. "They weren't coming to tell us, but you can read a member pretty well."

Pressure from outside special interests and the suggestions of future House rewards proved too powerful to overcome. When the vote was held on June 11, the amendment was defeated 280–153. Not only did it fall nine votes short, but twelve Democratic co-sponsors switched and voted no.

"To lose by nine votes and have twelve co-sponsors of the bill vote no — that's pretty tough," Stenholm said. "It was one of those cases where we had the votes, and then it was 'Now you see it and now you don't.' That was one of the toughest defeats I've ever taken. Because when you have co-sponsors of legislation that had sent out press releases that had answered all of their mail that they're for it, and then turn around and vote no, that's tough."

The twelve Democrats who switched their votes became known privately as the "Dirty Dozen." Here are their names:

Frank Annunzio of Illinois (retired in 1992)
Albert Bustamente of Texas (lost reelection bid in 1992)

Joan Kelly Horn of Missouri (lost reelection bid in 1992)
Gerald Kleczka of Wisconsin (won in 1992 and 1994)
Tom Lantos of California (won in 1992 and 1994)
Matthew Martinez of California (won in 1992 and 1994)
Austin Murphy of Pennsylvania (won in 1992 and retired in 1994)
Richard Neal of Massachusetts (won in 1992 and 1994)
Jim Olin of Virginia (retired in 1992)
Patricia Schroeder of Colorado (won in 1992 and 1994)
Robin Tallon of South Carolina (retired in 1992)
Jim Traficant of Ohio (won in 1992 and 1994)

Delaware Gov. Tom Carper, who was part of Stenholm's team to win approval for the balanced budget amendment in 1992, said the top Democratic leaders and the special interests stuffed defeat into the jaws of victory.

"The party leadership — the whips, the leaders, and the interest groups — they all did a better job than our whip organization," he explained. "Too many in our group took too lightly the ability of leadership to derail the balanced budget amendment."

Carper said many amendment supporters fell for a Foley ruse. About a month before the vote, Speaker Foley said he thought the amendment was likely to pass. Foley was hoping to lull amendment supporters into a false state of security and galvanize core Democratic special interest groups at the same time. It worked.

"The Speaker said the amendment was very likely to pass, and we believed him," Carper said. "We didn't work the issue hard enough. Most of the thirty or so members in our whip organization took victory for granted. We were lucky if a third of the whip organization turned up for the meetings."

He also credited the lobbying of powerful members of the Appropriations Committee, which distributes money for all federal projects. Carper said appropriators hinted that projects Democratic co-sponsors wanted might get a friendlier hearing if they switched their vote.

"I'm sure they talked to some of the sponsors and said 'You've asked for X,Y, or Z, and whether you get it depends on your willingness not to support the balanced budget amendment,'" Carper said. "That can be a very powerful message to someone in a marginal district with a high-profile project."

Siding with the leadership, however, cost some members dearly. It was pivotal in Democrat Joan Kelly Horn's loss to Republican Jim Talent in suburban St. Louis, Missouri. In an example of powerful House Democrats mowing down vulnerable moderate freshmen Democrats, Majority Leader Richard Gephardt and powerful Democrat Bill Clay gobbled up virtually all of Horn's Democratic precincts during redistricting, leaving her to fend for herself in mostly Republican St. Louis suburbs. Gephardt then demanded Horn vote against the balanced budget amendment she cosponsored, a flip-flop that proved devastating back home.

LABOR PAINS

Sometimes you have to be a real insider to see the Culture of Hypocrisy. The next instance would be hard for all but the closest Capitol Hill watcher to detect. It weakens the institution just the same.

Rep. William Ford from Michigan was, until his retirement in 1994, the extremely powerful and liberal chairman of the Education and Labor Committee. This committee oversees all education and labor laws in this country, and Ford, a no-questions-asked labor backer, has driven the committee to extreme positions on labor laws for years. From 1974 until 1988, Ford pressed for passage of a law to give factory workers sixty days' notice before a plant could close. The bill passed in 1988 when then–Vice President Bush persuaded President Reagan to take this potentially damaging issue off the radar screen.

Ford's victory proved illusory, however, for the loyal workers on the Education and Labor Committee. After becoming chairman in 1990, he fired at least six committee staff employees without the sixty-day notice. One of them was Louise Wright, the office manager who had worked for the committee for thirty years. Her annual salary was $26,275. The other aides had less seniority; none had worked for the committee more than four years.

On May 24, 1988, when Ford was debating the sixty-day plant-closure law on the floor, he said this about dismissing workers with little or no notice: "Mr. Speaker, there isn't an American worker anywhere in this country who wouldn't want and doesn't deserve to be told sixty days before his or her job is eliminated."

Except in Congress, which exempted itself from the plant-closure legislation when it passed in 1988.

Ford's memo notifying the six committee aides of their dismissal arrived in mid-December. They were told their jobs would be vacant December 31, 1990. Ford gave the employees one-half month's severance pay.

The plant-closing law required notification from businesses closing plants with more than fifty employees or if the closure was to affect at least 33 percent of the work force. The Education and Labor Committee had a staff of 130 in June 1990. Ford believed in the principle of fair notice to employees until it came time to notify his own employees.

Within Congress, a committee chairman is something like a chief executive officer. He or she controls a small corporation and oversees a budget and large staff. After years of decrying the insensitive treatment of union workers by corporate CEOs, Ford took jobs from dedicated employees overnight. This example of forcing the private sector to do one thing while doing something else oneself is but one of the ways the Culture of Hypocrisy undermines the image of our government.

DO AS I SAY, NOT AS I DO

This example deals with an issue that evokes strong voter passions: campaign finance reform. Most voters believe elections cost too much and that political action committees funnel far too much money to candidates who are trying to hold on to their seats in Congress.

The average incumbent spent about $595,000 on his or her campaign in 1992. Pressure to reduce the cost of congressional campaigns built dramatically after that election. The 110 new members of Congress arrived in Washington after spending less than most incumbents. The simple question they posed to the entrenched incumbents of both parties was: If we can do it, why can't you?

Well, they never got a clear answer. Instead, they got a bill pushed by the most powerful Democrats in the House that makes a mockery of reform.

And why not?

The lawmaker whom Democratic leaders appointed to write the bill, Sam Gejdenson, Connecticut Democrat, was fresh from a reelection campaign in which he spent $1 million to defeat Ed Munster, a Republican challenger who spent $119,461. He defeated by less than four thousand votes a challenger whom he outspent ten to one! And this is the lawmaker who will reform the law to make it easier for challengers to compete with incumbents!

Who is kidding whom?

In 1992, Gejdenson had produced a weak bill that called for an overall limit of $600,000 on campaign expenditures. When he was in a tough race, however, he spent $400,000 more than the limit in his own bill!

During consideration of campaign finance reform in the 103rd Congress, it became clear to senior congressional aides that Gejdenson was the biggest foe of change. In private meetings Gejdenson routinely lobbied against reduced PAC contributions. This was a key sticking point between the House and Senate (the Senate wanted to ban PAC contributions while the House wanted to preserve them). Gejdenson's opposition as leader of the reform effort prevented Speaker Foley from developing a coherent House position. That delayed action for months. Ultimately,

Gejdenson relented in the closing days of the 103rd Congress. By then, unfortunately, momentum had been lost and the reform bill died days before Congress adjourned. (In 1994, Gejdenson beat Munster by twenty-one votes even though he outspent him $1,413,379 to $424,064.)

In Washington, protectors of the status quo often co-opt efforts to reform the system. Those, like Gejdenson, who advocate a $600,000 spending limit are suggesting no real reform at all while trumpeting their legislation as a revolutionary change.

As in the last case, only those closest to Capitol Hill would have been aware of this example. It is, however, another example of the gap between rhetoric and reality in the nation's capital.

STATIC REFORM

President Clinton arrived in Washington promising to be an "agent of change" and an "outsider." Unfortunately, he too has adapted rapidly to the Culture of Hypocrisy.

Clinton won the tie-breaking vote of Sen. Bob Kerrey of Nebraska on his budget bill in 1993 after hinting he would consider cutting the "automatic pilot" entitlement programs.

A few months later, the President promised Kerrey he would form a high-level presidential commission to propose cuts in entitlement spending. Impressed, Kerrey began discussing the concept with Sen. John C. Danforth, a Missouri Republican who had announced his retirement and had nothing to fear in proposing cuts in these popular programs.

The two grew excited by the prospect of a full-blown presidential panel that could provide the political muscle to persuade reluctant voters and even more skittish politicians that reforming entitlements was the only way the nation could begin to solve its deficit woes.

It wasn't long, however, before Kerrey and Danforth got the feeling something was wrong. The President was dragging his feet. Soon, leaks from the White House indicated that senior political advisers such as George Stephanopoulos and James Carville opposed entitlement cuts.

The idea of taking a serious look at cutting these programs began to dissipate. The President asked congressional leaders to appoint ten members from the House and Senate, five from each party. He did nothing to encourage Democratic leaders to appoint lawmakers with new ideas or a proven interest in tackling entitlement spending. Instead, he let them appoint the very lawmakers who had made a career out of creating, expanding, and protecting the very programs they were now being asked to cut.

Consider the following: From the House were John Dingell, powerful chairman of the Energy and Commerce Committee, which oversees

Medicare and Medicaid, and a self-described "New Deal Democrat"; Dan Rostenkowski, indicted former chairman of the Ways and Means Committee, which has shielded retirement COLAs from all but the slightest cutbacks over the years; Martin Olav Sabo, a Humphrey Democrat who has devoted his life to expanding the scope of social programs; Kika de la Garza, a Texas liberal who grew up in poverty and is fiercely loyal to farm and social programs; and Eva Clayton, a black freshman from North Carolina whose liberal credentials make her a reliable "pro-entitlement" vote for congressional leaders.

Is this a serious list?

When Republicans got wind of the Democrats appointed to the committee, they concluded — correctly — that no reforms were on the horizon and immediately lost interest. So did Danforth. He skipped the low-key White House ceremony announcing the commission. Everyone else in Washington immediately concluded the commission was nothing more than a political smoke screen.

After meeting with members of this "reform" commission, Danforth tried to leaven his depression with a bit of humor: "I've asked myself what would I bet that this commission will actually succeed. I've come up with a stick of gum. A stick of gum. That's what I'd be willing to bet that this group would actually change the law and help the country. Occasionally I've left a meeting feeling upbeat and said to myself, Maybe I'll bet *two* sticks of gum. Then I'll see someone else and say to myself, It's now down to a Chicklet. A Chicklet is all I'll bet."

During the waning days of the 1994 campaign, both parties attacked one another for possessing secret plans to cut Social Security, Medicare, Medicaid, farm subsidies, and other popular programs (in fact, the very programs Congress must reduce to eliminate the deficit). Democrats said the Contract with America meant an assault on these programs. Republicans said Clinton's own Budget Director Alice Rivlin had outlined options to reach a balanced budget that included cuts in all of these programs. Both parties disavowed any serious cuts. Both parties promised they would not cut what the public wanted to keep.

The entitlement reform commission was an effort to give the Congress real reform to chew on, but all the signs from campaign 1994 suggest voters will see more deception, less leadership, and bigger deficits.

In the end, the commission could not agree on any specific recommendations. The best it could accomplish was a letter to the President stating the obvious — entitlement costs are out of control. Even so, six of the thirty-two members refused to sign the letter. Among those who would not sign were Clayton, Dingell, and Sabo.

FOLLOW THE LEADER?

Several House leaders succumbed to the Culture of Hypocrisy during debate over the North American Free Trade Agreement (NAFTA). The trade deal was among Clinton's top international and economic priorities. It also demonstrated his willingness to confront the Democrats' most influential constituency: big labor. Clinton rightly decided that all three nations (the United States, Mexico, and Canada) needed to lower trading barriers to build stronger economies throughout North America. He also saw NAFTA as an essential link to wider trade talks to lower tariffs for the 125 nations involved in the global trading compact known as the General Agreement on Trade and Tariffs (GATT).

It was a gamble for Clinton. A loss on NAFTA would have meant a return to isolationist trade policy and would have dealt Clinton a severe setback in the eyes of our international trading partners. It also would have undercut all GATT negotiations, leaving the United States virtually powerless to force European nations to lower tariffs and subsidies.

Top Democrats in the House didn't see it that way. While Speaker Foley supported NAFTA, he did nothing to block the defections of Majority Leader Richard Gephardt and Majority Whip David Bonior (the No. 2 and No. 3 House Democrats). Gephardt and Bonior lobbied hard to defeat NAFTA. They were joined by other top Democrats, such as deputy whips John Lewis of Georgia and Barbara Kennelly of Connecticut. Bonior led the public opposition while Gephardt conducted a stealth campaign within the Democratic caucus against the free trade pact.

Bonior and Gephardt's defection struck me as hypocritical because they both led the effort to pass the Clinton budget. They said the budget bill was crucial to Clinton's success as President and that anyone who opposed it (on whatever grounds) was bringing his or her party loyalty into question. They said Democrats had no right to abandon the President at a time when he most needed to govern. These arguments and other commitments from the White House to pursue deeper spending cuts persuaded me and many others to vote for the Clinton budget.

Those of us who supported NAFTA believed Democrats should show the same loyalty that Gephardt and Bonior demanded for the budget vote. We argued that it was important for Clinton to show the nation and the world he wouldn't be cowed by big labor, that he was willing to incite a core party constituency for the good of the nation. We also argued that improved trade was critical to the nation's domestic and international economic well-being. Private conversations with Democrats opposed to NAFTA only strengthened our conviction. They repeatedly said that NAFTA was a good deal for the United States but that they couldn't support it because they feared retribution at home from the AFL-CIO and other large labor unions.

Instead of confronting big labor's scare tactics, many Democrats used them to frighten junior members away from NAFTA. Unlike with the budget, this time when the President asked top Democrats such as Gephardt and Bonior to compromise for the good of the nation, they ignored him. This episode again revealed the do-as-we-say-not-as-we-do attitude that is so prevalent on Capitol Hill. With the help of House Republicans, the House passed NAFTA by a comfortable margin.

It was the only time the White House reached out to House Republicans, and it worked. In this episode House Minority Whip Newt Gingrich proved an able and trustworthy advocate for the White House and free trade. He surprised those of us who, judging by his previous behavior, feared he would scuttle NAFTA in an attempt to wound Clinton politically. Gingrich proved he can put partisan considerations aside and do what's right for the country. I only wish he would do so more often.

MIS-BEE-HAVIOR

It would be unfair to exempt myself from the Culture of Hypocrisy. I fell prey to it many times. The worst example is my silly devotion to a wasteful agricultural subsidy for beekeepers.

The subsidy started during World War II, when sugar was scarce, and the military was using beeswax to waterproof ammunition. I voted for the subsidy for years even though I knew it was unnecessary. The subsidy kept honey prices high to ward off cheaper imports and to maintain stable pollination patterns throughout the nation. This caused two problems: A handful of the largest and most profitable beekeepers garnered most of the subsidies; and the subsidies encouraged overproduction because the government had also agreed to buy surplus honey.

I talked myself into this hypocritical position in the same way most lawmakers do. I spent all of my House career on the Agriculture Committee, which oversees all farm subsidies. I felt the honey program was so small in comparison to the entire committee budget that it wasn't worth cutting. The subsidy cost $89 million in 1986, the most expensive year on record. The nation spent $59 billion on agriculture programs that year, meaning the honey program made up less than two-tenths of 1 percent of the agriculture budget. In most years, the subsidies cost $20 million.

The honey subsidy's biggest foe was Rep. Silvio Conte, a Massachusetts Republican. Conte grew up in Pittsfield and had represented western Massachusetts for thirty-two years — long after his district and the state had become one of the most reliably Democratic regions in the nation. Conte voted as a liberal Republican but pushed for several internal reforms — including waging a lengthy battle to shrink the size of the Capitol police force — and combed appropriations bills for shameless pork barrel waste, such as the notorious Lawrence Welk museum.

Conte was the best phrasemaker in the House. He could out-pun anyone. For years I listened to his pun-filled speeches against the honey subsidy and knew Conte was right. Still, I voted with my committee and backed the program almost every time.

In 1985 Conte sought to limit the honey subsidy to $250,000 per year. He would have preferred to kill the subsidy, but the best he could hope to get through the House was shrinking the subsidy. It was the one time I supported Conte.

I'll never forget his speech that year:

> I think everyone gets stung once or twice in their life, but this country is getting stung over and over again. Now the bees are getting into the act. Why, just last week in Hollywood, Florida, when the bees found out how the Americans are being robbed by this program they got out of their keeper's truck and refused to pay the toll on the Florida turnpike. I tell you these little fellers are in revolt over the way we raise the price on their diligently created product. Help me restore some dignity to the little bee and let's swat this program once and for all.

Conte's attempt in 1990 to phase out the honey subsidy over four years failed on a vote of 215–178 (39 lawmakers didn't vote). I voted for the honey program and have regretted it ever since. Conte died later in 1990. He didn't live to see Congress kill the honey program, which it did in 1993 by a vote of 344–60. The vote fulfilled one of Clinton's campaign promises. The honey subsidy was the only program out of the nation's $1.5 trillion budget he proposed abolishing when he ran for the presidency. I voted to kill the program not so much to support the President as to honor Silvio Conte.

HALLMARK

The vast majority of lawmakers (myself included) have at times lapsed into hypocrisy. Voters would have more regard for Congress if legislators on a more consistent basis practiced what they preached. I want to highlight one House lawmaker who truly lives his convictions.

Tony Hall has found a unique way to bring his Christian convictions to politics without compromising the necessary legal and political barriers between the church and state.

Hall is a Democrat who represents Dayton, Ohio. Hall became a born-again Christian in the early 1980s and decided to devote most of his energies in Congress to alleviating world hunger. This is not an issue that starts many fires on Capitol Hill. Viewed through the lens of today's increasingly cynical political periscope, it's a loser; you won't succeed and you won't get any credit for trying. Hall was undeterred throughout the

1980s and redoubled his efforts after the chairman of the House Select Committee on Hunger, Rep. Mickey Leland, a Texas Democrat, died in a 1989 plane crash, attempting to deliver food to starving Ethiopians. Hall replaced Leland as Hunger Committee chairman. Among his other efforts, Hall called for United Nations intervention to aid starving Somalians in February of 1992 — nearly a year before the United States intervened.

Hall didn't ignore hunger at home. During his term in Congress he founded a Gleaners operation in Dayton (in which volunteers pick fresh vegetables that mechanical harvesting machines miss and deliver them to the poor), assisted a senior citizens food program, and founded Operation Food Share (which picks up unused but edible food from hotels, hospitals, country clubs, and restaurants and delivers it to Dayton food banks).

In early 1993, the House tried to abolish Hall's Hunger Committee as part of a meager first step toward reducing the number of House committees overall. It was easier to kill a committee such as Hall's because it had very little visibility and few members cared about it. Hall knew he didn't have the votes to stop the House. Instead of sulking, Hall staged a twenty-one-day hunger strike to increase congressional awareness of world hunger. Some people might have gone on a hunger strike to keep control of the committee, but Hall knew that doing so would undermine his real message: that Washington should do more to alleviate hunger — at home and abroad. Hall lost more than twenty pounds before a promise from the World Bank and the Department of Agriculture to do more to address world hunger. In the process, Hall exposed Washington's indifference to hunger. His courage and sacrifice shamed a political system that is infatuated with glossy, high-profile issues and bored by those issues that persist and refuse to yield to blithe thirty-second sound bites.

No single culture in Congress has disillusioned me more than the Culture of Hypocrisy. It has left me discouraged and sad and full of shame. How can our leaders do these things, I have often asked myself. How could we fail the Founding Fathers like this?

As I prepare to leave, the Culture of Hypocrisy is thriving. It seduces most who come here: Republicans, Democrats, members of congress, senators, and Presidents.

In this environment, even when Congress does do something right, the voters do not believe it. Every political utterance is now suspect. Jefferson warned that a culture of lies would lead to the truth no longer being accepted. That is the real cost of today's Culture of Hypocrisy.

Five

The Culture of Fear

We must not in the course of public life expect immediate approbation and immediate grateful acknowledgment of our services. But let us persevere through abuse and even injury. The internal satisfaction of a good conscience is always present, and time will do us justice in the minds of the people, even those at present the most prejudiced against us.

—Benjamin Franklin

THOSE WORDS are as true today as when they were first spoken by Benjamin Franklin. Doing what they know to be right often places lawmakers at odds with popular opinion and undoubtedly raises the ire of certain special interest constituencies. This leads to a Congress that is largely risk-averse. A Congress where lawmakers are too often driven to cast the "safe" or "popular" vote for fear of losing their jobs.

The truth is that popularity polls and special interest groups create a Culture of Fear in Congress.

Sadly, poll taking is an integral part of decision making within Congress. Instead of trying to shape public opinion, many lawmakers allow themselves to be shaped by it.

Many voters complain that lawmakers are withdrawing from the public, becoming — as is so often alleged today — out-of-touch with voters' concerns. Quite the opposite is true. The Culture of Fear is a reaction to the whims of an electorate that sends mixed signals and grows enraged when lawmakers fail to satisfy its irreconcilable demands.

FISHING POLLS

Contrary to the suspicions of many, Congress's problem is not that it doesn't respond enough, but that it responds too much. Too easily. Too submissively.

There are many ways in which Congress is isolated from the general public but awareness of and sensitivity to public opinion is not among them. Whether the electorate is agitated or sedated, members of Congress are constantly measuring its preference for or opposition to the issues of the day.

The sophistication of polling has institutionalized decision making to tranquilize anxieties rather than solve problems. Modern polling can and often does subdivide the language of policy into words that pacify or inflame. Members of Congress use the language according to their needs: inflame if they oppose a policy, pacify if they support it. By using the words that pollsters tell them "connect" with the voters, politicians play to the voters' uninformed hunches rather than appealing to their intellect and exploring new approaches. In a sense, politicians use polls to fish for the words and policies the electorate finds most enticing.

Lawmakers do not do this because they are born liars or congenitally venal. They do so because modern politics has taught them that their electoral popularity is intimately linked to their ability to respond and adapt to the passions of the day. If a lawmaker ignores a particularly hot topic or disagrees with the pulse of the people, he or she risks inciting political opposition he or she otherwise wouldn't encounter. Politics wouldn't be this way if voters did not make so many irrational demands and if politicians wouldn't oblige them. In this regard, voters and politicians have conspired against themselves.

This conspiracy feeds on itself. When lawmakers tell voters what they want to hear, voters grow ever more confident that they are right. This confidence breeds an intellectual and political rigidity that resists new ideas. Too often, politicians use polls to determine what people want to hear rather than telling them what they need to know.

Polling dominates decision making in the Clinton White House as it has in no White House before. In 1993 the Democratic National Committee paid pollster Stan Greenberg nearly $2 million to learn what the public wanted to hear, so Clinton would know what to say. (But consider this: If polling is designed to enhance a politician's appeal, why have Clinton's popularity ratings remained so low? Perhaps voters today are looking for leadership instead of poll readership.)

Greenberg's $2 million dwarfs the $216,000 George Bush spent during his first year in office. It's also more than Republicans spent during Ronald Reagan's White House years, when, it was widely assumed, polls drove much of the President's agenda.

According to figures at the Federal Election Commission, the White House pays Mr. Greenberg $50,000 a month as a political consultant and buys three or four polls per month — ranging from $10,000 to $40,000 apiece. The White House also buys three to four focus group sessions per month. In a focus group, a dozen voters are paid to discuss issues of the day, and a professional communicator tries to elicit their deepest feelings about the issues under discussion. The groups' conversation is recorded and videotaped, and pollsters study the tapes to measure the emotion and language voters associate with certain issues.

When Clinton delivers a major speech, Greenberg registers voter reaction on a handheld device called a Dial-a-meter. Greenberg also organizes focus groups to deconstruct the President's language to see which words appeal and which repel. These sessions led to a major scrubbing of the White House's health care pitch: The words *universal coverage* and *employer mandates* were replaced with *real insurance reform* and *health benefits guaranteed at work*.

Such polling led the President to embrace the so-called "Three Strikes and You're Out" portion of the crime bill. This is a classic example of using polls to craft language that will pacify voters while failing utterly to solve the underlying problem.

The "Three Strikes" provision in the bill will affect a fraction of all federal crimes and, as such, do almost nothing to deter violent street crime. But it's great rhetoric. Greenberg's polls showed that it's what voters wanted to hear. Something tough. Well, who can blame the voters? They are terrified to walk the streets at night and yearn for some recognition of their plight. Trumpeting "three strikes" made it appear that Clinton recognized their suffering and is willing to get tough. When it comes to polling for the White House these days, sound bites count for more than substance.

THE CRIME OF POLITICS

There are countless examples of how fear of voter disapproval has conspired to throttle real reforms or led to political pandering that only deepens voter frustration with government.

The crime issue is one of the best examples. At a political level, it erupted in late 1993 after Washington politicians saw that it proved pivotal in two elections: Republican Rudolph Giuliani's defeat of New York City Mayor David Dinkins, and Republican George Allen Jr.'s victory in the Virginia gubernatorial race against Mary Sue Terry. Increased media attention brought crime to the top of the voters' concerns throughout 1994.

A bizarre symmetry existed here. Voters were legitimately concerned about the rise of heinous and senseless crimes. However, the ghastly and random nature of this violence overshadowed the truth about the crime rate in America, that is, that the total number of crimes declined by 3 percent from 1992 to 1993. Nonetheless, voters had real and legitimate fears about violent crime.

Lawmakers in Washington feared reprisals if they didn't persuade voters they were in touch with their fears of violent crime and prepared to do something about it.

Simply put, voters were afraid of criminals, and politicians were afraid of the voters. What happened next is a classic and lamentable consequence of the Culture of Fear.

Everyone from the President to the most junior member of Congress began talking about fighting violent crime. President Clinton and Republican and Democratic congressional leaders developed new rhetoric and supposedly new policies to deal with crime. It seemed Washington was in a bidding war to see which party could offer the toughest crime-fighting measures.

Rarely did anyone mention that the federal government can do almost nothing to stop crime in the streets. Federal crimes represent 5 percent of all crimes committed in the country. With the exception of the 102nd Congress (1991–93), the Congress has passed a bill to fight crime in America every two years for the past twenty years. In fairness, this has put a crimp in federal crime. The laws have done little, however, to deter the street crimes that terrorize most citizens.

That's because states and cities fight street crime. They pay for the police officers on the street. They build the prisons. They enforce the laws that most criminals violate. With the exception of providing direct federal aid, Congress can do very little to help states and cities fight crime (and with a huge federal deficit, where would it get the money?). Even if fully funded by Congress (which is doubtful), the ballyhooed addition of one hundred thousand police officers contained in the 1994 crime bill won't do much for local communities. The officers will be added gradually over the next six years, and even the big cities will add fewer than ten officers per eight-hour shift.

Instead of telling voters this truth, Washington politicians instead passed another crime bill, thus falsely ratifying the fiction that the federal government can do something to stop crime in the streets.

In many instances, voters expect lawmakers to respond rapidly to their concerns and follow, as if they were domestic servants, the instructions of the vocal majority. This shatters one of the foundations of our representative democracy and the ways the Founding Fathers hoped Congress would respond to the people.

Personal servants have no right to deny or ignore the whims of their masters. Public servants have a far more complex political and, in this nation, constitutional obligation. They must measure the convulsions of public opinion in their districts against the needs and desires of the nation as a whole. Sometimes they will favor the district and other times they will side with the nation's needs. This is a lawmaker's legitimate role in national policy-making. Voters should be far more tolerant of this calling than they are today.

In *Federalist* No. 71, Alexander Hamilton explained the duty of America's new lawmakers:

> The Republican principle demands that the deliberative sense of the community should govern conduct of those to whom they entrust the management of their affairs; but it does not require an unqualified complaisance to every sudden breeze of passion, or to every transient impulse which the people may receive from the arts of men, who flatter their prejudices to betray their interests.

On far too many issues, voters have come to demand that lawmakers slavishly respond to the latest popular whim. Today's methods of measuring public opinion leave little room for contemplation. National television networks take polls on all variety of issues on a national, regional, and local basis. Rarely are these polls designed to broaden the understanding of an issue. Rather, they are meant to gauge the mood of the electorate. Polling measures opinions, not convictions. In most cases the issues involved are far too complex for the respondents to have a well–thought out position. Instead, they have feelings or "gut" reactions to certain ideas. This is what polls tend to measure.

Of course, opinions come and go, but convictions tend to stick. Polls collect feelings from a small number of voters and from these jumbled sets of feelings, professional pollsters derive a majority "opinion." Poll-conscious politicians adopt public positions to identify with the "opinions" registered by pollsters. In this way, when a segment of the population is aroused by a certain issue, it can force convulsive change. But this is not as good as it sounds.

CATASTROPHIC REVERSAL

Case in point: The Medicare Catastrophic Coverage Act. Enacted 1988. Repealed 1989.

Congress revoked a law providing catastrophic health insurance to the elderly not because the law failed to provide the coverage but because it forced those who received the coverage to pay for it.

On the catastrophic health insurance bill, lawmakers failed to heed Alexander Hamilton's wise counsel. The bill providing umbrella coverage to protect the elderly from the financial ravages of catastrophic illness initially drew broad bipartisan support in Congress. It was drafted with the support of the nation's most powerful advocate for the elderly, the American Association of Retired Persons. The bill capped the costs of hospitalization and doctor's bills related to catastrophic illness at $2,000 per year and for the first time provided benefits for those who spent more than $600 per year on prescription drugs.

Within one year, the law vanished.

Why?

An angry cohort of Americans, wealthy retirees primarily, objected to paying for the new benefits the law provided. Some already had catastrophic health insurance and resented having to pay higher Medicare premiums — in some cases as high as $800 per year — to extend this insurance to those without it. These enraged seniors took to the streets and hounded members of Congress who took part in writing the bill.

In one memorable encounter, a frothing mob hurled eggs at Dan Rostenkowski, then the chairman of the Ways and Means Committee, which drafted the law, and beat the roof of his car with wooden signs as if it was a snare drum.

This vocal cabal, representing a fraction of all those covered by the new law, forced Congress to undo in less than one year the single-largest expansion of the Medicare system since its enactment in 1965. It was a stunning and altogether regrettable display of how willing Congress is to respond to the loudest and most aggressive petitioners.

Regrettable?

Yes. Congress abandoned more than a law in this case. It killed a noble principle that was trying to reemerge after being rendered obsolete by the dawn of the Great Society. The principle was that new government benefits should be paid for, at least in part, by those who receive them, and those with larger incomes should pay a larger share of the cost.

This pay-as-you-go principle had been pushed to the verge of political extinction by the Great Society's ephemeral promise of infinite benefits and finite costs. Congress tried, courageously, to resurrect fiscal responsibility, but was bullied by just the kind of mob Hamilton and other Founding Fathers cautioned the Congress to resist. Instead of protecting the pay-as-you-go principle from a vocal revolt, lawmakers surrendered. Enough decided there was no point in defending the principle if it meant risking their jobs in the next election.

I do not object to voters dumping benefits they don't want to pay for. What disappoints me is the knowledge that the elderly would have gladly accepted the benefits if Congress had not made them pay — the deficit be damned.

Congress has taken this lesson to heart, and that explains why no significant attempts were undertaken to cope with health care difficulties for the aged or anyone else for the next five years. Much of the paralysis that affected the 1994 debate about health care reform resulted from the deep-seated fear politicians have about asking voters to pay for a benefit they say they want.

FALSE PROMISES

The Culture of Fear is most noticeable when Congress tries to wrestle with the budget. It is here that Washington politicians try to accommodate two demanding masters. What's left at the end of the day are efforts that pacify the electorate but fail to solve problems.

By overwhelming margins Americans say they favor amending the Constitution to require the President and the Congress to produce a balanced budget. When Presidents and the Congress attempt to reduce the deficit, either by raising taxes or restraining spending, many of these same voters oppose these measures.

Politicians know the only way to reduce the deficit permanently is by enacting both dramatic spending cuts and tax increases. For starters, the cuts must include a reduction in benefits to Social Security, Medicare, Medicaid, civilian and military pensions, and farm subsidies. The taxes must be broad-based since taxes on the wealthy alone will not raise sufficient revenue.

The polls show voters oppose cutting these popular programs by margins of nearly eight to one. The most powerful special interest groups in Washington are those determined to protect these benefits from *any* encroachment, whether it comes from the White House or the Congress.

Consequently, lawmakers avoid them as they would a growling dog in a dark alley. Taxes aren't an easy sell either.

The result of this silent stalemate is that Congress passes many laws to reduce the deficit (there have been seven since 1981), knowing they will fall short of the mark. Lawmakers do this to "prove" they are responding to voter concerns to reduce the deficit. By exempting popular programs from cuts and raising taxes only at the margins, however, these efforts simply confirm the electorate's belief (wrongheaded as it is) that Congress can balance the budget without radical reductions in spending or dramatically higher taxes.

In the days before the midterm elections in November of 1994, Democrats and Republicans fought over how each party's policies would affect the deficit in the future.

It began when more than three hundred House Republican candidates endorsed the Contract with America, a ten-point plan that included, among other things, a pledge to reduce taxes on families and the elderly while increasing defense spending and approving a balanced budget amendment.

Democrats accused Republicans of plotting to cut Social Security and Medicare. This accusation carried immense political punch because it played on voter fears of Republican hostility to these programs. Republicans said they never pledged to cut these popular programs. Democrats countered that these cuts were the only way Republicans could finance their other costly objectives, namely cutting taxes and raising defense spending.

In the midst of this partisan crossfire, Clinton's new budget director, Alice Rivlin, drafted a memo that outlined what Clinton would have to do to reduce the deficit significantly by the year 2000. It was swiftly leaked to the media. To no one's surprise, the Rivlin memorandum called for massive reductions in spending for Social Security and Medicare and higher taxes. Republicans seized on this memorandum as proof that Democrats had secret plans to raise taxes and slash government programs — actions Republicans had been accused of advocating, but, in fact, had never proposed.

Clinton swiftly disavowed the memorandum and pledged he would never reduce Social Security benefits.

The entire episode offered fresh evidence that neither party is willing to confront the difficult choices inherent in reducing the deficit. Instead, both parties prefer to posture for political gain and indulge in fantasy stories that pacify the public but ignore the danger deficits pose to all Americans.

The Culture of Fear dominates the budget debate.

WHERE'S THE TOTEM POLE?

There are many monuments in Washington. Almost all of them are made of marble or bronze. There are no totem poles. I think there should be at least one. One totem pole that tells the story of this nation's fiscal policy from 1981 to 1993.

You can find totem poles in the northwestern part of the United States and Canada. Some of the earliest inhabitants of the continent carved them. Not all totem poles tell stories, but the best-known ones do. More accurately, these totem poles convey the history of an entire family or tribe through pictographs — faces and symbols carved from top to bottom on a majestic wooden spire. Each pictograph carries a certain symbolic meaning or message. When combined with others, they explain many things about the development of a family or tribe. The totems build on various significant events to recount a family's or tribe's memorable triumphs and tragedies. They become a memorial to their struggle, a permanent narrative of their saga.

Only those who understand the prevailing customs of the family or tribe can translate the symbols their totems have left behind. To the uneducated, the pictographs may appear to be works of art or quaint tribal oddities . . . not the historical monuments those who carved them intended them to be.

Let me explain why we need a totem pole to the federal deficit and debt.

Within the vast culture of Congress, there is a small clan of budgeteers. These men and women devote much of their legislative career to studying the baffling jargon and stultifying methods of the federal budget. In the process, they develop customs quite separate from non-budgeteers and learn and embrace the Orwellian language of budgeting (a cut is an increase, a tax is a contribution, and spending is an investment).

This clan has left behind several budget "deals" between 1981 and 1993. All captivated those inside the Beltway; some even attracted attention beyond the Beltway. There was the Reagan Revolution, the Bush budget summit of 1990, and, of course, the Clinton budget of 1993. These budget fights teach us much about how and why this great nation currently faces deficits of nearly $200 billion and will continue to see deficits of this magnitude until the year 2000 and beyond. However, one failed budget deal, in 1985, tells the best story.

If we could have one totem pole, it should explain what those lawmakers who were part of the clan of budgeteers were thinking and contemplating in 1985.

I imagine there would be three symbols and the faces of three people to tell the story.

The symbols would be as follows:

1) The face of an old person (sex doesn't matter; simply a carving of a venerable elderly person wearing a slightly hostile expression).

2) A tank with a turret pointed in one direction and a rocket or missile flying above it aimed in the same direction.

3) A ballot box (nothing fancy, just a simple square box with a small opening in the top).

The faces would be as follows:

1) Sen. Bob Dole, Kansas Republican and Majority Leader of the United States Senate in 1985. His expression would be fierce and determined.

2) President Ronald Reagan. Instead of looking placidly confident, Reagan would appear frightened by some distant adversary just beyond his sight (his brow wrinkled, his eyes a bit narrowed, his mouth slightly puckered over a clenched jaw).

3) Tip O'Neill, the jolly elder statesman of Democratic liberalism. The Speaker of the House would be his typically cheerful self, looking as if he'd just told a great anecdote to a roomful of South Boston Irishmen.

The story this portion of the totem would tell goes something like this.

It's 1985 and the Senate Republicans are terrified of the federal deficit, which is projected to exceed $213 billion (at the time, a scandalously high figure). They pester their newly reelected President to seize his forty-nine-state landslide victory and blaze a new path toward deficit reduction, the missing peg of his three-legged design for national renewal in his 1980 campaign — economic growth, a strong national defense, and a balanced federal budget.

Reagan sets a one-year target of $50 billion in deficit reduction, but adheres to two core principles: continued increases in defense spending and no tax increases. Even when top advisers tell him Congress won't support his social cuts without some give on defense or taxes, Reagan remains nonplussed. His mantra remains *no taxes, more defense. No taxes, more defense.*

That means Reagan's budget, with its $50 billion in non-defense cuts, dies on arrival. Even Senate Republicans won't vote for it. While it's easy for the Republicans to decide what they're against, they can't decide what they're for.

The Senate budget debate drifts aimlessly from January to April — well beyond the deadline for putting the budget into law. In desperation, Republicans beg the White House to give a little on defense. Their fruitless labors to craft a new budget reveal one inalterable rule of budget politics: voters won't tolerate social spending cuts unless there's a cut in military spending. Again, Reagan says no.

The chief Republican in the clan of budgeteers is Pete Domenici of New Mexico. He was never very fond of the 1981 tax breaks, and ever since he has been trying to shrink the deficits they helped create.

Domenici comes up with a plan, which he sells to fellow Republican budgeteers. It's an ambitious and politically risky proposition. It promises $56 billion in immediate deficit reduction and nearly $300 billion in cuts over three years — by far the largest package of its kind since the Reagan tax cuts. If it passes, the deficit will fall to less than $100 billion by 1988.

There are no tax increases.

But instead of giving Reagan the 6 percent increase in defense spending, Domenici only gives him 4 percent. That's enough to keep pace with inflation. For the next two years, Domenici wants to cut Reagan's defense budget by 5 percent. His plan still allows for 3 percent growth above inflation in those two years.

On top of that, Domenici agrees to eliminate the thirteen civilian programs Reagan wanted to abolish and freezes Social Security benefits at 1984 levels.

The Social Security cut is far and away the most hazardous proposal. By eliminating a cost-of-living adjustment, Domenici proposes freezing the benefits of some thirty-six million Social Security recipients. By the mid 1980s, Social Security cost-of-living adjustments are the costliest and yet most passionately protected of all federal benefits.

They began in 1972, a presidential election year. First, Congress boosted Social Security benefits by 20 percent. Then it approved cost-of-living adjustments pegged to the annual inflation rate. Congress raised base benefits by 5.9 percent in 1973. In the election year of 1974, Congress raised base benefits another 21 percent.

This binge transformed Social Security benefits from a meager safety net into a steady fiscal hammock. The benefits lifted most elderly Americans out of poverty and propelled some middle class elderly into a life of leisure their parents could have only dreamed of.

Domenici times his proposal to take advantage of record low inflation, which was running at 3.7 percent in 1985. The Social Security freeze is scheduled to take effect in January of 1986. The proposed cost-of-living adjustment cut would cost the average family $81.40 per year (or $6.78 per month) and the average individual $66.60 per year (or $5.55 per month).

The ensuing debate, however, is not going to be about math. It is going to be about politics. And the bottom line is this: Domenici's plan reduces the buying power of 36 million elderly Americans, many of whom vote, while maintaining the Pentagon's buying power.

Nevertheless, Domenici's plan wins the instant support of Bob Dole, a World War II hero and native of Russell, Kansas. Dole's heartland Republicanism always feared runaway deficits. He believes voters will reward Republicans for taming the deficit while the economy is growing.

Dole sets about finding votes for the Domenici plan. It isn't easy. While most Republicans favor the concept of reducing the deficit, they have different ideas about how to do it. Some want deeper cuts in social programs. Others want deeper defense cuts. Still others want tax increases.

The Senate debates the budget for two weeks while Dole delays a vote on final passage because he can't find enough votes to win.

When Dole finally finds the votes, or at least thinks he has found them, he calls for a vote. The stakes are higher than they've ever been for Senate Republicans under Ronald Reagan. Republican senators have never voted on spending cuts of this magnitude. A Republican Senate leader has never forced such a compromise on Reagan. Never before have Republicans, especially the twenty-two who are to seek reelection in 1986, taken such a big risk in voting to scale back Social Security benefits.

It is 1:30 A.M. when the five bells ring, summoning senators to the chamber. Eyes bleary and faces flecked with fatigue, the senators — especially the Republicans — know they are witnessing something historic.

"I thought it was a major event," recalled Sen. John Danforth of Missouri, a moderate Republican who had long advocated deficit reduction. "I walked over to [R.I. Republican] John Chafee and told him 'This is big.'"

It will be close. Closer than close. It could end in a tie . . . or Dole might lose by one vote. To be safe, Dole retreats to the Republican cloakroom to alert California Republican Pete Wilson, who is at Bethesda Naval Hospital recuperating from emergency surgery to remove a ruptured appendix. (As a precaution, Dole had telephoned Wilson earlier and asked Wilson if he could vote if things got so tight that they might lose. Wilson had assured him he could.)

An ambulance ferries Wilson to the foot of the Capitol, and a small platoon of Senate officials watches as orderlies haul Wilson's stretcher from the ambulance, place him on a gurney, and roll him into the Capitol. Covered by a pale yellow blanket and visibly groggy, Wilson is wheeled into Dole's office. There, orderlies lift him into a wheel chair. They transfer an intravenous bottle from the gurney to a small aluminum pole on wheels.

As the vote count winds down, they roll Wilson into the Senate chamber. He is met by a standing ovation of senators and Senate staff. He sits slumped in the wheelchair, the intravenous bottle swaying silently above him on that thin aluminum pole. The vote is 48–48 when the clerk calls Wilson's name.

On the brink of delirium, Wilson brings down the house with a bit of deadpan humor: "What is the question?"

Wilson votes aye.

That makes it 49–48. Then Spark Matsunaga, a Hawaii Democrat, dashes from his office to vote against the budget.

49–49.

Vice President Bush, who is presiding over the Senate, casts the deciding vote.

50–49.

The budget passes. Dole wins.

But that's only part of the story.

On the other side of the Capitol, House Republicans are thinking the Senate Republicans are crazy. They don't see the benefits of lower deficits. All they see is the danger of cutting Social Security. House Republicans lost twenty-six seats in 1982 after Reagan *proposed* cuts in Social Security, and they are not going to take any more chances.

After the 1982 debacle, many Republicans publicly pledged to oppose all Social Security cuts. Reagan, in fact, made a similar promise in 1984. He tried to sidestep it by saying he had promised not to cut benefits but he had never agreed to support every increase in benefits.

Either way, House Republicans will have none of it.

"I remember getting calls right after the Senate vote," recalled Rep. Bill Gray, Pennsylvania Democrat, who was then the chairman of the House Budget Committee. "Republicans said 'Bill, if you don't accept the Senate version, we can help you in the House.' They'd already given the signal. House Republicans were already backpedaling."

Encouraged by the Republicans' timidity, Gray tries to coax liberal and moderate Democrats into accepting a $50 billion deficit-reduction package that, unlike all previous Democratic efforts under Reagan, contains no tax increases. Gray argues that Reagan's forty-nine-state landslide in 1984 proved Democrats had to confront the deficit without raising taxes.

"People were really asking serious questions about Democrats," Gray recalled. "They were asking, 'Are the Democrats dead?' I mean, we were in the grave, the benediction had been given, dirt was being thrown in. That was the atmosphere around here."

The Gray plan cuts defense by $30 billion and trims $20 billion from other domestic programs. It is a bold approach, one that forces liberals and moderates to compromise.

"Where I had the big problem was on the far left," Gray said. "Oh, God, we had some violent arguments. Hot arguing. I mean fighting almost. Literally, a couple of times I thought people would come to fisticuffs."

Liberals want $30 billion in defense cuts and $20 billion in higher taxes. Moderates want more in defense and some reductions in Social Security. Gray has to balance these desires against the orders Speaker O'Neill gives him when he asks permission to draft a no-new-taxes budget.

"Tip said, 'If you think you can pull it off, go work with the committee. But under no circumstances do you touch Social Security,'" Gray said.

Ultimately, Gray puts the package together. When it passes the House, only sixteen Democrats vote against it, making it the most popular Democratic budget passed by the House since Reagan's election.

Meanwhile, rank-and-file House and Senate Democrats turn up the heat on the Social Security issue. House Democrats wear buttons that say "Save Social Security. Vote Democrat." Senate Democrats sport buttons that read "SSSFRS," which means "Save Social Security From the Republican Senate."

For their part, House Republicans are plotting to undercut the Senate's handiwork. Republican Reps. Jack Kemp of New York and Trent Lott of Mississippi have Chief of Staff Don Regan set up a private meeting with Reagan to talk him out of the Social Security cut. Dole and Domenici are kept in the dark.

"It was Kemp and Lott together," said former Republican Rep. Vin Weber of Minnesota, a Kemp confidant. "They just went to Reagan, who basically believed the same things. I remember them saying, 'Making the case to Reagan was much easier than anyone thought.' Reagan was a Social Security Democrat and understood perfectly how that issue would be played against Republicans. And they persuaded the White House to oppose it, which killed it, of course."

The Kemp-Lott meeting foreshadows a now-famous deal Reagan and O'Neill cut at a White House cocktail party on July 9. Reagan will give up the proposed Social Security cut in exchange for more defense spending. Reagan gets what he wanted, more defense spending, while O'Neill gets what he wanted, more Social Security.

Senate Republicans get the shaft.

"We have lost the last best chance we had of seriously approaching a balanced budget in the foreseeable future," Republican Sen. Slade Gorton of Washington, a key Domenici ally, said after Reagan's capitulation.

Gorton and others feel betrayed.

"If the President can't support us, he ought to keep his mouth shut," says Iowa Republican Sen. Charles Grassley.

Senate Republicans are now in greater political danger than they have been at any time since Watergate. Almost all of them (forty-eight of fifty-two) voted to cut Social Security in hopes of reducing the deficit. Now they have the vote, which was politically hazardous, but no deficit reduction to back it up (which is doubly hazardous).

"Reagan blew their brains out," Gray said.

In politics, tough votes have to enforce tough policy. If tough votes don't create tough policy, politicians get stuck with all the negatives and none of the benefits. That is exactly what happened to the Senate Republicans.

Republicans lose control of the Senate in 1986 and the Social Security vote is pivotal in at least three of those races (it plays heavily in six of them).

Now, as a result, Republicans refuse to consider reducing Social Security benefits, even though it's the most credible way to reduce the deficit.

In 1995, Social Security benefits will consume nearly $330 billion or one-fifth of the total federal budget. Although these benefits are not the fastest rising of all the entitlement programs, they are the costliest. When Congress summons the courage to reduce these benefits, it will have found the key to cutting thousands of smaller programs.

That's because if they have the courage to cut Social Security, they can find the mettle to cut almost anything. All other programs are open for discussion if they can agree to cut the most politically popular program in the land. Republicans tried it in 1985. No one has tried it since.

SPECIAL INTEREST PRESSURE

To this point, I've discussed the congressional compulsion to satisfy public opinion. The other component of the Culture of Fear is the inordinate influence of special interests. While polls measure the distant echoes of public opinion, special interests amplify and direct their voice right inside a congressmember's or senator's office. They are organized to protect and enlarge whatever it is they receive from the federal government: tax breaks, subsidies, regulatory protection, and, most important of all, money. Special interest groups set up shop in Washington to keep an eye on the movement of any legislation that seeks to take from them what they have or, even better, get more than they've already gotten.

In his refreshing new book *Demosclerosis,* author Jonathan Rauch argues that special interests are primarily responsible for the lethargy and sloth of modern government. Even when new lawmakers arrive with new ideas, they often succumb to the special interest pressure that so dominates the nation's capital.

According to the American Society of Association Executives, about five thousand special interest groups existed in Washington in 1956. By 1993, there were more than twenty-three thousand. And there were sixty-four thousand state, local, and regional associations on top of that. The society's survey also suggests that a thousand new associations will be formed each year. The special interest industry employs five hundred thousand full-time workers, roughly the same number as are employed by the steel, computer, or airline industries.

Rauch argues, and I agree, that these special interest groups are not always an evil or even undesirable component of modern democracy. They can provide a valuable service by presenting information pertinent to decisions involving, say, a new tax, regulation, or spending program. Associations also develop codes of ethics for lawyers, bankers, and doctors, and safety standards for numerous manufacturing industries.

However, Rauch and I also agree that the cumulative effect of special interest politics poses a serious threat to modern democracy. Special interests too often choose stagnation over evolution. Congress responds to this pressure and holds on to programs and subsidies that long ago outlived their usefulness. The government now maintains virtually every program ever created, a policy that, Rauch points out, makes about as much sense as Ford Motor Company selling the same models it manufactured in the 1940s, 1950s, and 1960s.

The proliferation of special interest pressure has slowed the government's ability to respond flexibly, reasonably, and sensibly. Rauch has given this enervating phenomenon a pungent name: *demosclerosis.* The chronic disease demosclerosis threatens the life of our democratic republic. Just as arteriosclerosis weakens the human body, demosclerosis leads to a calcified government less able to respond to the needs of the nation.

Rauch writes:

> The same programs that made government a progressive force from the 1930s through the 1960s also spawned swarms of dependent interest

> groups, whose collective lobbying turned government rigid and brittle in the 1990s. Demosclerosis has thus turned progressivism into its own worst enemy. Yesterday's innovations have become today's prisons. One of the main paradoxes of demosclerosis, and one of its nastiest surprises, is that the rise of government activism has immobilized activist government.

According to a 1990 survey of the American Society of Association Executives, seven of ten Americans belonged to at least one special interest group; one of four Americans belonged to at least four. It reminds me of the words of that great political philosopher Pogo: "We have met the enemy and it is us."

MARCHING ORDERS

A more contemporary example of the Culture of Fear occurred in the spring of 1994 when it came time for Congress to affirm a budget cut it had already approved.

Early in 1994 the House and Senate passed a bill reducing the federal workforce by 10 percent over six years, affecting 272,000 employees. The cuts were projected to save at least $22 billion. The administration began to decide which agency personnel it would cut. Meanwhile, the House Veterans Committee — chaired by Mississippi Democrat Sonny Montgomery (elected in 1966) — approved a bill to exempt the Veterans Health Administration from any personnel cuts.

Then Clinton budget director Leon Panetta said the exemption "would make it impossible for the administration to carry out the downsizing" of the federal workforce. That didn't matter to most members of Congress and certainly not to the House leadership. Instead of fighting for a cut the administration sought and the House passed (391–17, by the way), House leaders did nothing to mobilize members against the pressure they knew was going to arise from the veterans groups. This despite the Veterans Administration's open acknowledgment that it had already identified ways to reduce its workforce. What's more, the Veterans Administration had more than 212,000 full-time employees, making it the largest non-defense agency in the government and larger than six federal agencies combined. In other words, if the Veterans Administration were exempted, deeper personnel cuts would be required in other agencies or, worse yet, Clinton's planned workforce reduction could unravel.

Veterans groups wanted the exemption and put the word out: Vote against us at your peril. I served on the Veterans Committee. I served for six years in the Navy Reserve and two of my brothers served during the Vietnam era. I appreciate the valuable service veterans have given this country. But their demands, just like every other special interest group, can sometimes be excessive. As Rauch points out in his book, the veterans lobby strangled a commonsense reform initiated by Ed Derwinski, Bush's Secretary of Veterans Affairs. Presiding over a monopoly hospital system that included many underused facilities, Derwinski proposed opening veterans hospitals to nonveterans. In some parts of the country, Derwinski argued, VA hospitals were the only ones for miles around and most had plenty of open beds. Derwinski suggested opening up the excess space to nonveterans on a three-year trial basis. Under the plan, no veterans would ever be denied medical care, veterans would be admitted before nonveterans, and the VA budget would remain the same. Nonetheless, veterans groups killed the proposal in short order.

In like manner, they also mobilized in early 1994 to shield the Veterans Health Administration from any personnel cuts. When the vote came, the House approved the exemption 282–118 (33 lawmakers did not vote).

I was leading the charge to defeat the exemption because I thought the administration should have flexibility in deciding which agencies should absorb the cuts. Besides, it's hypocritical to support a nonspecific 10 percent workforce reduction and turn right around and oppose the application of that cut to an agency with enormous clout in Washington. As I lobbied for support, I ran into the maddening political calculus begat by the Culture of Fear.

I had the following unforgettable exchange with Rep. Ron Coleman, a Texas Democrat who occupies an office down the hall from me.

> Coleman: How did this bill ever get to the floor? This is irresponsible.
>
> Me: Can you vote no?
>
> Coleman: I can't do that. This is an election year. Veterans already have enough reason to be upset with me.

I also heard this from Texas Democrat Jack Brooks before he voted for the exemption: "Sometimes you have to rise above principle."

These two reminded me of Sen. Henry F. Ashurst, Arizona Democrat. When asked once if he sided with special interests or his constituents, Ashurst said, "When I have to choose between voting for the people or the special interests, I always stick to the special interests. They remember. The people forget."

MONEY TALKS

Generally, special interests influence lawmakers because they represent a sizable block of voters, which could prove crucial at election time. It is also true that most special interest groups distribute thousands of dollars in campaign contributions to legislators who vote their way. As they say, money is the mother's milk of politics. Anyone who runs for office, whether it's for the city council or the presidency, needs money to bring his or her message to the voters. Money is not the most important factor in a successful political career, but it helps.

Let me tell you a story about my first encounter with the Culture of Fear as it pertains to the availability of special interest money and the price you have to pay to get it.

As I neared the end of my first term in Congress, I was beckoned to the Washington, D.C., offices of the AFL-CIO, the single-largest source of labor union donations in America. In 1984 it donated more than $18 million to Democrats. Before giving some of that $18 million to me, they wanted to discuss my performance in Congress.

The meeting was arranged by Neil Peterson, a labor lawyer who was very close to Sen. Hubert Humphrey, a liberal Democrat with deep roots in and sympathy for the labor movement. I was to meet with John Perkins, the AFL-CIO's point man in distributing political donations. It was felt that a face-to-face meeting might smooth over some differences on a few issues. It was also understood that without their financial support, I would have a difficult time raising money. I was heading into a fierce reelection campaign against a well-funded opponent, and every dollar would be important.

Perkins clearly wanted to tell me to my face that my labor record was weak. After my first year in Congress, the AFL-CIO calculated that I had supported them 70 percent of the time. "Most other Minnesota Democrats support the AFL-CIO almost one hundred percent of the time," I remember Perkins saying.

With a certain silkiness developed after years of "playing the game," Perkins mentioned there were several labor votes coming up and that he would watch me closely. The implication was simple: no improvement, no money. By Washington standards, this was an incredibly blunt exchange. Usually, special interests know that lawmakers raise money from many sources and their contribution is not necessarily going to sway them. Contributions are designed to keep the lines of communication open so they can get their message to a lawmaker when they need to.

Big labor is different. The AFL-CIO gives more money to more Democrats than any other group in the country does. Its tentacles reach into the deepest levels of party activities. The AFL-CIO can do a lot more than throw money around. It can encourage primary opposition in the next election. It can influence party leaders in Washington to punish lawmakers. It can send negative signals back to their home states, which means they might have to spend time patching fences with their state or local union workers.

No other special interest group in the Democratic Party can cause as many problems as the AFL-CIO. That's why its agenda drives so much of what Congress does. That's doubly true in the House.

Instead of promising to do better and thanking him for his time, I admit I got my back up and I lectured him on the need to reduce the deficit.

I got the distinct impression that Perkins didn't care if I used that kind of rhetoric back home as long as I voted right when I was in Washington.

Here is one of the great secrets of the most powerful special interest groups in Washington: They don't mind if lawmakers "vote their district" so long as they vote with the Washington insiders when it really matters.

Frequently, the special interests work closely with Democratic leaders in Congress to draft amendments so lawmakers can cast votes that look good back home but are inconsequential in the legislative process. Republicans and their pro-business special interests play the same game.

As soon as it dawned on Perkins and the others that I actually believed what they initially dismissed as campaign rhetoric, the atmosphere grew very tense.

I knew the meeting had not gone well, and I faced, with some apprehension, the prospect of being cut off by big labor. As I left the meeting, I was convinced Perkins wouldn't give me any money for my reelection campaign, even though the Republicans were targeting my race and I was vulnerable. I recall some of my top advisers telling me I'd been foolish to argue with Perkins when so much money was at stake (labor unions gave only $52,175 to my first campaign, but my second campaign would require more money). Without labor, I couldn't raise the needed amount.

As it turned out, my voting record fell to 38 percent in my second year. Nevertheless, the AFL-CIO endorsed me and gave me $130,237. This was no act of capitulation. Perkins knew my Republican opponent would have been a nightmare. In spite of labor's displeasure, my opponent attacked me back home for being a labor lackey by voting with them 70 percent of the time during my first year. Even though Perkins didn't see all that he wanted in my voting record, he knew labor would get even less consideration if the Republican were elected.

After 1984, I never got another endorsement from the AFL-CIO until 1992, my last campaign. Ironically, my voting record going into that campaign was only 42 percent. From 1986 onward, they cut off all PAC funds and even denied me a local endorsement from the Minnesota AFL-CIO.

Interestingly, I cultivated a much better relationship with big labor after they cut me off. Since no money was changing hands, we knew and accepted where each other stood. There were no veiled threats and no pleas for dispensation. When we agreed, we did so amicably. The same was true when we disagreed. Although I didn't realize it at the time, standing up to labor was among the most liberating experiences of my political life.

Most lawmakers don't take their orders from big labor or other special interest groups. Yet, few could honestly say that campaign contributions play no role in decision making. That doesn't necessarily mean that taking PAC money makes a lawmaker evil or unethical.

PAC money can be a serious problem if the demands of the special interests take precedence over the desires of the politicians' constituents or the needs of the nation. Then the relationship becomes poisonous. Then money can corrupt. It's a fine line. Often, lawmakers have no idea when they've crossed it.

The best check on a lawmaker is his or her own conscience. The second-best check is the vigilance of the voters. Later, I'll show you how to keep track of your lawmaker's voting record and campaign contributions. Then you can judge for yourself.

Money can corrupt . . . if we allow it.

MANN OVERBOARD?

No issue in my life in Congress provoked big labor more than the North American Free Trade Agreement. Unions from across the nation made NAFTA a political trip-wire for Democrats. Vote for it, Democrats were warned, and labor unions will spring into action to defeat you.

Many Democrats took these threats seriously. In all, 102 House Democrats voted for NAFTA, while 156 voted against the agreement. For the most part, Democrats from big labor states tended to follow labor's lead and opposed the treaty.

Freshman Rep. David Mann of Ohio did not. And big labor vowed to make him pay.

As soon as Mann announced his support of NAFTA, labor unions throughout his district mobilized to find a well-known Democratic challenger for the upcoming primary.

Mann, fifty-five, represents Cincinnati and its outlying suburbs. The district is part of the pro-labor Ohio matrix, but it lacks the sizable labor presence of more industrialized cities such as Akron and Cleveland. Clinton beat Bush by 155 votes in Mann's district in 1992 while Ross Perot captured 14 percent of the vote.

Labor unions supported Mann's 1992 candidacy with $56,000 in contributions. Volunteers made thirty thousand phone calls for Mann, and the AFL-CIO paid for one hundred thousand pro-Mann fliers. Mann defeated a little-known Republican challenger by less than nine thousand votes. His meager victory margin convinced him voters wanted a moderate Democrat in Washington. That's what he tried to be.

Mann defied White House and congressional leaders (and most freshmen Democrats) by voting against Clinton's $16 billion economic stimulus bill because it would have increased the deficit. He voted against the

President's budget because it lacked enough spending cuts, and he refused to support extended unemployment benefits that would increase the deficit. On fiscal matters, Mann showed laudable fortitude and judgment.

Despite these disagreements, Mann supported the White House on 81 percent of the votes taken in 1993. His principled opposition to deficit spending and support of NAFTA, however, put him at the top of big labor's enemies list.

One month before the Democratic primary, the Ohio AFL-CIO sent thousands of fliers to Mann's constituents.

"In 1992, union workers backed David Mann's election to Congress," the fliers said. "Then he turned his back on us. When you hear the word 'betrayal,' think of David Mann."

Richard Walsh, the AFL-CIO's national political director, told the *New York Times* that Mann got what he deserved. "There's a sense of betrayal here," Walsh said. "We're not afraid to punish our enemies."

Enemies?!

A Democrat who sides with a Democratic President 81 percent of the time is big labor's enemy?

Ludicrous.

Mann's only sin was to oppose big labor's protectionist and budget-busting agenda. Labor tried to unseat him by coaxing William F. Bowen, a state senator since 1970, into the race. Political observers in Cincinnati thought Bowen would have a tough time defeating a Republican in the general election, but the AFL-CIO wanted to make an example of Mann.

Mann lost an expected $150,000 in donations from the AFL-CIO and had to scramble to raise money from Cincinnati corporations willing to overlook his Democratic voting record and reward him for supporting NAFTA. Clarence Frost, the AFL-CIO's regional director, told the *New York Times* the union would mobilize all twenty-seven thousand members in Mann's district and import others to make telephone calls and distribute anti-Mann fliers.

"We're going to do everything we can, that's legal, for Senator Bowen," Frost said.

This opposition demonstrated how difficult it is for members of either party to confront their interest groups and vote for policies they believe will best serve their district and the nation.

Mann won the primary by 667 votes. I know that doesn't sound like much but, in the context of the AFL-CIO's all-out assault, Mann's victory sent a vital signal to other moderate Democrats: You can chart an independent course and win. (Mann lost in the general election in 1994. His defeat is likely to encourage Democrats from similarly competitive districts to kowtow to big labor. Mann's defeat proved what big labor always tell Democrats — a Democrat can never do enough to please big business, but a pro-labor Democrat will never lose labor's support.)

This all-or-nothing attitude is typical of the AFL-CIO and other special interest groups. By opposing Mann in the primary, the AFL-CIO contributed to his defeat in November. As a result, they got an anti-labor Republican in Congress. Pretty smart, huh?

SHOOT TO KILL

My final story involving special interest pressure involves one of the best-known and feared interest groups in Washington, the National Rifle Association (NRA).

I'm not convinced that gun bans will effectively or efficiently reduce crime. Throughout my career, I've always tried to balance the possible benefits of gun restrictions with the constitutional right to own firearms. Usually, I've come down on the side of gun owners.

Last year I found the case for limits on gun purchases a bit more persuasive. In early May of 1994, the House voted to ban the manufacture, importation, and sale of nineteen types of semiautomatic weapons. The same bill included a ban on sales of bullet magazines capable of carrying more than ten bullets. The Bureau of Alcohol, Tobacco and Firearms estimated that at least 869,000 of these weapons were in circulation nationwide. Generally, criminals don't use these weapons to commit murders, rapes, or robberies. Instead, they have become the weapons of choice for street gangs. They are compact, powerful, and capable of firing dozens of bullets in seconds. They are far more lethal than the pistols most police officers carry. Not surprisingly, a majority of police departments supported the assault weapons ban.

I did too. I concluded the right to own these types of weapons was less important than making it more difficult for criminals to buy them. Unlike many of the ban's vocal proponents, I never said it would dramatically reduce crime. I don't know if it will or not. I think it's possible. That possibility was more important than protecting the rights of citizens to own weapons that have no reasonable use in hunting, target practice, or self-defense.

Powerful figures in the House lined up with the NRA in staunchly opposing the measure. The two biggest House opponents were Rep. Jack Brooks, Texas Democrat and chairman of the Judiciary Committee, which controls all crime bills, and Speaker Tom Foley of eastern Washington state, where gun rights are sacrosanct. The two worked together to put the assault weapons ban on the slipperiest footing possible.

Foley scheduled a debate quickly, and Brooks prevailed on the Rules

Committee (the one that does in so many reformers) to deny all amendments. These actions did two things.

One, they undercut the ability of legislators to combat effectively the up-and-ready pressure from the NRA. While most Americans supported the gun ban, legislators knew that this support was far more amorphous than the vocal minority opposed to it. NRA lobbyists prowled the halls in the days leading up to the vote. To augment its efforts, the NRA set up national phone trees. Gun owners and hunters from across the country peppered House offices with calls.

Furthermore, Brooks's decision to block all amendments meant those who sought minor changes were more likely to oppose the bill. Several lawmakers, myself included, wanted to offer an amendment that would lift some paperwork requirements. Brooks rebuffed us. Brooks made the assault ban as unappealing as he could to undecided lawmakers.

The Foley-Brooks gambit failed. Barely. The House approved the ban on a vote of 216–214. The vote, which typically lasts only fifteen minutes, lasted twenty minutes, while those who favored the ban tried to overcome a 214–213 vote. Proponents needed 216 votes. The three members who cast the deciding votes underscore my argument (which I will make in more detail later) that most lawmakers find it easier to vote courageously when one of three conditions is at play: they are new to Congress and less frightened by the entrenched interests; they have decided to leave and are no longer beholden to the entrenched interests; or they have built a political career around votes that defy the entrenched interests.

Freshman Sanford Bishop Jr. is a black Democrat who represents southwest Georgia, and Democratic history is as much a part of this region as the soft-pine trees and peanut farms that provide much of the area's income. Franklin Delano Roosevelt first vacationed there, at the Warm Springs resort, in 1924. That year, seventy-five miles farther south, Jimmy Carter was born in Plains. President Roosevelt died at Warm Springs in 1945. Jimmy Carter, of course, became our nation's thirty-ninth President in 1977.

Bishop had intended to oppose the gun ban, and his press secretary had already prepared a press release explaining his opposition. Moments before leaving to cast his vote, however, Bishop gathered his staff. They joined hands and Bishop led them in a prayer asking for God's guidance. Bishop voted yes.

"What really turned me around was the thought of what it would mean for the people who are in fear [of gun violence]," Bishop said.

That was a tough vote for Bishop. His district is also home to Fort Benning, where Gen. George Marshall conducted the maneuvers that revealed which of his officers were prepared to be generals in World War II.

Loyalty to the military remains important in this largely rural district that has traditionally been leery of gun control. Bishop found it possible to chart a new direction because he wasn't wedded to the gun lobby and because he took the time to clear his head and listen to his conscience.

Another lawmaker to switch his vote was Rep. Andy Jacobs, an Indiana Democrat. Elected in 1974, Jacobs has steered an independent course in the House and is among its most frugal and irreverent members. In 1992 he had the fourth-lowest congressional payroll in the House, and he refuses to hire as many staff members as House rules allow.

Jacobs has also clashed with top Democratic leaders, usually over his refusal to follow in lockstep behind them.

In 1987, he assumed the chairmanship of the Ways and Means Subcommittee on Social Security but irritated his chairman, Dan Rostenkowski. In 1989, Jacobs opposed the House pay raise. Jacobs's independent streak led to an unsuccessful plot to strip him of his chairmanship of the Social Security subcommittee. If he had deferred to Rostenkowski and backed the pay raise, I'm sure no one would have plotted to oust him.

Jacobs accepts no PAC contributions and spends little on his campaigns — even against well-funded opponents. After Jacobs led the Ways and Means Committee effort to limit doctors' fees, the AMA poured $300,000 into the campaign of his Republican rival. The Republican outspent Jacobs ten to one, but Jacobs won with 58 percent of the vote.

Jacobs worked as a police officer while in law school and knew enough about firearms to fear the new multi-bullet magazines criminals were using on assault rifles. Jacobs didn't support the assault weapons ban, but wanted to halt sales of the multi-bullet magazines.

"The banning of the rifles wouldn't save lives, the banning of magazines would," Jacobs told *USA Today*.

Jacobs could afford reversing his earlier position because he had built a reputation for independence with his constituents and within the House.

Rep. Douglas Applegate of Ohio, a Democrat who retired last year, cast the deciding vote. Applegate opposed the Brady Bill, which imposed a five-day waiting period for handgun purchases. Congress had passed the Brady Bill earlier in the fall of 1993.

Applegate opposed gun-control measures throughout his sixteen years in Congress, earning him a top rating from the NRA. When Applegate's top Washington aide ran for the seat he was vacating, however, the NRA endorsed his opponent. Applegate switched his vote for two reasons: First, he was retiring and no longer faced retribution from the NRA; second, he sought revenge for the NRA's refusal to support his hand-picked successor.

"I came to the conclusion it was the right thing to do," Applegate told reporters. "It was my own conscience."

In the case of the assault weapons ban, there were three lawmakers who could, for very different reasons, resist the pressure that typically protects the status quo. The vote showed that sometimes special interests can lose.

Today's politicians would do well to remember John Quincy Adams. John F. Kennedy, in his book *Profiles in Courage,* described Adams's political philosophy this way: "He denied the duty of elected representatives, 'to be palsied by the will of their constituents.'" Adams refused to achieve success by becoming what Kennedy termed a "patriot by profession" by pretending "extraordinary solicitude for the people, by flattering their prejudices, by ministering to their passions, and by humoring their transient and changeable opinions."

Six

The Culture of Power

The essence of government is power: and power lodged as it must be in human hands will ever be liable to abuse.

—James Madison

POWER is a complex and difficult thing to wield, which is why most people wield it so poorly. Its seductions are innumerable, its thrills unmatched. Unlike New York, the nation's capitol is not driven by the pursuit of money. Unlike Hollywood, it is not driven by the pursuit of fame. Washington's number one commodity is power. It's traded and acquired almost daily, and the stock of a politician rises and falls based on the power he or she acquires.

Irish philosopher and statesman Edmund Burke's description of power in the mid-eighteenth century loses none of its potency in describing the modern Congress:

> Those who have been once intoxicated with power, and have derived any kind of emolument from it, even though but for one year, can never willingly abandon it.

Power is not evil. It's much like a weapon; weapons become evil when used in evil ways. If used properly, they can defend innocents from bloodthirsty aggressors.

The same is true of power. In the right hands, power can achieve great and noble results. The powers Franklin Delano Roosevelt used to aid the British and French in the early stages of World War II proved invaluable in their struggle for survival. The powers Abraham Lincoln wielded during the Civil War proved crucial to saving the Union at its moment of maximum peril.

The downsides of power are equally well known. Richard Nixon's resignation occurred because he abused power in many ways unrelated to the Watergate burglary. He used the FBI, the CIA, and the IRS to punish political opponents. Ronald Reagan abused his power to prosecute an undeclared war in Nicaragua by selling weapons to the Iranians and illegally diverting the profits to the Nicaraguan contras.

Within Congress, power is never wielded as publicly as it is by a President. This chapter is about power and those within Congress who know how to use it. There are only a handful of lawmakers who abuse power, and, to be truthful, their numbers are smaller than they were only a generation ago.

When Rep. Paul N. McCloskey Jr., a California Republican, retired in 1982, just as I was running for Congress, he issued this warning about the way power corrupted Capitol Hill:

> Power is something one should not enjoy too long. A lot of my colleagues, after they've been in Congress awhile, feel that somebody owes them a salute. I've seen people who made Congress a career — who had to be elected in order to be successful — that were not necessarily the best public servants. The longer you are in a position of power, the more likely you are to become corrupted, demand power as a matter of right or become lazy.

Some lawmakers fall prey to this power dynamic and begin to view their power not as a privilege but as a right. This often leads them to act ruthlessly or capriciously. Some abuse it to impose legislation a majority in Congress would normally oppose. Others use it to smother legislation a majority in Congress supports. Still others use it to protect themselves from legitimate investigations of unethical conduct.

That these abuses are less frequent than before does not excuse them. Common sense tells us that every abuse weakens Congress and demeans public service in the eyes of the voters.

TURF: ACQUIRE IT, PROTECT IT

Twentieth-century German author Konrad Heiden said this of power: "Unused power slips imperceptibly into the hands of another."

Those who wield power in the modern Congress believe this, and many of their exertions are meant to protect their power rather than enhance the laws of the land.

One of the most powerful figures during my twelve years in Congress was Rep. John Dingell, a Michigan Democrat and chairman of the Energy and Commerce Committee.

"Big John" intimidated virtually everyone in Washington. He intimidated administration officials and captains of industry. He intimidated fellow power brokers in the House and legions of junior lawmakers. Some veterans of Congress say Dingell operated as if he were the Pope of his committee: He was the absolute power with the final say on all matters of procedure and doctrine who rewarded loyalists and punished rebels.

Since rising to the chairmanship in 1981, Dingell sought to expand his influence. The *National Journal*'s Richard Cohen and Burt Solomon have said that Dingell "claims jurisdiction over anything that moves, burns or is sold." So far, the list includes air pollution and securities markets, consumer protection and toys, and railroads and defense contracting. Dingell oversaw 40 percent of all House bills each year. Forty percent! Dingell had the largest staff and biggest budget of any House committee. He used his staff and budget to conduct intensive investigations of defense contractors, academic research, prescription drugs, lobbying, environmental cleanup, and abuse of government contracts.

To his credit, Dingell's investigations have uncovered serious malfeasance in Washington. They led to the indictment of former Reagan aide Michael Deaver on charges of illegal lobbying; the ouster of Anne Burford as EPA director; and the discovery of defense contractors billing the Pentagon $640 for toilet seats and General Dynamics billing Uncle Sam for dog kennel fees.

In this way, Dingell has served a valuable public service. But he just as frequently abuses his power by stalling legislation or killing it to protect an industry close to his heart, namely the auto industry.

Dingell's constant quest for more power has led him to claim jurisdiction over bills that rightfully belong to other committees. He has clashed with other chairmen over cable regulations, telecommunications, product liability, and banking regulations. Dingell's stratagems have, in some cases, single-handedly derailed legislation supported by committees with dominant jurisdiction. For example, Dingell alone has blocked new laws to allow commercial banks to get involved in investment activities.

"We used to say that John Dingell views jurisdiction like a Texas rancher views land," said former Rep. Tom Tauke, who served on Dingell's committee. "A Texas rancher doesn't want to own all the land in the world. He just wants to own all the land that borders his. He's always looking to expand and consolidate his power."

Dingell sat on legislation to deregulate the price of natural gas in 1984. He refused to bring the bill to a committee vote because he feared proponents of deregulation had the votes to pass amendments that would aid the natural gas industry and injure states such as Michigan that consumed a lot of energy.

When Dingell did convene the committee to vote on the bill and amendments, a proponent of deregulation walked over and said, "John, we've got the votes." Dingell said, "Yeah, but I've got the gavel."

After losing the first two test votes on deregulation, Dingell adjourned the committee and delayed consideration of the bill for another year. He didn't bring it before committee until he wrested concessions from committee members that were less favorable to the natural gas industry.

The new chairman of the Energy and Commerce Committee is Thomas Bliley Jr. of Virginia. He will possess many of the same powers Dingell did and early on showed how he would use his power to protect his parochial concerns. Bliley said the committee would halt ongoing investigations of the dangers posed by passive cigarette smoke and the ethical questions surrounding the tobacco industry's hard-sell approach to American teens. Not surprisingly, the Phillip Morris tobacco company operates one of the largest cigarette plants in the world in his district.

CLEAR THE AIR: DIRTY DEAL

Dingell has been studying the intricate levers of House power since he was a child. He came to Washington at age five, when his father was elected to Congress. When his father died, Dingell won his seat in 1955 at age twenty-nine.

Dingell is a master of parliamentary tactics, and he uses them to get his way. In the grand scheme of things, oratory is incidental to the legislative process. Laws are made by those who have mastered the arcane process of ushering a bill through the subcommittee, the full committee, and the Rules Committee. Dingell does this better than anyone in the House. He can also use his subcommittees and full committees to hold hostage legislation he opposes. A consummate inside player, Dingell knows that by controlling the process he can also control the content of legislation.

Dingell once told the Rules Committee, "If I let you write substance and you let me write procedure, I'll screw you every time."

Dingell used his vast powers to bottle up the Clean Air Act for more than a decade. The Clean Air Act was designed to tighten federal regulations on automobiles and coal-fired factories and other sources of air pollution.

The first Clean Air Act was passed in 1970. The law was intentionally written to force the auto industry to make cars that emitted fewer pollutants — even though Detroit had not yet developed the technology to do so. (The law eventually led to the invention of catalytic converters.) This "technology-forcing" legislation caught Detroit by surprise and drastically increased the cost of automobiles at the same time when lower-priced and more energy-efficient imports were hitting the market.

While the first Clean Air Act took great strides toward cleaning up the nation's air, it wrecked havoc on the auto industry. Industry leaders were further chagrined by the way other industries — steel companies and electric utilities in particular — used friends in Congress to dodge similarly stringent regulations. From Detroit's point of view, the first Clean Air Act failed the fairness test. But it did lead to drastically lower auto pollution. Congress added still stricter auto emission standards to the Clean Air Act in 1977, further increasing the price of cars and weakening Detroit's hold on the market.

It is often said that in politics, where you stand depends on where you sit. Dingell's congressional district sits on the southern and western edges of Detroit and was once home to more than eighty thousand jobs directly or indirectly tied to the auto industry. Dingell's second wife, Deborah Insley, is an heiress to the family that founded Fisher Body Corp., which General Motors purchased in 1919 to enhance its assembly line output. Before and after marrying Dingell in 1981, Insley worked in General Motors' Washington lobbying office.

Environmentalists in Congress started pushing for new Clean Air amendments in 1981, the year Dingell rose to the chairmanship of the Energy and Commerce Committee. Dingell feared new regulations would further injure the auto industry, which, by this time, was still struggling to incorporate the new air pollution standards and beat back foreign competition. Dingell wanted to give Detroit a breather and made sure his committee — which had primary jurisdiction over Clean Air Act amendments — took no substantive action against air pollution throughout the 1980s.

In this regard, Dingell was the nemesis of his party leadership and a valuable ally of President Reagan. Most Democrats wanted tougher air pollution regulations. The Reagan administration opposed them. (Remember Reagan's famous assertion during the 1980 campaign that trees caused pollution?)

In 1982, an Energy and Commerce subcommittee chaired by Rep. Henry Waxman, a liberal Democrat from pollution-choked Los Angeles, tried to pass some minor Clean Air amendments that could have opened the door for a broader legislative assault on all forms of air pollution. Dingell persuaded allies on Waxman's subcommittee to defeat the amendments, but Waxman forced Dingell's full committee to debate and vote on them.

Waxman then started lobbying various business groups by suggesting their support for tougher pollution standards might shield them from more stringent standards later. Some of the groups responded and encouraged lawmakers sympathetic to their needs to side with Waxman. When Dingell lost two early and relatively minor votes on amendments he opposed, he adjourned the committee and halted all committee action for months.

After the 1982 confrontation with Waxman, Dingell forbade substantive committee action for nearly two years. (Dingell and Waxman clashed repeatedly throughout the 1980s on the Clean Air Act. The rivalry made it even harder to move the bill because both power brokers were fighting over policy *and* turf.)

"The [Clean Air] legislation didn't move, and that was in large part due to John Dingell," Tauke said. "If you had had somebody who was sympathetic to [the Democrats' environmental] views, I'm sure that it would have moved through committee and it would have moved to the floor. Undoubtedly, people will argue Dingell has distorted policies to protect the auto industry."

Dingell's determination to protect the auto industry helped Reagan avoid a bruising battle with Congress and prevented Democrats from pursuing their environmental agenda.

President Bush broke the logjam in 1989. His administration made passage of the Clean Air Act a top priority and recruited Senate Majority Leader George Mitchell as its top legislative ally. With Bush and Mitchell pressuring Congress, Dingell could no longer hold up the Clean Air Act by himself. Although he continued to do battle with Waxman, the two found common ground long enough to move the bill through the House. Mitchell forged compromises in the Senate and beat back a fierce campaign by Sen. Robert C. Byrd of West Virginia to water down new pollution standards he feared would harm his state's coal industry.

Bush signed the Clean Air Act amendments in 1990. The bill was in some ways more stringent than Bush would have preferred and more lenient than some ardent congressional environmentalists originally sought. Bush's leadership and willingness to work with other powerful Democrats isolated and eventually overcame Dingell's stalling tactics. Together, Bush and other leading Democrats forced Dingell to join in passing the nation's first significant anti-pollution regulations since 1977.

GROUNDED FOREVER?

Dingell's obduracy is not unique. There are other obstinate committee chairmen who snuff out legislation a majority in Congress supports. They refuse to hold a hearing on an idea or allow a bill or an amendment to escape their committee. These actions single-handedly deny the full House or Senate the opportunity to vote to express their will. The power to silence is just as profound as the power to amplify. Some committee chairmen use both powers to further their agenda . . . while vanquishing the nation's agenda.

In this regard, the current chairman of the House Judiciary Committee, Texan Jack Brooks, reminds me of one of his predecessors, New York Rep. Emmanuel Celler, who served in Congress for fifty years and chaired the House Judiciary Committee from 1955 to 1973. When asked once where he stood on a particular bill, Celler said, "I don't stand on it. I am sitting on it. It rests four-square under my fanny and will never see the light of day."

That's exactly what Brooks did for nine years to a bill that would reduce product-liability lawsuits against the manufacturers of small aircraft.

Rep. Dan Glickman, Kansas Democrat, had introduced legislation every year since 1986 to limit to fifteen years the amount of time a small aircraft maker could be held liable for damages resulting from a plane crash.

As it stands now, small aircraft companies such as Cessna, Piper, and Beechcraft are targets for product-liability lawsuits whenever their planes crash — even when pilot error or other factors are to blame. Three of the nation's largest small-craft manufacturers — Cessna Aircraft Co., Beech Aircraft Co., and Learjet Inc. — are based in Kansas.

Small airplane manufacturers attract lawsuits because their products last a long time and they are perceived to have big enough pockets to pay hefty settlements.

Hundreds of lawsuits were filed in the 1980s, and small aircraft makers saw their product liability costs soar. The industry spent $24 million on liability suits in 1977 and $210 million in 1986, forcing many industry leaders to shut down production lines. By the end of the 1980s, the cost of defending product liability cases became the most expensive cost of manufacturing an airplane. Rising liability costs help drive the price of U.S.-made small planes above the threshold most consumers were willing to pay. Foreign competitors unencumbered by never-ending liability exposure soon took over the lost U.S. market share.

As a result, the U.S. production fell from 17,811 in 1978 to 880 planes in 1993. In 1980 there were twenty-nine U.S. manufacturers of small aircraft. In 1994 there were nine. In that time, nearly one hundred thousand industry jobs disappeared. Those who left the industry complained bitterly of the product liability costs and being blamed for tragedies that were truly the fault of pilots, bad weather, and other circumstances.

Until the mid-1980s, apprentice pilots in the United States trained inside the cockpits of Cessnas, Pipers, and Beechcraft planes. Now they crawl behind the controls of Aérospatiale planes made in France. Aérospatiale is now the largest importer of training flight aircraft in the United States.

The makers of Beechcraft planes recently asked their lawyers to analyze the 203 lawsuits filed against them alleging faulty designs in the mid-1980s. In every case, federal aviation investigators blamed the crashes on bad weather, pilot error, air traffic control errors, or faulty maintenance. Design flaws were never cited as a contributing factor in a single crash. Yet, the plaintiffs' lawyers alleged design flaws were to blame in 100 percent of the crashes. Settlements cost Beech an average of $530,000. Cases the courts dismissed cost Beech upward of $200,000 each to prepare.

In one case, Beech was sued when one of its nineteen-year-old Beechcraft planes crashed into a tree. The suit alleged design flaws, but federal investigators showed the pilot was flying at dusk and ignored warnings from the ground not to duck under the clouds to view the field. Investigators blamed pilot error and the judge dismissed the case. Still, while not a fault, it cost Beech $100,000 in legal fees simply to prepare its defense.

Brooks had refused for eight straight years to hold a hearing on the Glickman bill. Brooks is one of three committee chairmen to claim jurisdiction over the bill. In cases where bills are referred to more than one committee, if one chairman objects, the bill dies. Brooks had objected every year . . . denying Glickman a hearing and a floor vote.

"Turf is the essential operating mechanism in Congress," Glickman said. "It's almost the gospel of the Hill. Committee chairmen jealously guard their turf. The ruling sect here is made up of careerists."

Brooks opposed the bill because the nation's trial lawyers opposed it. Trial lawyers are frequent contributors to Democrats and are especially generous to Brooks. In return, Brooks is one of the trial lawyers' staunchest allies in Congress. The other is Sen. Howard Metzenbaum, Ohio Democrat. Metzenbaum chairs a crucial Judiciary subcommittee and had also bottled up a Senate version of the Glickman bill sponsored by Republican Sen. Nancy Landon Kassebaum of Kansas.

Finally, in 1994 the Senate passed Kassebaum's bill 91–8.

That prompted Brooks to promise a hearing on the bill. Brooks still refused to bring the bill to the floor, perhaps because 294 House members cosponsored the bill (more than enough to win a floor vote). Brooks's refusal to move the bill to the floor forced Glickman to pry it out of the committee by using something called a discharge petition.

You may remember talk about discharge petitions in the summer of 1993. Under House rules, a bill locked in committee can be brought to the floor immediately if a majority of members (218) sign what is called a discharge petition. This is a rarely used tactic because it directly confronts powerful committee chairmen and undermines the senior House leaders who typically side with chairmen in such disputes.

Glickman was a part of the Democratic inner circle due to his chairmanship of the Intelligence Committee. He served in the House for eighteen years and did not consider himself a bomb thrower. Brooks's one-man war against Glickman's bill had driven him to extremes, and he was prepared to use the discharge petition. In deference to other committee chairmen, however, Glickman asked Republican Rep. Jim Hansen of Utah, a top ally, to file the discharge petition on his behalf.

"I have been personally admonished and advised by some in the House this isn't a wise thing to do because as a committee chairman, I need to work within the system," Glickman told *Roll Call,* the twice-weekly newspaper that covers Congress more aggressively than any other publication in Washington. "I respect the institutional process, but do you think if they were about to close down NASA, Jack Brooks would allow that? If they were about to close down McDonnell Douglas in St. Louis, wouldn't [Majority Leader] Dick Gephardt object to that?"

Facing the threat of losing a showdown via the discharge petition, Brooks relented in late June and allowed Glickman's product-liability bill to reach the floor. The House passed the bill by a lopsided margin. The discharge petition made the difference in dislodging Glickman's bill. The bill is now law. (Ironically, Brooks and Glickman lost reelection bids in 1994.)

RISKY BUSINESS

In 1993 a freshman Democrat discovered the difficulty of challenging power brokers in her own party. Karen Thurman of Florida tried to score a stunning victory for environmental reforms in her second year in Congress. She was joined by another freshman, Republican John Mica of Florida. (I served with John's older brother Dan on the Veterans Committee when I first came to Congress.) Three-term Democrat Gary Condit of California was also a key Thurman ally on this issue.

Thurman, a ten-year veteran of the state senate, was the leading advocate for an overdue law that would require the Environmental Protection Agency to study how much it would cost businesses to comply with new regulations.

Since its inception, the EPA has created new regulations without ever weighing the costs of compliance on the business sector. Businesses and developers must conduct impact studies to see what effect their new projects will have on the environment. Thurman wanted the EPA to do the same for business, arguing that just as runaway development can harm the environment, runaway regulation can harm jobs and local economies. Thurman is no industry sycophant. Florida has seen the ravages of pell-mell development but has also felt the lash of overzealous regulators. Thurman had studied the issue in the state legislature and had won plaudits from both sides of the aisle.

When Clinton sought to elevate the EPA to cabinet status, he provided a suitable vehicle for Thurman's cause. In April of 1993 the Senate approved the so-called "risk assessment" amendment to its EPA cabinet bill by an overwhelming vote of 95–3.

When Thurman tried to introduce similar language in her Government Operations Committee, the chairman, John Conyers, ruled it out of order. He opposed the policy and was reading the rules quite tightly to prevent Thurman from even getting a vote on the idea.

Thurman retreated and researched ways she could reword the amendment to qualify for committee consideration. What she didn't know was that Conyers was eyeing her every move on behalf of Henry Waxman, another powerful figure on the Government Operations Committee. Waxman opposed the "risk assessment" amendment and wanted Conyers to bury it in his committee so he wouldn't have to be bothered with it. As soon as Conyers got wind of Thurman's plan to offer a new amendment, he cut a deal with New Jersey Republican Dick Zimmer to offer a milder version of Thurman's amendment.

That way Conyers could bring the mushy Republican amendment before the committee, see it passed, and then dump it later when the House and Senate met to work out differences in the two bills.

Conyers sprang into action as Thurman was about to seek recognition. He called on Zimmer, who offered his amendment. The chairman accepted it without a vote. Within seconds, Thurman's entire amendment was decimated. Six months of research and effort went for naught.

This taught Thurman a valuable lesson about the loyalty of committee staff. When Thurman informed Conyers's committee staff of her intentions to resubmit her amendment, which she thought was the proper thing to do, she had no idea she was dealing with the enemy. Thurman's disclosure sealed her fate. It allowed Conyers to set the trap that dropped her amendment into a pit of legislative quicksand.

"I was livid," Thurman said. "I blew up at the committee staff."

When the EPA cabinet bill was about to reach the House floor for a vote, Thurman decided to make one more stab at sticking her language in the bill.

But it was an uphill fight. By that time, the Clinton administration had issued an executive order establishing some of the "risk assessment" procedures for the EPA. But executive orders do not carry the weight of law.

Still, Thurman and dozens of other Democrats wanted the "risk assessment" language in the House bill. They were joined by most Republicans, who favored the policy and didn't like the EPA cabinet bill in the first place because they believed it would give the EPA more power.

Sensing the EPA bill might be in trouble with freshmen legislators, Vice President Gore and EPA Secretary Carol Browner hastily called a meeting to lobby them against adding any "risk assessment" language.

Throughout the meeting, Gore and Browner gave short shrift to the policy ideas behind Thurman's amendment. This enraged the freshmen, who thought Gore and Browner were issuing marching orders and ignoring their strong support for a new approach to reviewing the consequences of EPA regulations.

"It was a total kiss-off on policy, and they totally pissed off the freshmen," said Eric Fingerhut, an Ohio Democrat who, like Thurman, had at times clashed with party titans while pushing new ideas.

Afterward, Fingerhut ran into Lorraine Miller, the top White House lobbyist for the House of Representatives. Miller asked how the meeting went.

"I told her there were a lot of angry people in there," Fingerhut said.

Thurman decided to bring the "risk assessment" amendment to the floor. To do that she first had to win a crucial procedural battle with House leaders, something freshmen rarely attempt and almost never win. Thurman had to defeat the rule that the Rules Committee (one of my foes in the Penny-Kasich fight) had approved for the EPA bill. The "rule" prevented debate on a "risk assessment" amendment.

House leaders wrote the rule with the help of the committee and subcommittee chairmen who didn't want to see the "risk assessment" language prevail. Among them were Conyers and Dingell. House leaders frequently cave in to pressure from powerful committee chairmen to block floor consideration of ideas they oppose. Instead of allowing ideas that command strong support within the House to reach the floor for debate — as the Founding Fathers recommended — House leaders often derail them with crafty procedural maneuvers.

That was the plan, and Thurman feared it would work. She was even losing support among the industry lobbyists who desperately wanted the "risk assessment" language. They were afraid Thurman would lose the rules challenge and that would be viewed as a defeat for "risk assessment." They were content to rely on the lopsided Senate vote and try to win in the House-Senate conference committee.

Virtually alone, Thurman pressed on. After giving her speech, she returned to her office convinced that she would lose. She asked her press secretary to prepare a statement emphasizing that her defeat would not deter her. But as the votes on the rule began to come in, it was clear Thurman would win.

Many freshmen Democrats teamed up with most House Republicans and defeated the leadership's punitive rule that had sought to block Thurman's amendment. It was a staggering defeat for the House leaders and sent a clear signal that, on some issues, the freshmen would not roll over.

Thurman's victory was short-lived, however. Instead of bowing to the will of the House and letting Thurman's amendment come to the floor, House leaders pulled the bill and bottled it up for months. A lengthy stalemate ensued. The leadership withheld action on the EPA bill, denying Thurman another chance to pass risk assessment. An ally of hers, Rep.

Gary Condit, California Democrat, succeeded in attaching the risk assessment language to the U.S. Department of Agriculture authorization bill. This small victory looms large in the developing story of how freshmen lawmakers are changing Congress.

OVERRULED

What House power brokers did to Thurman is typical of the way the modern House tries to scuttle ideas they oppose. In general, most of the dominant committee chairmen in the House were liberal Democrats. They tended to dislike compromises with Republicans and resisted middle-of-the-road Democratic alternatives to their "pure" liberalism. These committee chairmen exerted profound influence on the Rules Committee, often with Speaker Foley's acquiescence. As a result, the Rules Committee frequently prevented alternative ideas from reaching the floor.

This process muted the House's ability to debate openly various issues and reach the consensus necessary to build better policy for the nation. Historically, powerful committee chairmen used their clout to draft bills to their liking. When their bills came to the floor, however, the chairmen allowed amendments and gave lawmakers with different approaches an opportunity to present their case and vie for majority support. If the alternative ideas won a majority vote, they were added to the chairman's bill. If the alternatives lost, at least the lawmaker sponsoring the idea had the satisfaction of knowing he or she was heard in a fair and open democratic process. More important, the House had other choices than those dictated by the powerful chairman.

When members are unable to influence bills in committee, their only recourse is to take their ideas to the House floor. But the Rules Committee has typically blocked them. Often, the Rules Committee approved "closed rules." A closed rule means no amendments are allowed on the floor. A less lethal limit on debate is what is called a "restrictive rule." Restrictive rules allow only a select few amendments on the floor. Closed and restrictive rules deny lawmakers a fair fight on many legitimate ideas.

This process betrays a basic deliberative function of the House. Former Speaker Sam Rayburn (who ran the House in all but two years from 1940 to 1961) believed open and fair debate was crucial to maintaining Congress's credibility. In a radio address on November 1, 1942, Rayburn said,

> It is out of the airing of conflicting opinions in hearings, debates and conferences that a people's Congress comes to decisions that command the respect of a free and democratic people.
>
> . . . Not all the measures which emerge from the Congress are perfect, not by any means, but there are very few which are not improved as a re-

> sult of discussion, debate and amendment. There are very few that do not gain widespread support as a result of being subject to the scrutiny of the democratic process.

In the modern Congress, House leaders seldom bring a bill to the floor unless they are sure it can pass in the form they prefer. They often manipulate the legislative process in order to win on their terms.

Republican leaders have vowed to increase greatly the number of open rules and return to a House more recognizable to Sam Rayburn. I hope they succeed. And I hope they maintain this openness even if it means risking defeat sometimes. Because that's not what those in power did when I was in Congress.

Leaders in the modern Congress believe, almost as an article of political faith, that losing a floor vote means they've failed politically. They dread bringing a bill to the floor that the majority of the House won't accept. They take this kind of rejection very personally. It's almost as if every bill they bring to the floor is a reflection of their worth. To reject the bill is to reject them.

It's one of the many pointless games played in Washington. Everyone is obsessed with winning. And if you're not up, you're down. The Congress is like one giant tote board on which lawmakers keep constant track of each other's petty successes and failures.

This attitude is completely at odds with what most voters want and expect from Congress.

House history shows that the decline in open debate is new.

In the 95th Congress (1977–1978), the Rules Committee approved 211 rules for floor debate. Of those, 179 were open rules, meaning that a lawmaker could offer any amendment germane to the bill on the floor. Another 32 rules were "restrictive," meaning either no amendments or a select few were allowed.

In the 102nd Congress (1991–1992), the Rules Committee approved 109 rules for floor debate. Of those, only 37 were open, while 72 were restrictive. That means from 1977 to 1992 the percentage of open rules has declined from 85 percent to 34 percent and the percentage of restrictive rules has risen from 15 percent to 66 percent. The House leaders' muzzling techniques have led to a 400 percent decline in open debate!

This strategy forced the House in 1993 to debate several significant pieces of legislation under restrictive rules.

The Rules Committee allowed only three of the thirty proposed amendments to the Family and Medical Leave Act. It allowed only one of nineteen proposed amendments to the National Voter Registration Act. It allowed only eight of fifty-one suggested amendments during debate of the $496 billion Clinton budget and tax bill. (Nineteen of these rejected amendments were offered by Democrats. This revealed that the Democratic leadership isn't simply trying to shut down Republican proposals.) And only six of fifty amendments were allowed during debate of the $2.3 billion spending bill for congressional operations. (In this instance, forty-four rejected amendments came from Republicans seeking cuts in congressional operations. Some of these amendments appeared to have been drafted for political rather than substantive reasons.)

The inclination of Democratic House leaders to limit debate penalized Democrats and Republicans. But Republicans found it even harder than Democrats to get a fair shake.

"We're willing to take the losses if it's a fair fight," said Rep. Jerry Solomon, New York Republican and ranking member of the Rules Committee. He often watched in impotent frustration as the Rules Committee, which, remember, was stacked 9–4 against him, dismissed numerous Republican amendments.

"The American people do not see their views being represented," Solomon said. "The vast majority of Americans think the same way. They are moderately conservative people. That is the will of the House. If you took all of those people that are more moderate in both parties, you're talking about two-thirds of the House. You would have a final outcome that is going to be what the vast majority of Americans support. All anyone wants is a fair fight and a chance to win. If you lose, you lose. But at least it's fair." Solomon is now chairman of the Rules Committee, and I trust he will use his influence and his 9–4 committee majority to open up the House floor to wider debate.

THE MOST EXPENSIVE THIRTY SECONDS OF MY CAREER

Power exerts itself in many ways. Sometimes a powerful member of the House will blindside you, as Conyers did to Thurman. Other times, the power play will occur in broad daylight . . . and there is nothing you can do to stop it.

That happened to me once. It nearly cost the taxpayers $500 million.

It was 1989, and I had a golden opportunity to break through and actually pass a $500 million budget cut on a spending bill for housing and veterans programs that grossly violated budget rules.

Without getting too technical, here's what was wrong with the bill: It provided more than $80 billion for veterans, housing, and environmental programs plus funds for space exploration and the Environmental Protection Agency. Well, that figure was $500 million above what our new budget said it should be.

Bear in mind, these budget limits were very generous. They allowed for more than a 7 percent growth in total discretionary spending for the next year. No one, I mean no one, was starving under these new rules.

For once, some powerful Democrats wanted to cut excess spending. Leon Panetta, who is now Clinton's chief of staff, was chairman of the Budget Committee at the time. He was the most authoritative voice of budget matters in the House.

Panetta wanted the $500 million in excess spending killed. He and the ranking Republican on the committee, Bill Frenzel of Minnesota, asked me to sponsor an amendment to take the $500 million out by requiring an across-the-board cut of all programs in the bill — everything from veterans and housing programs to NASA and the EPA. They promised plenty of leadership support. I was thrilled. It looked as if I might actually win one!

I alerted all of my budget allies within the party and notified the outside budget watchdog groups. I knew from experience that budget cutting is tough business, even if there appears to be lots of support. Some advocates for cuts have trouble locating their spine when it comes time to vote. Pressure from special interest groups turns many stout, chest-thumping budget-cutters into meek, invertebrate budget-busters when the roll is being called. I wanted a big cushion of votes on my side so as not to risk losing. Panetta helped greatly by signing a letter to other Democrats supporting my $500 million cut.

The stage was set.

As I got to the House floor, I noticed several other amendments were pending on the bill and that some floor votes would certainly be necessary. Debate started shortly after noon and was expected to drag on as these lesser amendments were discussed.

As I sat there scanning all of the research material I had collected in preparation for the debate, a sick sensation gripped my stomach. I realized I had another meeting to attend. At 2 P.M. a strategy session had been scheduled to discuss an upcoming vote to kill the B-2 bomber, a Pentagon boondoggle of the highest (or lowest) order. A bipartisan group in the House was determined to kill the project for good, a move that would save the taxpayers tens of billions over the next decade. Ron Dellums, a California Democrat and senior member of the Armed Services Committee, had specifically asked me to attend the session, and I didn't want to miss the meeting (scheduling conflicts like this make life in Congress maddening).

As I scanned the floor I looked to see how many members were waiting to speak and calculated the time those speeches would take. I also calculated how long it would take to conduct the roll call votes it appeared would be necessary. I gambled that I would have enough time to go to the B-2 meeting and still make it back to the floor to push for my $500 million in cuts.

Just to make sure, however, I talked to Rep. Bob Traxler, Michigan Democrat, who was chairman of the appropriations subcommittee that drafted the bill I was attacking. Traxler came to Congress in 1974 and had served in the state legislature twelve years before that. He was a pro. His job, as he saw it, was to protect his bill from people like me. Democrats were pulling at him from all sides: Some wanted more money for NASA, while others wanted more housing projects, while still others wanted more for the EPA or veterans. Traxler gave a little to all sides, which is why his bill was $500 million over budget.

He didn't view being over budget as a problem. To him, my amendment was the problem. As far as he was concerned, his committee had approved the bill, and that was all the authority he needed. He didn't want a bunch of nattering budget-cutters taking $500 million out of his "delicately balanced" bill.

Traxler was prepared to do anything to protect his turf. I should have known that. Well, I guess I did, but in this case I believed the stage was set and there was little Traxler could do to stop my amendment. I was wrong.

I asked Traxler if there would be time for me to attend my B-2 meeting. I said I'd be willing to skip the meeting if he thought my amendment would come up soon.

When I said it looked as if there would be at least two roll call votes (which usually take about twenty minutes each), Traxler nodded in agreement. When I said it looked to me that there would be at least an hour's worth of debate before my amendment, I recall him saying, "Oh, easily."

I didn't trust Traxler completely, but I felt more comfortable after this exchange. I decided to rush to the B-2 meeting, get a sense of who was there and the upcoming strategy and bolt back to the floor. I didn't want to miss the opportunity to cut $500 million in excess spending.

According to House rules, a member cannot offer an amendment unless he or she is on the floor. If the amendment is called and the member is absent, the amendment is stricken and all chances of having it debated are lost. It's a one-shot deal. No second chances. The member can't get another number like at a corner deli.

After Traxler said I should have enough time to attend the B-2 meeting, I dashed outside the Capitol, crossed the street to the Longworth Office Building, and joined in the B-2 strategy session. It was clear from the wide array of Democrats and Republicans present at the meeting that the B-2's days were numbered and that a budget breakthrough was near.

Meanwhile, back on the House floor, Traxler sprang into action.

As soon as I left the floor, he encouraged those present to allow three noncontroversial amendments to pass on voice votes (thereby saving forty to sixty minutes). Traxler also persuaded other lawmakers to drop controversial portions of other amendments to further accelerate the process. Traxler sagely compressed more than an hour's worth of floor action into roughly fifteen minutes. He was clearing the decks as fast as he could, hoping to get to my amendment before I got back to the chamber.

Bill Green, the Republican who was co-managing the debate, could have thwarted Traxler's gambit, but he didn't. Green represented Manhattan and was as liberal as many New York Democrats. A former employee for the Department of Housing and Urban Development, Green wanted to protect housing programs in the bill.

I fidgeted for less than thirty minutes inside the standing-room-only B-2 meeting when my beeper went off. My frantic staff was watching the floor action, and it had just dawned on them what Traxler was up to. They were warning me to dash back to the floor.

Breathless, I reached the floor and discovered that Traxler had moved so quickly that I wasn't present to speak on behalf of my amendment.

I was thirty seconds late.

If I'd been there thirty seconds earlier, I could have saved my amendment from Traxler's double-cross. But I blew it.

So it disappeared, and with it a very good chance to cut $500 million from the deficit. They were the most expensive thirty seconds of my life.

I glared at Traxler, who was smiling giddily at his tactical triumph. He won. I lost. I was furious at my own stupidity. How could I have trusted the word of the man whose bill I was trying to cut?

He kept the money in his bill and I got the most painful lesson of my congressional life.

Thankfully, the $500 million was later deleted when House and Senate members worked out differences in their two bills. Traxler had won the battle but not the war.

In a surprising turn of events, within two years Traxler and I teamed up to propose elimination of the Space Station Freedom. The multibillion-dollar space project was beginning to crowd out other priorities in his committee's budget. This time, he offered the budget-cutting amendment, and I was there — on time — to speak and vote for it.

As evidenced by the Traxler story, powerful committee leaders can and do exercise power to protect their agenda, even if it means publicly sabotaging another lawmaker.

MORE ARMEY, FEWER BASES

There are times, however, when a lawmaker with a good idea can single-handedly overcome the opposition of other powerful figures in Congress. One House member deserves all of the credit for one of the most significant congressional reforms of the 1980s.

Texas Republican Dick Armey, who is now the Majority Leader in the 104th Congress, changed the way Congress closes military bases. He took parochial politics and executive branch abuse out of the process and put base closures in the hands of an independent commission. Before Armey's changes, local pressure discouraged Congress from closing military bases, and the White House sometimes used the threat of closing military bases as a weapon against congressional opponents. From 1977 to 1987, Congress did not close a single military base. It did vote to open thirteen new ones, however. The system was broken.

Until Armey began his crusade in 1987.

At the time, the United States had about four thousand military installations. Most had been built during World War II, when the military needed to house some twelve million soldiers and support personnel. The military had only 2.1 million active-duty soldiers in 1987, and roughly four hundred thousand of those were stationed overseas.

Elected in 1986, Armey, a former college economics professor, found no economically justifiable reason to keep so many bases open. He also discovered that fears of permanent job losses due to base closures were unfounded. A Pentagon study of a hundred base closures from 1961 to 1977 showed that communities successfully converted military bases into colleges, office parks, and airports. Overall, more people were employed after the bases were closed than when the bases were open.

Armey proposed scrapping a cumbersome environmental impact study Congress had required for each base closing. The regulation wasn't meant to protect the environment nearly as much as it was meant to keep the bases open. The environmental studies invariably sparked lawsuits and counterlawsuits that stalled the process of closing bases for years.

Instead, Armey wanted to allow Congress to appoint an independent commission to recommend which bases to close and to force Congress to accept or reject the base-closure list on an up-or-down vote. The process would prevent lawmakers from lobbying to protect a single military installation. Under Armey's proposal, Congress would close either all of the bases on the commission's list or none of them.

Armey said Congress was looking for ways to reduce Pentagon spending, and closing bases appeared the most politically salable and economically defensible approach. Armey opposed slashing personnel budgets or weapons systems — many of which were made in Texas. If politics could be removed from base closing decisions, Armey argued, Congress could close dozens of bases every two years and save taxpayers billions in the process.

Armey's idea solved two huge headaches for lawmakers. First, it held them blameless (and thereby rendered them safe) if their base was put on the closure list; if the independent commission chose to close a base in their backyard, well, voters certainly couldn't fault their congressman. Second, the independent commission took away one of the more insidious weapons Presidents could use to pressure lawmakers into voting the President's way. Many lawmakers knew what it was like to get a call from the White House and learn that their vote could determine the fate of a base in their district.

While some in Congress were intrigued by Armey's idea, he found few immediate allies. Armey was not on the Armed Services Committee, which would decide the matter, so most lawmakers assumed his legislation would die there. Others wondered if Armey had a secret agenda.

"In every conversation I can recall on base closing," Armey said, "I first had to respond to the question 'Dick, which base are you trying to shut down?' I had to convince people I had no pet project here."

One lawmaker, however, proved invaluable to Armey's efforts . . . even though he opposed his legislation.

California Democrat Ron Dellums, the chairman of the subcommittee that controlled all military construction, granted Armey's request for a hearing on base closures and his legislation. The hearings drew widespread attention to the redundancy of many military bases and Armey's relatively pain-free approach to closing those bases with the least military use.

"He had an amazing commitment to the proposition that a person had a right to be heard," Armey said of Dellums. "By conventional standards, [holding hearings] was an enormous act of generosity."

Dellums opposed Armey's concept because he thought it gave away too much congressional authority. Dellums wanted Congress to close bases on its own and still thought such a thing was possible. Armey was convinced that lawmakers would keep the bases open forever if they could.

Armey brought his base-closing amendment to the floor for the first time in 1987. Had it not been for an intense last-minute lobbying effort by Democratic leaders, Armey's amendment would have passed on the first vote. Newly elected Speaker Jim Wright and Majority Leader Tom Foley switched nine votes on the floor, and Armey's amendment lost by seven votes (199–192). The leaders did not appear as motivated by a desire to stop base closing as they were to stop any Republican amendment from passing on the floor.

"It had nothing to do with the issue," Armey said. "What it had to with was their new leadership team showing Democrats 'We're in charge here and this Republican is not going to win something by three votes.'"

In 1988 two powerful Democratic chairmen — Jack Brooks of Texas and Walter B. Jones of North Carolina — did try to bury Armey's base-closure amendment. They claimed their committees — Brooks on Judiciary and Jones on Merchant Marine and Fisheries — had jurisdiction over the bill. Brooks and Jones had large military bases in their districts they wanted to protect. And even though no one knew which bases an independent commission would recommend for closure, neither chairman wanted to take any chances.

The two chairmen delayed action on the bill for months. When the committees finally passed the Armey bill, it had been watered down so severely that Armey barely recognized it. The issue would have died there because Aspin, the Armed Services Committee chairman, also opposed Armey's bill. Armey forced a confrontation with Aspin and had his original amendment resurrected one day before the House began debate on the defense bill.

"I had to stand up to Jack Brooks," Armey said. "And more than anybody else, I had to be willing to face down Aspin a couple of times."

The Rules Committee could have blocked Armey's new amendment but did not. The House passed the measure 223–186 in July of 1988. The Senate accepted the language, and President Reagan signed the bill in September of 1988.

Later that year, Armey bumped into Majority Leader Wright at a function in Fort Worth, Texas (both lawmakers represented parts of Fort Worth at the time).

"I took the moment to ask him, 'Why didn't you stop me with my amendment on base closing?'" Armey said. "And he said, 'Well, first of all you were doing a great job on that. You were good-natured, but you worked hard on it, and people appreciated how hard you were working on it. And we thought you deserved your vote.' Wright stopped for a moment, grinned, and delivered the *real* answer: 'And we didn't think you could win.'"

By the end of 1992, Congress had agreed to close 125 military bases and realign another 100. The independent base-closure commission is due to recommend additional base closings this year. So far, base closings are projected to save taxpayers upward of $5 billion a year by the year 2000.

Armey's experience disproved a couple of common myths in Congress. First, Armey succeeded *because* he was not a member of the Armed Services Committee, not in spite of it. By being an outsider, Armey could think creatively about military policy without fear of alienating his chairman or irritating other committee members.

Most members on powerful committees defer to established leaders and tolerate age-old practices because the cost of rebellion is too high. Independent-minded lawmakers are frequently ostracized by committee colleagues when they don't follow the chairman's lead. Most members want to serve on committees that can deliver benefits to their district. Losing favor on these committees can cost a lawmaker prestige in Washington and vital political support back home. The pressure to conform, therefore, is immense.

"It's much better to be a committee outsider," Armey said. "You go on the committee because . . . its activity is important to your district in one way or another. You are there because you want that committee to do more of what it does and especially more of it in your district. It creates a co-dependency. If you're not on the committee, the committee can't discipline you."

BREAKING THROUGH THE POWER

The most important reform the public should pursue for the modern Congress, in my opinion, is not term limits for all members, but term limits for committee chairmen.

Currently, members can serve as committee chairmen for as long as they are reelected. They are seldom challenged for these positions. I have often remarked that committee chairmen keep their jobs until they die or are indicted. I've witnessed only a handful of chairmanship contests in my twelve years in Congress. It's risky challenging a chairman because failure is often met with ruthless retribution. Unlimited committee tenure concentrates too much power in the hands of too few people. The solution is not to deprive them of all power, but simply to require them to hand it over to others after a certain period of time.

My idea is to limit chairmanships to four or six years. The Intelligence and Budget committees already abide by such a limit, and it is generally agreed that these committees perform remarkably well. If supported by a majority of his party's caucus, a chairman could rotate to another committee. This rotation would increase the level of general-interest awareness among chairmen and committee members alike. When members stay on the same committee for years, their worldview tends to shrink. This causes two problems. First, they become wedded to the status quo on the committee and hostile to new approaches. Second, by remaining on the same committee for years, they are unable to understand fully the complexities of other issues before Congress. They lose sight of the big picture. It's a classic example of not seeing the forest for the trees.

What you end up with is a system with built-in barriers to reform and to new approaches to old problems.

Here's an example of what I mean. The House's Energy and Commerce Committee is among the most sought-after assignments in the House. Once members land a spot on this coveted committee, they almost never give it up. Members stay on Energy and Commerce for years and grow comfortable with its issues and its hidebound ways. Their "expertise" influences dozens of other members whose long tenure on their own committee — Agriculture, let's say — leaves them poorly versed in policies that come from Energy and Commerce. What's left is a system of institutionalized insularity. Lawmakers tend to think about their committee before they think about the larger needs of the nation. All legislation is viewed through the lens of a particular committee's needs and wants.

"The problems arise when you have one person in control of a committee who therefore year after year after year can shape the legislative agenda and block legislation," said Tauke, who is now a lobbyist for the telecommunications giant NYNEX. "[Chairmen] also then have a tendency to protect their committee turf. When they protect their committee turf, they thwart the kinds of reforms that have been talked about for a long time. The biggest obstacle to that is that the chairmen are protecting their turf for their career — not for a couple of years. If [a chairmanship] were a five-year or four-year or six-year deal, they would say, 'Let's do what's right because I'm going to have a different committee next time around.'"

Republicans have pledged to limit the chairmanship of all House committees to six years. I hope they stick to it and I hope Senate Republicans follow their lead. If this reform is carried out, voters should consider letting it work for a while before pressing for limits on the terms of all members of Congress.

I would like to see this issue rise on the campaign trail. If voters ask candidates who are seeking reelection or are running for the first time if they support term limits for committee chairmen, they will be forcing a dialogue on real reform. In my opinion nothing would improve the current Congress more than breaking the permanent grip of power a few people hold over legislation.

POSTAGE DUE — JUSTICE OVERDUE

One of the most insidious aspects of power is the aura of invincibility it creates around some lawmakers. The recent imbroglio involving Rep. Dan Rostenkowski of Illinois is a lamentable example.

Rostenkowski is a product of the ward system of Mayor Richard Daley's machine in Chicago. Rostenkowski volunteered for Washington in 1958, an oddity at the time for those inside the Daley machine. Most ambitious Chicago politicians wanted to be aldermen and dole out Daley's patronage. Back then, Washington was a demotion, not a promotion.

But Rostenkowski saw it differently. He had watched how southerners had consolidated power in Congress. They arrived early and stayed on until they became committee chairmen. From that perch they could pass or kill lots of laws.

It was time for someone from Chicago to get there early and make his way to the top, Rostenkowski told Daley. The mayor agreed and sent him to Congress, where for years he was known by the demeaning moniker "Daley's man in Congress."

Rostenkowski stands six feet two inches tall and weighs well over two hundred pounds. His domineering physique is made all the more intimidating by his booming voice and gruff demeanor. Rostenkowski does not walk through the capitol; he thunders through it. You can hear him coming from quite a distance. His leather soles slap the smooth and infinitely cool Capitol marble tiles like a gavel being slammed in anger. This burly, bejowled street pol oversees that most inane and incomprehensible of all legislative galaxies in Washington: the U.S. tax code.

Rostenkowski has chaired the Ways and Means Committee since 1981. Within the House, he is considered the second-most powerful lawmaker, second only to the Speaker. Running a close third is Rep. John Dingell of Michigan, chairman of the Energy and Commerce Committee.

I have admired Rostenkowski's strong leadership through the years on many issues: Social Security reform in 1983, tax reform in 1986, welfare reform in 1987, the Caribbean Basin Initiative, the Canadian Free Trade Agreement, and the North American Free Trade Agreement. On many occasions, he has demonstrated an ability to work with Republican Presidents and build bipartisan coalitions within Congress.

Nonetheless, throughout his career Rostenkowski has faced questions about his ethical standards.

After rising to the top of Ways and Means, Rostenkowski began to rub elbows with the corporate captains of America and their well-heeled lobbyists. The huge salaries of these corporate chieftains and the limitless expense accounts of their lobbyists deepened his distaste for limits on a lawmaker's outside income and made Rostenkowski an even stronger advocate for pay raises. Why should a Washington kingpin like me feel like a pauper, a bum next to these corporate captains? he must have thought.

Limits on the amount of money lawmakers could earn in outside income didn't take effect until 1990. Before that, Rostenkowski raked in something we call "honoraria." An honorarium is a fee received for giving a speech. Most lawmakers (myself included) have accepted a fee from time to time. However, some have made tens of thousands of dollars annually from speaking fees. Throughout the 1980s, Rostenkowski was at the top of all lawmakers who gave speeches for pay. In 1990, he hauled in $310,000, or three times his congressional salary.

House rules prevented Rostenkowski from keeping more than $27,000 per year, so the remainder went to charities. Rostenkowski's speeches were often delivered at luxurious resorts with picturesque beaches or championship golf courses. Rostenkowski was part of what is affectionately referred to in Congress as the "Golf Caucus." In Rostenkowski's case lobbyists were usually picking up the tab.

Rostenkowski argues that these hand-in-glove vacation getaways do nothing to cloud his vision about which tax loopholes to protect, which to close, and which to open. Maybe not.

Close relationships with lobbyists are pandemic in Washington and, thus, hardly worthy of an ethics committee investigation. Until recently, the rules governing these relationships have been intentionally vague. In 1994 the House and Senate attempted to tighten rules on the gifts lawmakers receive. At this writing it's unclear what the final outcome will be, but it appears certain that fewer gifts will be showered on lawmakers in the future.

Rostenkowski has for years bullied his way past reporters and government watchdogs who have questioned his ethics. His power has kept many critics within Congress at bay.

Rostenkowski was finally on the run.

A federal grand jury indicted Rostenkowski on May 31, 1994, on seventeen felony counts of corruption. Federal prosecutors said Rostenkowski defrauded the government of more than $500,000. The indictment said Rostenkowski embezzled at least $50,000 from the House post office for postage stamps he converted into cash. The indictments also accused Rostenkowski of hiring fourteen "ghost" employees who performed little or no work and — in one instance — remitted their salary to Rostenkowski; defrauding taxpayers of $40,000 by purchasing gifts from the House Stationery Store and giving them to his friends; and by bilking the Congress for over $73,000 for fraudulent automobile lease agreements.

The Rostenkowski investigation began in April 1991 when post office employee Edward Pogue stole more than $7,000 and fled to Puerto Rico. Eventually, four post office employees, including Pogue, pled guilty to embezzlement. The scam worked this way: lawmakers would purchase stamps supposedly for office mail and subsequently return the stamps in exchange for cash. The post office employee supervised the exchanges and never recorded the return of the stamps. These four employees now have lost their jobs and have established criminal records because they followed the orders of powerful members of Congress.

The federal indictments accuse Rostenkowski of being one of those powerful lawmakers. Rostenkowski has denied all charges. He rejected his defense attorney's attempts to negotiate a plea bargain arrangement with federal prosecutors.

What is so galling is that these employees did what some power broker told them to do. And long before any power brokers were brought to account, these workers paid a heavy price.

Democratic leaders circled the wagons around Rostenkowski from the very start, knowing his vital role in aiding Clinton's tax bill and health care initiative through Congress. The diffidence of my own party leaders illustrates the sad state of the Culture of Power. We protect those in positions of power more than we protect the supposedly sacred standards of conduct we promise to uphold when we are sworn into Congress. A little-known trade lawyer, Michael Patrick Flanagan, a Republican, scored a stunning defeat of Rostenkowski in the 1994 election. The Democratic leadership could protect Rostenkowski from some foes, but not from the voters.

THE EXCEPTION TO THE RULE

Some lawmakers wield power with restraint. They allow the nation's will to supersede their own political agendas, even though they have the power to do just the opposite. They stand as radiant examples of how Congress can and should work, of how power can reflect the will of the many instead of the will of one.

California congressman Ronald Dellums arrived as one of the most ideologically liberal — at the time, some said radical — lawmakers in what was unquestionably a volatile political era.

He arrived in Washington in 1970 after serving for four years on the Berkeley City Council, among the most liberal governmental entities in the nation. Dellums believed the progressive catechism of the 1960s: that America's customs remained racist even though most of its laws no longer were; that poverty was the result of disinterest or design on the part of financial and political powers in America; and that the U.S. military and intelligence complex too often compromised liberties at home and abroad and drained money from the federal budget that could address domestic needs.

Dellums's political agenda still reflects this creed. The way he has used his considerable power in Washington, however, shows how a lawmaker can serve the nation and his conscience at the same time.

In 1983 Dellums rose to become chairman of the military construction subcommittee on the House Armed Services Committee. That meant he oversaw a multibillion-dollar budget responsible for building many of the military projects he believed were unjust and redundant. Dellums would have preferred to slash the military construction budget and could have used his new power to harass the power centers in Congress more sympathetic to the Pentagon.

Instead, Dellums presided over development of a bill that reflected the will of his subcommittee, though not his own. He recognized that most members of Congress and the majority of the public supported more defense spending. During committee deliberations, he made his objections known but allowed the process to work.

When floor debate on the military construction bill was just about over, Dellums said something that was both memorable and honorable: "I have now discharged my institutional responsibilities," Dellums said. "Now I remove that hat. I must oppose this bill."

For the next five years as chairman of the military construction subcommittee, Dellums drafted a bipartisan bill, brought it to the floor, and then opposed it. He allowed the will of his subcommittee and the will of the House to prevail — even though he fundamentally disagreed with the policies being written into law.

Dellums became the chairman of the Armed Services Committee in 1993. The 1960s antiwar protester was now the second-most influential voice on military policy in Congress (most observers consider Sen. Sam Nunn of Georgia to be number one). Again, Dellums allowed the committee to write a bill that was less aggressive in reducing defense spending than he would have preferred. Nevertheless, when the bill came to the floor, Dellums supported it. It was the first defense bill he had voted for in twenty-three years in Congress.

"When I announced to the committee that I would vote for the bill, my voice cracked," Dellums recalled. "I was choked up. It was an opportunity to lead my colleagues in a way I had not been allowed to lead in the past. I don't believe in the 'power chairman.' I believe in democracy with a small *d*. I believe the role of the chairman is to maintain the integrity of the process and protect the rights and prerogatives of the members."

Dellums did another thing few chairmen do. He appointed freshmen to conference committees. This is where much of the hidden power of Congress truly resides. Conference committees resolve the many and oftentimes significant differences in House and Senate bills. Usually only senior members serve on these special committees because they can trust one another to carry on the same old policies with the same old compromises. It's a clubby, protective, and static environment. It's the place where innovations approved by the House or the Senate often die. The senior members typically kill these new ideas in favor of the comfortable and familiar. Conference committees are the least understood, least documented, and least democratic political organisms in the Congress.

Dellums tried to shake that up a bit by appointing freshmen to these committees. Most other chairmen keep the freshmen away because they aren't sure if they will be on the chairman's team. They don't want any surprises in conference. They want to get their way and get out. Freshmen might interfere, so they are usually excluded.

Dellums wanted freshmen to be heard.

As I said before, I don't always agree with Dellums's politics. That's not the point. What matters is he never abuses the immense power he has acquired. He wields his authority fairly and with deference to the will of the committees he has led and the House in which he has served. He's an example of someone who has used power far less radically than many others whose ideology is far more conservative than his.

PUBLIC SERVICE AT ITS BEST

I have also worked with lawmakers who rose above the temptations of power and struck an inspiring balance between the desire to pursue a personal agenda and the obligation to serve the national agenda.

There is no better example than Rep. William Natcher, a Kentucky Democrat whose service from 1953 to 1994 defines the best in public service.

Natcher never abused his power. Natcher never played the you-fund-my-program-I'll-fund-yours spending game in Congress. Natcher never hired a press secretary. Natcher never hired a chief of staff. Natcher never bought a FAX machine. Natcher never accepted a campaign contribution. Natcher rarely spent more than $10,000 on a reelection campaign. Natcher never ran a television or radio commercial.

What did Natcher do? Natcher memorized Robert's Rules of Order and followed them scrupulously when asked to preside over heated House debates. Natcher arrived at the office every morning at 7 A.M. and opened his own constituent mail. Natcher did all of his own research and reading. Natcher wrote his own speeches. Natcher kept a diary of every day in office. Natcher paid for the leather binding of each three-hundred-page volume of the diaries at the Government Printing Office (all fifty volumes will soon be released). Natcher hired a staff two-thirds smaller than was allotted to all House members.

Oh, by the way, Natcher cast an unprecedented 18,401 consecutive floor votes in the House. You can look it up in the *Guinness Book of World Records*.

Once, when a snowstorm prevented his plane from taking off for Washington from Bowling Green, Kentucky, Natcher hired a taxi and made it in time for a House vote. In 1991 his wife of fifty-four years, Virginia Reardon, fell ill. Natcher flew from Washington to Bowling Green, Kentucky, and back every day to comfort his wife and fulfill his House duties. He was eighty-one at the time. Mrs. Natcher died later that year.

Natcher never missed a vote until 1994, when the illness that led to his death kept him bedridden. House leaders did all they could to preserve Natcher's amazing streak, suspending all floor votes on March 2, 1994, in hopes Natcher would retire rather than see his streak broken. Natcher declined to retire, and his streak ended the next day.

In 1992 Natcher had a chance to catapult himself over an ailing colleague and capture the chairmanship of the full Appropriations Committee. He refused. That year the sitting chairman, Jamie Whitten, eighty-two, suffered a stroke, and his mental faculties and physical strength deteriorated rapidly and perceptibly.

Natcher had been the second in seniority on Appropriations since 1989. Whitten's failing health provided a perfect opportunity to seize the chairmanship. Natcher declined. He even balked when senior House leaders tried quietly to persuade Whitten to hand over the chairmanship. Whitten resisted, and Natcher waited patiently for his turn. The time came in December of 1992 when Democrats did not renominate Whitten for another term as chairman.

For thirteen years Natcher chaired the Appropriations subcommittee on Labor, Health, and Human Services. With the exception of the defense subcommittee, no other committee spent more than Natcher's. Yet Natcher never used his power to funnel wasteful projects to his district. Unlike others in positions of power in the House, Natcher never denied other lawmakers the right to offer amendments to cut spending under his jurisdiction. Above all, Natcher was fair. Natcher let the House work its will in committee and on the floor.

Michael Barone and Grant Ujifusa said it best in the 1994 *Almanac of American Politics:* "He is one of a kind — one of the few who make the House work, a splendid old stickler for doing things the way they are supposed to be done. He is, above all, meticulous and attentive to detail; he abhors waste and disorder; he is appalled by anything that smacks of corruption."

Sadly, Natcher died March 29, 1994, of heart and lung ailments. He was eighty-four.

At his funeral, which President Clinton and dozens of House members attended, the Rev. Richard Bridges, pastor at Natcher's church in Bowling Green, Kentucky, warned those who might try to succeed this paragon of political virtue: "If his name were to appear on the ballot at the next election, he would be reelected. Because most of us would rather vote for a dead Natcher than a living somebody else."

Seven

The Culture of Isolation

Whenever you are to do a thing, though it can never be known but to yourself, ask yourself how you would act were all the world looking at you, and act accordingly.

— Thomas Jefferson

MEMBERS OF CONGRESS are isolated from the ways in which the laws we pass affect the lives of people outside the Beltway because of the congressional cultures that so dominate the lives of lawmakers in Washington. Many lawmakers cannot understand why voters detest the perks and benefits we glibly take for granted.

In short, some lawmakers forget where they came from.

A colleague of mine, Democrat Romano L. Mazzoli of Kentucky, announced his retirement from the House shortly after I did. Ron, as his friends call him, came to Congress in 1970 after serving one term in the state senate. He understands the Culture of Isolation better than most lawmakers because he's been able to resist its many temptations:

"The lowest common denominator is D-Day, the lowest common denominator is the six o'clock news, the lowest common denominator is the front page of the hometown newspaper. And yet, around here we so frequently forget about the lowest common denominator. After all, we're up there in the stars. I mean, we come here, we're big shots. I mean, prime ministers come calling. Presidents call on the phone. I mean, it's big deal time. And you forget you're from Keokuk [Iowa] or Shively, Kentucky."

ABOVE THE LAW

For example, Congress exempts itself from most labor and safety regulations it imposes on the private sector. Some lawmakers fail to understand the "real world" that must adhere to the laws Congress passes.

Former South Dakota Sen. George McGovern wrote a startlingly candid essay for the *Wall Street Journal* on June 1, 1992, about how little his life in Congress prepared him for the rigors of the marketplace. McGovern's first business venture, a hotel and restaurant in Connecticut, had just fallen into bankruptcy. In the process, McGovern found reason to lament many of the labor, health, and safety laws he advocated as a senator but found so burdensome as a businessman.

"In retrospect, I wish I had known more about the hazards and difficulties of such a business," McGovern said. "I also wish that during the years I was in public office, I had had this firsthand experience about the difficulties businesspeople face every day. That knowledge would have made me a better U.S. senator and a more understanding presidential contender."

McGovern's experience underscores the danger of a legislature exerting so much influence over American commerce while possessing little "real life" knowledge of how the laws affect those who must comply with them.

Here is a list of some of the laws that apply to you but not to Congress.

Workplace safety. The Occupational Safety and Health Administration (OSHA) can fine private businesses for unsafe working conditions. It cannot investigate or fine Congress. And yet, a 1992 Government Accounting Office inspection of 25 congressional work sites found 140 safety violations. Of these, 50 were described as "serious." The report estimated the potential liability at nearly $1 million. Still, Congress is exempt from OSHA scrutiny.

Discrimination and harassment. Congress is exempt from all civil rights and sexual harassment laws. Congressional employees can appeal only to in-house committees run by members of Congress (not exactly a fair and impartial process). Complaints immediately bring an employee's "loyalty" into question and pit his or her word against the word of a lawmaker.

Wage and hour regulations. In the private sector, the Fair Labor Standards Act of 1938 requires employers to pay overtime for more than forty hours of work per week. The Senate is exempt from this requirement. The House began paying overtime in 1989 after it was revealed that House employees were working seventy-two-hour work weeks stuffing envelopes for taxpayer-subsidized congressional newsletters.

Congressional leaders contend that the Constitution's separation of powers doctrine exempts Congress from complying with these laws. The leaders fear the executive branch could abuse its oversight powers by leveling inflammatory accusations against political opponents. Congress has set up in-house committees to review wage complaints, but the hearings are rarely public, and the committees have shown little interest in punishing lawmakers.

Meanwhile, extraordinary demands are still placed on certain House employees. On January 20, 1994, the government's Office of Personnel Management ordered all nonessential federal offices closed due to record snowfall in the Washington area. Nevertheless, all one hundred employees of the House Folding Room were ordered to work. Twenty-five braved the treacherous driving conditions and tromped to work stations in the bowels of the Capitol to fold taxpayer-subsidized congressional newsletters. The other seventy-five were docked a day's pay (a day of annual leave or accrued vacation). Speaker Foley had said only "essential" Capitol Hill employees were required to report to work on January 20. For the rest of the federal government, "essential" employees were those involved in law enforcement, security, and vital maintenance functions. All other government employees were given a day off. A backlog of congressional newsletters prompted House officials to summon the "essential" Folding Room employees to work, according to *Roll Call* newspaper.

Congress was considering bringing itself under these and other laws in 1994. This reform is long overdue and a consequence of heightened voter interest in the differences between laws Congress passes for others and laws it passes for itself. Left to itself, the Congress would never have undertaken these steps. This is a classic example of how voters can change Congress by forcing members to discuss and take positions on matters they would just as soon ignore.

Congress failed to pass this reform in 1994. It died, as did many elements of the reform agenda, as a result of partisan squabbles and irresolute congressional leadership. Republicans have pledged to apply these laws to Capitol Hill early in the 104th Congress.

DIVERSE VOICES

Rep. Maxine Waters, a California Democrat, complained that Congress was failing to meet minimum affirmative action hiring goals the public sector has been required to meet for years.

In November of 1991, Waters interrupted a Veterans Committee hearing to fault chairman G. V. "Sonny" Montgomery for hiring only two black staff members on a committee with a staff of thirty. It's hard to describe how unusual this frontal assault was. Committee members almost never criticize their chairmen. When they do, it's almost always in private. To air her grievances in public was as bold a move as I'd ever seen from a freshman legislator. Montgomery was not a racist, and Waters never implied that he was. She said, however, that black staff representation was appallingly low. Waters was right, and her outburst highlighted the lack of minority representation on most congressional committees. Montgomery soon hired two more black committee staff members.

Waters and I first met when she joined the Veterans Committee, on which I served, after her election in 1990. When some colleagues referred to her as Maxine in public, she tartly informed them she considered their behavior disrespectful and asked that they refer to her as Mrs. Waters. When she arrived for a meeting of all House Democrats, she claimed a front-row seat even after being told it was customarily occupied by a powerful committee chairman. No one made her move.

Waters represents South Central Los Angeles, one of the poorest districts in America. Her district exploded in flames, looting, and gun shots in April of 1992 after four Los Angeles police officers were acquitted in the Rodney King case. Waters saw the riots far differently than most Americans, myself included. She flew home immediately and saw to it that water service was restored. She used her office to provide other assistance. But she did little to calm her constituents or discourage them from more violence. She called the wanton lawlessness a "rebellion" and came to the defense of the four African American men accused of stoning white truck driver Reginald Denny. She said Denny's attackers were no different from the Los Angeles police officers who beat Rodney King.

After returning to Washington, Waters crashed a White House meeting of congressional leaders and President Bush in the aftermath of the South Central riots. She told Speaker Tom Foley she would be there whether he wanted her there or not (after all, it was her district). That left Foley no choice but to make room for this audacious freshman at the White House conclave.

Waters's perspective reflected an upbringing few Americans and even fewer members of Congress can relate to. She was born in St. Louis, one of thirteen children in a family that subsisted on welfare and lived in public housing. She bused tables in a segregated restaurant and married soon after graduating from high school.

Waters moved to Los Angeles in 1961 and worked in a garment factory and raised her two children while her husband launched a successful car dealership. After the Watts riot in 1965, she decided to get involved in the community, becoming an assistant teacher in the fledgling Head Start program for disadvantaged children. She joined several other community organizations and worked full-time for Head Start. She won a seat in the California assembly in 1976.

While in the assembly, Waters was a loyal follower of Speaker Willie Brown, a liberal Democrat. She led the effort to divest California's pension funds from South Africa and was a vocal supporter of Jesse Jackson's 1984 and 1988 campaigns. Waters won her seat in Congress after Rep. Augustus Hawkins retired in 1990.

Waters's intensity and impatience forces complacent lawmakers to view issues differently. Waters doesn't win many legislative battles, but she never loses without leaving the system with a different perspective than it had before. Even though our political beliefs are quite different, I admire Waters's willingness to speak her mind and confront some of the capitol's creaky traditions. I joined with her in an effort to prevent trade schools from defrauding the student financial aid program set up to aid low-skilled minority students. Sadly, Congress buckled to pressure from trade school lobbyists and we lost.

Another new Democrat, Cynthia McKinney of Georgia, brings a similar passion to House politics.

McKinney arrived in Washington at age thirty-seven as the first black woman ever elected to Congress from Georgia. House employees frequently mistook McKinney for a tourist. Elevator operators routinely tried to shoo McKinney off elevators reserved for House members. Maybe it was the metallic-gold tennis shoes. McKinney often dresses for House business in casual and sporty outfits that look better suited for a college professor (she did work on her Ph.D. at the Fletcher School of Diplomacy at Tufts University during her first term).

McKinney's casual garb deceives many. She is a passionate supporter of abortion rights and highly suspicious of defense spending and foreign entanglements. As a member of the Georgia legislature, McKinney gave a lengthy speech denouncing the Gulf War, prompting two-thirds of her colleagues to walk out.

In her first term, McKinney gave a thundering speech in defense of abortion rights for poor women. It occurred during debate over providing federal funds for poor women seeking abortions. Congress had prevented such funding for sixteen years under something called the Hyde Amendment, in honor of the prohibition's sponsor, Rep. Henry Hyde, an Illinois Republican. Many women spoke during the debate, none more effectively and passionately than McKinney:

> Mr. Chairman, for far too many women in this country, the legal right to choose is meaningless because they have had no practical access to the full range of reproductive services. All available data confirms that what Henry Hyde has succeeded in doing has been to create devastating consequences in the lives of low-income women. The Hyde amendment is nothing but a discriminatory policy against poor women who happen to be disproportionately black. By denying poor women abortion services while at the same time paying for childbirth and sterilization, the federal government is practicing discriminatory policies. This is about equity and fairness for all women, and quite frankly, I have just about had it with my colleagues who vote against people of color, against the poor, and vote against women.

I didn't agree with McKinney's reasoning. But I know it had a profound effect on the debate that day and is recalled by many lawmakers on both sides of the abortion issue. That's because McKinney's speech was unrehearsed. (She scribbled the text on the House floor.) As a black single mother who represents a poor district, McKinney reacted to the Hyde Amendment from the perspective of her many low-income constituents, whose voice deserves to be heard on the House floor. Whether or not one agrees with her, McKinney has challenged Congress to view issues from another perspective, and that is the essence of representative democracy.

Like Waters, McKinney's intensity sheds new light on familiar issues. Both lawmakers have helped shake Congress out of the complacency the Culture of Isolation breeds.

THE GIFTS THAT KEEP ON GIVING

Lobbyists give lawmakers gifts all the time. They pay for lawmakers' trips to ski resorts, tropical islands, and championship golf courses. They take them to all-star games and Super Bowls, the opera and music concerts. They take them to the finest restaurants in Washington. Happens all the time. Until recently, few in Washington thought there was anything wrong with it. Few thought the gifts compromised their judgment.

Then some newcomers suggested that accepting gifts, dinners, show and sports tickets, and vacations probably clouded lawmakers' judgment and set a horrible example. In the Senate, the rabble-rousers were Democrats Russell Feingold of Wisconsin and Paul Wellstone of Minnesota.

Congressional veterans disagreed. When it comes to reforms, they almost always do.

The Senate devoted two weeks of debate to the question. Under consideration was a bill to prohibit gifts worth more than $25. The ban meant lobbyists could pay for a show at the local movie theaters (medium popcorn and drinks only), dinner at Denny's, or golf outings at courses with windmills and red schoolhouses.

But that's about it.

Unless, of course, the lawmakers wanted to pay for their own opera tickets, their own filet mignon and champagne, and their own greens fees at Augusta National.

Here are some memorable excerpts from the Senate debate:

Louisiana Democrat Bennett Johnston, serving his twenty-second year in Congress, complained he would miss out on some swanky events.

> JOHNSTON: I assume we cannot go to the Opera Ball? Do you say that we cannot go to the Symphony Ball, Ambassador Ball, the National Guard Ball, the Opera Ball?

WELLSTONE: I would say you can go to any opera you want to; you pay for it just like ordinary people pay for it when they go to the opera. It's just that simple.

When Johnston argued the gift ban would make it more difficult to meet with constituents over lunch or dinner, Feingold offered these commonsense suggestions.

FEINGOLD: One is to not have them in connection with a meal. The second is not to eat, not to have lunch. And the third is to pay your own way.
JOHNSTON: For this, bring a brown bag.
FEINGOLD: That is right. These are all options.

Johnston said paying for lunch and dinner would force some senators to skip charity dinners and other pleasant outings.

JOHNSTON: If I had to pay $150 for something every time I went to those [functions], most senators except the wealthy ones will not go.
FEINGOLD: There's nothing in the [gift ban] proposal that would make your life more difficult.
JOHNSTON: It would make things a lot more expensive, in my view, to do things that are ordinary parts of being a senator as far as I am concerned.

Wellstone, a former college professor, put the entire debate in perspective:

WELLSTONE: If people do not believe in our process, they are not going to believe in any of the outcomes of the process. If they are going to think that there is a lot of wheeling and dealing and gifts and trips and all the rest — which is not for them; they do not get these free gifts and trips and all the rest of it. But they think that is a part of the culture here — they are not going to believe in our policies. They have to feel like this process is more accountable. They have to feel like it is more open. They have to feel like we are focused on the common good or the public good.

In spite of the objections raised, the Senate's gift ban passed 95–4.

The House passed its version of the gift ban. A compromise version passed the House but a Republican filibuster killed it in the Senate.

HELLO, I MUST BE GOING

There is another side to the Culture of Isolation. It's the individual isolation of life within Congress. There are so many committees in Congress (146 in the House alone), that members are routinely dashing from one meeting to another. Once they arrive, they have almost no time to confer with other members or even immerse themselves in the testimony being given. In 1988 the average House member served on six committees and subcommittees. The average senator served on eleven committees and subcommittees.

A recent study of sixty bills passed by three of the most influential House committees showed that lawmakers often missed the most important part of the legislative process — the markup. That's when the bill is being drafted in its final form in preparation for full House debate. And many of those who did attend did so only briefly. After leaving, they gave their "proxy" votes to the chairman for him to cast as he saw fit. This is not because legislators are slackers. It is an unavoidable consequence of the overlapping nature of scheduling on Capitol Hill.

On the Energy and Commerce Committee, one of the most influential in the House, 24 percent of the members didn't attend the markup of its bills in the 1983–85 session. Thirty-four percent left "proxy" votes behind. On the Education and Labor Committee, 30 percent of the Committee members didn't attend markups for its bills in the 1981–83 session. Forty-five percent of those members left behind "proxy" votes. The results were similar for the Agriculture Committee.

Congressional scholar Richard L. Hall describes the absenteeism this way: "Members often duck into a markup for a brief moment, leaving their proxy behind them with little knowledge of the way in which it will be used. In practice, though, proxy voting tends to augment the power of the active, not preserve the authority of the absent."

This phenomenon occasionally allows an outnumbered Democratic committee chairman to kill Republican amendments even when all committee Democrats are absent.

In the spring of 1994, Rep. William Ford, chairman of the Education and Labor Committee, called for a voice vote on a Republican worker safety bill. When Ford asked for the "nays," he was met with dead silence. When he asked for the "yeas," several Republicans piped up. It sounded as if Ford was beaten. But not so.

"In the opinion of the chair," Ford declared, "the nays have it."

Republicans demanded a roll call vote. Ford then plucked more than two dozen proxy votes out of his pocket and prevailed on a vote of 28–15.

The pell-mell pace on Capitol Hill leaves most lawmakers exhausted. In addition to having committee responsibilities, members typically meet with constituents, attend fund-raisers, give outside speeches, answer calls from the local and national press corps, attend party caucuses, and attend meetings with lawmakers informally organized to pursue a specific legislative goal (the numerous meetings to work on the Penny-Kasich bill are a good example).

Frequently, every hour of every day is blocked off. There is no time for independent research. No time to discuss issues with other lawmakers. There's almost no time to think. Life within Congress is a treadmill. Members get on it every morning and walk all day long. Just like the treadmill at your local gym, the treadmills on Capitol Hill don't go anywhere. The belt keeps moving, but the lawmakers rarely get anywhere. I've never seen another institution where individuals can work so hard and yet get so little done.

Most lawmakers I know can't wait for a floor vote. That's one of the few times during the day when lawmakers can talk to one another. It's also one of the few times when they can ignore their schedule . . . but only for a few minutes. If it weren't for floor votes, most lawmakers would seldom see one another. There is so little time to talk to one another in Congress that most lawmakers learn about each other primarily through press releases and interoffice letters, better known in Congress as "Dear Colleagues."

Consequently, too often there is a highly impersonal nature to our relationships in Congress. This isolation makes it much, much harder to forge consensus on tough issues. Regrettably, it makes it easier to assume the worst about an opponent's motives or to engage in fiercely partisan attacks.

PENCHANT FOR PENSIONS

The Culture of Isolation also leads lawmakers to become dependent on the perks of office.

Some of the harshest criticism I encountered to the Penny-Kasich proposal came from members upset about our attempt to scale back the congressional pension. There was no issue that caused the Penny-Kasich group more heartburn. (We debated provisions to cut members' pensions for nearly an hour.)

Three lawmakers specifically sought me out to explain that they would oppose Penny-Kasich on that basis alone. The most memorable confrontation was with Rep. Bob Livingston, Republican of Louisiana, who is now the chairman of the Appropriations Committee.

Elected in 1977, Livingston was counting on a big pension after retirement and objected to any attempt to cut those benefits.

Livingston pulled John Kasich aside on the House floor and swore at him at the top of his lungs. His obscenity-laden diatribe was so loud I could hear it from the other side of the chamber. I hustled over to give Kasich a hand, and Livingston lit into me, his face red with rage. He said Kasich and I had a lot of gall sticking *our* hands into *his* pocket. Kasich and I stood there impassively. We'd heard these complaints before —

although never at this volume — and were sure to hear them again. It dawned on me that the passion Livingston found to protect his generous pension was far more genuine than any he'd ever mustered to reduce other government spending — even though he had carefully cultivated an image back home as a budget skinflint. Rep. Jim Bilbray, a Nevada Democrat, was one of the first lawmakers to complain about the pension reduction. He said it was so bad he couldn't support the bill. I knew better. Bilbray wouldn't support big budget even if the pension cut had been taken out. Bilbray lost in 1994.

BAD BOUNCE

The Culture of Isolation led the House into one of the most embarrassing episodes in modern history: the bank scandal.

Common sense in politics, as in life, recommends that when you've done something wrong, the best response is to swiftly admit your mistake, seek forgiveness, and move on.

The House bank scandal was an acid test of the relationship many House members felt they had with their constituents. A good number were afraid to submit to it. And the congressional leadership did everything in its power to protect them. Few events in modern congressional history so vividly illustrated Congress's desire to shield itself and its most powerful members from hostile public scrutiny. It illustrated the Culture of Isolation at its worst.

As we now know, Speaker Foley first learned of abuses at the House bank on December 19, 1989. That's when an audit from the General Accounting Office, the investigative arm of Congress, revealed that House members were routinely cashing checks they didn't have the funds to cover.

I don't know why Foley didn't act immediately to clean up the bank (he did ask some outside bankers to recommend changes but never followed up). But it's not hard to imagine the reaction he got when he began sounding out members about shutting down one of their most favored perks. It's safe to assume that by not acting, Foley was doing what most members wanted.

I won't bore you with all the gory details of the bank and those among my colleagues who essentially milked it for hundreds of thousands of dollars in interest-free loans. I just want to tell you the story of how the public forced the Congress to do the right thing, despite the intensely muscular efforts by top congressional leaders to keep most of the scandal's details under wraps.

The House bank saga started when the GAO, in September of 1991, issued its third report on the flagrant abuse of checking procedures at the

House bank. Both parties had ignored the two previous reports. The checks just kept bouncing. The third GAO report revealed that members had floated 8,331 checks in one year, which meant an average of 160 checks were floated per week and that, on average, each member overdrew at least 19 checks in that one year. A total of 276 current members wrote no bad checks, which meant some members were floating dozens of checks.

Unlike the first two GAO reports, the third drew widespread media attention in *Roll Call,* which sparked interest in the broader Washington media. Suddenly, the House was being asked to account for its unaccountable banking practices.

Foley at first resisted calls from junior House Republicans to close the bank. Again, he was deferring to the wishes of many Democrats (and in all probability, many in the Republican Party).

"In this case, the fact that there were a sizable number of members involved [led to the resistance to act]," said Rep. Jerry Lewis, a California Republican and one of the first to call for full disclosure of all House bank accounts. "There were members on the Republican side with some considerable influence who had some problems, there was resistance. On the Democratic side, they were very frightened of the political fallout because of the numbers there. They were very hesitant."

Foley reluctantly joined with House Republican Leader Bob Michel on October 3, 1991, to sponsor a resolution to close the bank and begin an internal and secret investigation of members "who routinely and repeatedly" wrote checks in excess of their account balance "by a significant amount."

This was necessary, the speaker said, because "no member should be permitted to cash checks with insufficient funds, an opportunity not afforded to citizens of the country generally."

Asked if the results of the investigation, including the names of those who most abused the bank, should be shared with the public, Foley said no.

"This is now a matter that is over and done with," Foley said.

Wishful thinking.

That was October 1991. By the second week in March of 1992, the House bank saga had become a cause célèbre. Few things in life concentrate the mind quite like bouncing a check. Everyone can identify with the sick feeling you get in the pit of your stomach when you get the notice in the mail. Those who have inadvertently written a bad check know how you try to avoid shopping at the store where you bounced the check for a while, even if the "bounce" was an accident. News reports claimed that House members intentionally bounced checks. In reality, no checks bounced, and there was no check-kiting scheme. Nevertheless, it is true

House members enjoyed scandalously generous overdraft protection unavailable to anyone in the private sector.

Voters everywhere were thunderstruck and angry that House members could float checks with impunity. They instinctively knew this was an example of Congress out of touch because at the members' bank, they never once had to juggle the bills or confront the gnawing nausea that comes when a check is bounced or an overdraft penalty is assessed.

Despite the palpable public rage, House leaders still, as late as the second week in March, intended to keep most of the information on "check bouncers" under wraps. They had no intention of letting the public learn everything about how many floated how much for how long.

Instead, the leadership accepted the recommendation of a six-member panel selected from the fourteen-member House ethics committee. This bipartisan panel (three Democrats and three Republicans) was itself meant to be an agent of damage control. Its members knew better than anyone else how hard it would be to explain the bank shenanigans. They had seen the bank records and realized that — for many members — public disclosure would be politically damaging.

In reaction to voter and media inquiries, about ninety members, myself included, had already checked carefully our bank records to see if we had any overdrafts. I called in all the reporters representing Minnesota newspapers and told them what I thought to be the facts. I had three bad checks totaling less than $100. The checks had been held a few days awaiting another deposit and cleared once the deposit was made.

Like most members, I was never notified of the overdrafts by the bank. Evidently, as a courtesy to members (I consider it an outrage), overdrafts were not handled as they would have been at a normal bank. The important thing was to clear the air, admit my mistake, and apologize to my constituents. I did it. Afterward, I thought my troubles were over.

During its probe, the ethics panel discovered the following: 355 current and former members floated checks during those three years; nearly twenty thousand bad checks had been written; some checks were for more than $100,000; some members overdrew their account for dozens of months.

"I was rather shocked," said Rep. Matthew McHugh, the New York Democrat who led the bank investigation. "I don't know how some of the folks slept at night, given the kind of books that they kept."

Despite the breadth of the scandal, McHugh's committee recommended naming only twenty-four abusers. Of these, nineteen were still in the House, four had retired, and one, Texas Democrat Mickey Leland, had died in a plane crash in Ethiopia, where he was delivering aid to starving children.

The panel named those who had done the following: overdrawn their account in at least eight months by an amount exceeding their net monthly salary, which at the time was approximately $6,000.

If, for example, a member had overdrawn his or her account for only seven months by his net monthly salary of $6,000, he or she would not be publicly identified. In other words, a member who had floated $42,000 in checks in only three years would be spared the embarrassment of public disclosure.

It's painfully clear that McHugh's committee was trying — undoubtedly at the congressional leadership's bidding — to shield the House from the damage of full public disclosure. In essence, the top leaders feared that voters would be unwilling or unable to distinguish between members who accidentally floated checks — the bank's procedures were sloppy, after all — and those who willfully abused the system.

The full ethics committee endorsed this flimsy standard by a vote of 10–4. Foley immediately embraced it and urged Democrats to stand with the committee so the House could put the embarrassing spectacle behind it.

But the dissenters helped galvanize the public.

"The reputation of the House of Representatives is at stake," said Rep. John Kyl, an Arizona Republican and one of the four to oppose the McHugh standard. "A person who wrote over eight hundred and fifty bad checks would not be deemed an abuser under the majority's definition, and we don't think that is defensible."

But Foley's support for the McHugh standard seemed to sway many members. Most thought it possible to hide behind the legitimacy of the ethics committee and the Democratic leadership.

What they didn't realize was that Congress had no credibility to draw upon. Most voters had already concluded a coverup was underway, and they were interested in only one thing: full disclosure.

Robert Merry, the executive editor of *Congressional Quarterly,* a weekly publication that chronicles all floor and committee action in Congress, compared the House's strategy to the fairy tale of Br'er Rabbit and Tar Baby. When Tar Baby wouldn't respond to Br'er Rabbit's friendly chatter, Br'er Rabbit, following his own instincts, hit Tar Baby. With each blow, Br'er Rabbit found himself stuck ever more closely to Tar Baby.

"They have followed their instinct," Merry said of the House leaders, "which is to protect House members, or at least as many as possible, from their constituents. The instinct of incumbency has become its own trap, and the more the House strikes at this tar baby the more stuck it will become. Escaping to the brier patch will require not sly tricks, but a basic faith in the wisdom and judgment of the voters."

In other words, common sense.

But the leadership and many House members refused to see the bank scandal for the tar baby it was.

The House was to vote on March 13 on the recommendation to identify only the twenty-four worst bank abusers. On March 9, a Monday, Foley confidently predicted the House would endorse the limited disclosure plan. Majority Leader Gephardt and Majority Whip Bonior agreed and were part of an intense lobbying effort to support limited disclosure.

By now, Republicans were pressing for full disclosure, even though several of their own members were the worst abusers. This was not altruistic. The Republicans knew the bank scandal would hurt more Democrats than Republicans because Democrats outnumbered them 268–166. They calculated it was worth losing a few GOP check floaters in exchange for the heads of more Democrats.

On March 10, the House Republicans gathered to decide whether to push for full disclosure. Their leader, Michel of Illinois, refused to lobby one way or the other. An institution man, he knew that full disclosure would damage the House's already shaky public standing. But he knew just as well that opposing disclosure would incite younger, more partisan Republicans and threaten his already tenuous hold on the top leadership post.

Congressman Lewis, who was chairman of the GOP conference, said he was going to offer a floor motion for full disclosure whether Michel wanted him to or not.

Seven freshmen Republicans, later dubbed the "Gang of Seven," had been pushing for full disclosure from the first. One of them, Jim Nussle of Iowa, infuriated Democrats by placing a grocery bag over his head and, in full view of the C-SPAN audience, dramatically yanked it off his head and said he was too embarrassed by Congress to show his face in public. Their theatrics were partly responsible for the Republicans' push for full disclosure. Nussle supervised the GOP transition to power in the 104th Congress.

On Tuesday, March 11, the ethics committee report was released.

Of its arbitrary definition of "abusers" it said: "No doubt, many who are unfamiliar with how the House bank operated for many years will find this definition of 'significant amount' [of floated checks] generous. It is."

Officially, the ethics committee reported — without naming names — that a hundred members wrote forty-five or more overdrafts (or more than one a month for the thirty-nine-month period under investigation). Many wrote hundreds of bad checks. One member floated 996 checks . . . more than one every working day.

Unofficially, more information was leaked to enterprising investigative reporters.

The *Washington Times* reported on March 12 that sixty-six members floated 19,373 checks worth about *$10.8 million*. Many members had negative balances of more than $1,000 for hundreds of days. The *Times* published a graphic on its front page with account numbers — but no names — of the sixty-six worst abusers, the number of checks floated, and the amount the accounts had been overdrawn.

What had been shrouded in secrecy was now one step from becoming public.

The *Times*'s graphic gave every reporter in Washington (some six thousand) the power to call a member of Congress and ask specifically if they had an account number on the list of the sixty-six worst abusers. It also revealed that there were flagrant abusers who, under the ethics committee's recommendation, would never be identified.

Suddenly, members realized if this much information could be leaked in one day, it was only a matter of time before all would be leaked . . . and the scandal exposed in all its sordid dimensions.

The political calculus that made limited disclosure a safe bet now made it political suicide. Now, the only way members had to protect themselves was to vote for full disclosure and take their chances. The members' decision was not based so much on a sudden infatuation with the public's right to know but on the grim and cold-blooded calculation that there no longer was a place to hide.

On top of that, members started to hear that the ethics committee records were showing that members had floated more checks than the bank had originally identified. I was furious and so were many others. We'd already come clean, exposed our mistakes, and moved on. We'd already paid our political penance. We thought we'd done the right thing, even though the leadership was still trying to cover the tracks of the worst offenders.

As soon as reporters got wind of this, they began retracing their steps. They called members again to see if they had floated more checks than they'd originally disclosed.

It's hard to describe the poisonous atmosphere the bank scandal created. Members feared for their political lives. The primary season was just starting, and many worried that disclosures about bank abuses would sink their reelection campaigns. Careers were at stake here. No one was sure how the voters would react. Even those of us who confessed our overdrafts wondered how it would all play out. We all felt as if we were in the crosshairs.

Like many members who had already gone public, I called the ethics committee to see what the new records showed. They told me I had floated seven checks. That did it. I snapped. I was beyond rage. I was nearly blinded with anger. I knew I would have to call in the Minnesota reporters a second time and apologize all over again. Even though I'd disclosed everything I was aware of earlier, it would look as if I had been part of some cover-up. The value of the additional four checks, by the way, was $40.

This was a radicalizing event for those members who had tried to deal with the bank scandal in an honest manner. We now understood that the leadership's attempts to protect the worst abusers had created horrendous political problems for those who hadn't abused the system and who had tried to come clean.

Like many other members, I was in no mood to let the leadership shield the worst abusers while I stood there with egg on my face.

"I am hopping mad," I told reporters at the time. "I want heads on a stake — those who are the most flagrant abusers."

Democrats and Republicans gathered separately to decide what to do. At this point, there seemed to be little choice. Full disclosure was coming; only the details were left to debate.

As those who knew the details explained to the rest of us what full disclosure would mean, members started venting their spleens. Some still tried to hold out for limited disclosure to protect themselves, while others pressed aggressively for full disclosure to show their constituents they weren't as bad as the others. It was every man for himself. Party labels were worthless. Loyalty to leadership was nonexistent. It was political chaos.

"Both Republicans and Democrats had caucuses that more closely resembled brawls," said Rep. Fred Grandy, an Iowa Republican and member of the smaller ethics committee that conducted the investigation and recommended limited disclosure. "Once they found out what full disclosure meant, there was open trembling."

After the caucuses, the House recessed while the leaders worked out the wording of the full disclosure resolution. After hours of ugly, venomous debate, the House voted 391–36 to name the twenty-four worst abusers within ten days.

Before doing so, House Minority Whip Newt Gingrich called the bank scandal a fitting metaphor for the Democrats' corruption of power. He said the bipartisanship that brought the full disclosure measure to the floor arose out of Foley's desperation to put the scandal behind him. Democrats hissed Gingrich as he spat out his invective. As soon as the scandal passed, Gingrich said, Foley and other Democratic leaders would resort to the same "cover-ups" and "abuses of power" that led to the bank scandal.

As Gingrich walked backed to his seat, it was as if all the oxygen had been sucked from the chamber. Republicans and Democrats sat in silent, clenched-jaw rage . . . infuriated with each other, themselves, and the dreadfully embarrassing spectacle they were making of the U.S. House of Representatives.

Unbeknownst to many Democrats, at least some of the rage on the Republican side was reserved for Gingrich. Many senior Republicans knew Gingrich had been pleading for months in private meetings to keep the scandal under wraps. They concluded that he, too, had overdrawn his account and was willing to hide behind the ethics committee's cover-up.

"I sat back astonished at Newt's involvement there. I was just amazed," Lewis said. "Because of what had gone on in those other discussions. He'd been very resistant in private sessions. I was really quite surprised. It was really incredible. He actually jumped up out of the back of the room and went down to the well [to attack the Democrats]."

At 1:15 A.M. on March 13, the House voted 426–0 to also name the 277 current and 54 former members who had overdrawn their accounts. This list was to be released ten days after the worst abusers were identified.

Most of the worst "check bouncers" pleaded for political mercy. Some got it. Others didn't.

A few of the worst violators, however, offered no apologies. They merely outspent their opponents in the next election.

Democrat Charlie Wilson of Texas floated eighty-one checks for $143,000 and exceeded his net monthly salary in eight of the thirty-nine months under investigation. He laughed it all off.

"It's not like molesting young girls or young boys," Wilson said. "It's not a show stopper. If my constituents didn't forgive sloppiness and a certain amount of eccentricity, I wouldn't have been here in the first place."

Wilson won his bid for reelection. He spent $1.1 million. Of that total, more than $683,000 came from political action committees, or PACs. His opponent, Republican Donna Peterson, who once posed for a photograph castrating a calf she had named Charlie, spent $344,000.

Republican Duncan Hunter of California floated 399 checks worth about $129,000. At first he denied the overdrafts; then he blamed them on his charitable contributions; then he said he had a right to write the overdrafts because he was a busy and important lawmaker (at the time, Hunter was chairman of the Republican Research Committee and a member of the GOP leadership).

Finally, Hunter, a former helicopter pilot in Vietnam, decided to meet the enemy head-on. He sat behind a card table at the local courthouse for three days with a copy of each overdrawn check. He defended each overdraft to anyone who had a question.

Oh, by the way, Hunter defeated his Democratic opponent Janet Gastil 53 percent to 41 percent after outspending her $559,970 to $164,480.

In the end, while 110 new members were elected to Congress in 1992, the bank scandal was a deciding factor in only a few House contests.

THE REBEL IN THE RAMBLER

There is a bright side to the Culture of Isolation. It doesn't last forever. Sooner or later, the scales fall from the voters' eyes.

That happened to two Washington luminaries in 1992.

The people who replaced them are among the few freshmen of 1992 who can legitimately lay claim to the title "political outsider."

On the night the House voted to disclose the names of all who had been caught in the bank scandal, Republican Guy VanderJagt of Michigan could barely contain his glee.

VanderJagt, you see, was chairman of the multimillion-dollar National Republican Congressional Committee. This committee is designed to defeat as many House Democrats as possible each election year. The chairman raises millions of dollars every year toward that end. He mixes with all sorts of big-wallet Republicans and flies all over the country stumping for the party's best and brightest challengers.

VanderJagt, elected in 1966 and chairman of the committee since 1975, thought he'd struck the mother lode.

"There will be many, many members who will be taken out, lose their reelection because of their record of bounced checks," VanderJagt said, leaving no doubt which party he believed would take the biggest hit. "I am absolutely overjoyed."

VanderJagt was right. Many, many members lost in 1992.

He was one of them.

But not because he bounced any checks. Because he'd lost touch.

It all started in 1990, when ABC television secretly videotaped VanderJagt and other powerful lawmakers gamboling on a Caribbean island with lobbyists on a trip sanitized in press releases as a seminar on tax law. VanderJagt by that time had become the third-most senior Republican on the Ways and Means Committee, which writes tax law and was chaired by Illinois Democrat Dan Rostenkowski.

That episode nearly cost VanderJagt his seat in 1990.

In 1992, the situation looked brighter. VanderJagt hadn't dipped as much as a toe in the tar pit of the bank scandal because he had no bad checks. And he had scared off the man who appeared to have been his toughest competitor, state senator William VanRegenmorter. Some 150 Republicans tried to draft VanRegenmorter for the GOP primary, but former President Gerald Ford (who represented Michigan in the House from 1949 to 1973 and served as Minority Leader from 1965 to 1973) persuaded him to sit out the race.

Then VanderJagt did something his constituents could not understand.

In the aftermath of the bank scandal, VanderJagt endorsed fellow Michigan Republican Bob Davis's bid for reelection — even though Davis had floated 878 checks worth more than $350,000. (A lot of good it did

Davis. His dismal reelection chances later led him to retire.) You could almost hear the sound of VanderJagt's previously spotless House checkbook plopping into the bank scandal tar pit. Voters soon decided that VanderJagt, an ordained minister, had confused righteous indignation with partisan grandstanding.

And along came Peter Hoekstra.

All of thirty-eight years old, Hoekstra had never held a public office of any kind. He was vice president of one of the nation's largest office furniture manufacturers. Like many Americans, he'd grown frustrated with politics. For a while, he didn't even vote.

Then he decided, if politics was to change, people like him would have to do it. Impulsively and quite illogically, Hoekstra decided to skip over the school board, the city council, the state legislature.

He took on VanderJagt.

He knew VanderJagt could raise more money in a week than he could raise in a year. He knew that VanderJagt would spend as much as it took to win. He knew VanderJagt could produce the slickest radio and television advertisements in the land (the ones in his 1990 campaign were produced in the Netherlands). He knew the party insiders would shun him and embrace VanderJagt.

All of this happened. And none of it mattered.

Though a novice, Hoekstra quickly mastered the art of political jujitsu, the Japanese martial art that relies on turning an opponent's strength to one's advantage.

But first, Hoekstra had to deal with GOP party regulars, none of whom were interested in his candidacy. Both parties dislike untested "citizen politicians" entering the fray. They fret about their loyalty and reliability when it comes to upholding party traditions . . . regardless of how moribund they've become. When he announced his candidacy, GOP insiders bluntly told Hoekstra to drop out and work as a party volunteer for a while until he got the hang of politics. When he refused, a GOP county chairman sent a memo to Republicans throughout the district showing Hoekstra had voted in only 33 percent of all elections held since 1985. The chairman advised the Republicans to leak the memo to reporters covering Hoekstra's campaign.

Hoekstra turned all of this to his advantage.

- Hoekstra acknowledged that VanderJagt was well known. So he planted twenty-five hundred yard signs with his name *and VanderJagt's*.
- Hoekstra saved up all of his annual vacation, and spent four weeks pedaling his ten-speed bike through all nine counties (some 270 miles) in the 2nd Congressional District.
- After his vacation, Hoekstra drove to campaign events in a 1964 Nash Rambler, a homely antique that rolled off the assembly line the year

VanderJagt won a seat in the state senate and two years before he entered the House.

- Hoekstra admitted VanderJagt had more clout in Washington and promised to leave Congress after twelve years and return to the life of a businessman.
- When confronted on his voting record, Hoekstra admitted he'd become disillusioned with the system but decided sitting on the sidelines wasn't doing any good (an argument many voters could identify with).
- When campaign documents released less than a month before the primary that VanderJagt had spent $311,000 to Hoekstra's $10,000, the novice shrewdly reminded voters he refused to take contributions from political action committees. He then pointed out that about $250,000 of VanderJagt's contributions came from PACs and that Hoekstra volunteers paid the purchase and postage of twelve thousand postcards they sent to friends in the district.

It worked.

Hoekstra scored a stunning upset in the August primary and defeated his Democratic opponent in the November general election.

THE RESOURCEFUL RECEPTIONIST

The other true outsider is Democrat Blanche Lambert of Arkansas.

She upset twelve-term incumbent Bill Alexander after at first being dismissed as a frivolous amateur with no money, no name recognition, and no platform.

Sound familiar?

To one degree or another, these criticisms were all true. Lambert had no political experience. At age thirty-two, some would say her political experience was limited to answering phones as Alexander's receptionist from 1983 to 1985 and working as a research assistant for a few Washington lobbying firms. Lambert hadn't lived in the 2nd District for eleven years and was totally unknown in political circles. She had no fund-raising base. From the beginning, her campaign centered on Alexander's infatuation with Washington power and increasing disinterest in district business.

After surviving two scary primary battles in 1988 and 1990, it looked like Alexander was in the clear.

Then the news came.

House bank records showed Alexander had floated 487 checks and had overdrawn his checking account by more than his monthly salary in nineteen of the thirty-nine months examined. His overdrafts exceeded $208,000.

Lambert's "out of touch" rhetoric no longer looked contrived. It looked prescient.

And all the bad memories of Alexander's Washington blunders flooded back to the voters on the western side of the Mississippi Delta.

- They remembered that Alexander requisitioned a military plane in 1985 for a one-man trip to Brazil with the ostensible purpose of studying gasohol (an emerging energy source in his district). Alexander defended the junket by saying five other lawmakers intended to go but didn't make it. It was never clear if the other five lawmakers wanted to go in the first place.
- They remembered that when House leaders tapped Alexander for the No. 4 position in the Democratic leadership, that promotion led him to devote far more time to national party chores than the district's needs.
- They remembered the lawsuit filed against Alexander to recover a $308,000 personal debt.
- They remembered Alexander's ties to businessmen involved in a Florida research firm funded by the Appropriations Committee, of which he was a member.

In essence, Lambert collected all of these blunders in one biting indictment: Alexander's gone Washington.

She drove home her message by driving throughout the district in a red jeep accompanied by enthusiastic volunteers and escorted by her uncle. She reminded voters that her brother represented the seventh generation of Lambert farmers and stressed that her roots ran deep in the Mississippi Delta, where her family had sown rice, cotton, and soybeans.

Lambert swamped Alexander 61 percent to 39 percent in the Democratic primary and cruised to victory over her Republican opponent in the November general election. Just as Alexander was when he arrived, Lambert is widely viewed as smart, resourceful, and full of promise. Although it's never easy to predict such things, it's my guess Lambert will stick to the basics and evade the temptation to "go Washington."

The voters pegged Alexander correctly. He had lost touch: At a Washington party in mid-1994, someone asked Alexander what he thought about the new congressman from his district. "Do you mean Jim Moran?" Alexander said. Jim Moran is the House Democrat who represents Alexandria, Virginia, the Washington, D.C., suburb Alexander had come to think of as his home.

My friend Kentucky Congressman Ron Mazzoli believes that Alexander's experience is the rule rather than the exception.

"So many of our members don't go home," Mazzoli said. "They can't go home. They've either fouled the nest they grew up in. Or they have so long severed relationships with their friends that they don't really have any relationships at all. They haven't really lived there. They go home, but in the meantime their agents and acolytes go home and the media mavens and spin doctors who do their campaigns for them [go home]. But they're not really hometowners anymore. So they live as a kind of a breed. Literally, a privileged class. Until this place starts resembling Hometown U.S.A. — how we act and handle things — it's going to be very tough to recapture the [public's] support."

Eight

The Culture of Partisanship

Let me now . . . warn you in the most solemn manner against the baneful affects of the spirit of party.

— George Washington, Farewell Address

FOUR YEARS after Washington spoke those words, Thomas Jefferson, then vice president, wrote to Martha Jefferson Randolph in Philadelphia about the partisan strife consuming national politics: "Politics and party hatreds destroy the happiness of every being here."

Jefferson knew what he was talking about. He had spent the previous four years organizing farmers, planters, and artisans into an opposition party against John Adams's Federalists. Adams had put the young nation on a war footing with France and a hysterical Congress had enacted the Alien and Sedition Acts, which had rendered any disagreement with Federalist policy a federal crime and given Adams unlimited authority to imprison "seditious" editors. Jefferson led the counterattack and won the presidency in 1800.

I don't know if the depth and intensity of partisanship is worse now than it was in 1800, but I know there's more of it now than when I arrived in 1982. This is a dangerous trend.

Partisanship is not about differing political philosophies. It's about parroting party dogma. It's about questioning the motives of political opponents instead of analyzing their arguments. It's about plotting strategies to score political points for the good of your party instead of seeking compromise for the good of all. It's about ideological litmus tests that reward robotic party purity.

Partisanship distorts political debate. It minimizes the opportunity for compromise. Party purists believe that to compromise is to capitulate; to negotiate with the opposition is to surrender. This all-or-nothing approach frequently produces *nothing* instead of *something*. While I was in Congress I saw partisans in both parties destroy several middle-of-the-road compromises and delay action for years on laws that would have improved the lives of many. Unfortunately, the national parties and their special interest allies rewarded this confrontational behavior.

When he retired in 1992, Ed Feighan, an Ohio Democrat, said this about the state of partisanship in the modern Congress:

> I have never had to endure such a mean-spirited, ugly and dehumanizing atmosphere as the one which now prevails in Washington.

Understandably, voters have come to believe that special interests and partisanship channel the energies of Congress into banal and ceaseless conflicts that create fictitious solutions while deeper problems are papered over. Voters see the sound and fury of political gamesmanship replacing the less glamorous but purer pursuit of the national interest. They are correct. Partisan behavior in Congress is far more prevalent than it used to be and is responsible for an unpardonable waste of energy and talent.

"There is an element of partisanship that wasn't there before," said former Rep. Vin Weber, Minnesota Republican. "There was more of that [bipartisanship] in the past. The notion that Republicans and Democrats are the governing class and they put their partisan differences behind them after the election and try to solve the government's problems . . . there was more of that in the past. That clearly has receded a great deal."

This chapter is about partisanship and the damage it does.

The Republicans' rise to power gives me little hope for a swift end or even modest reduction in partisanship. The new House Speaker, Newt Gingrich, said immediately after the Republicans' takeover of the House that he would "cooperate" with the Clinton administration but not "compromise." Only Gingrich can discern the difference. What Gingrich meant was that when the President agreed with him, he would cooperate. When the President did not agree with him, he would not compromise. I wonder if it has ever dawned on Gingrich that the most sacred document of this nation — the Constitution — was the product of a magnificent and hard-fought compromise. I wonder if he appreciates how much would have been lost had those who ratified the Constitution held so blindly to his dictatorial approach to legislative politics? His comments give me little hope for this Congress's ability to address the nation's problems adequately. What I fear is an even louder clash of partisan tongues.

UNHOLY ALLIANCE

In 1990, President Bush tried, at great political cost, to reduce the deficit. After months of secret negotiations, the White House and congressional leaders agreed on a plan that advertised $500 billion in deficit reduction over five years. The crucial vote occurred on the first week of October. Across the Atlantic Ocean, one epoch in world history was dying and another was being born.

On October 3, East and West Germany became, simply, Germany, in a rapturous political embrace made all the more powerful because it symbolized the beginning of the end of the Cold War.

Germany's reunification stood in stark contrast to the divisiveness and partisanship on display in the U.S. Congress.

As Germans toasted their triumph over deep ideological divisions and fifty years of political antagonism, Bush and the Democratic leadership couldn't sober up a majority of lawmakers in Congress long enough to give up their addiction to deficit spending.

President Bush and the Democratic congressional leadership unsuccessfully tried to sell a package of tax increases and spending cuts to the ideologues in both parties. Bush had given up his 1988 campaign pledge not to raise taxes to get the ball rolling on negotiations to create a bipartisan package. In exchange, Democratic congressional leaders anted up some savings on programs they valued most: Medicare and Medicaid.

But it wasn't good enough for the extremists in both parties. On October 5 the House overwhelmingly voted to kill a bipartisan plan to reduce the federal deficit.

The White House and congressional leaders cut this deal after six months of talks at Andrews Air Force Base in suburban Maryland. Why did things take so long? Mainly because senior members of Congress and White House officials wasted a lot of time lecturing on each other's failed budget policies. Frequently, participants sought refuge at the dessert cart in the back of the main conference room.

"They made the mistake of having a soft ice cream machine out there without a check on it," said former Republican Rep. Bill Frenzel, a participant in the talks. "Jesus, they put whole plates of that stuff away. It was self-serve. It was a metaphor for the entire budget process."

The deal advertised $500 billion in deficit reduction over three years. Both sides knew that was hype only a Madison Avenue executive could love. The budget was worth $300 billion in deficit reduction. Perhaps. A central flaw in both sides' math was the prediction of 4 percent economic growth per year for the next five years. This projection ignored the anemic 2 percent growth of 1989 and the frightening signs of recession throughout the economy. While these cheerful projections made no economic sense, they made perfect political sense. When the government projects strong economic growth, it can project large tax revenue receipts because more profits and earnings are spread throughout the economy. By projecting higher revenue, both sides avoided even more painful choices on taxes and spending cuts.

Nevertheless, the remaining elements of the deal infuriated extremists in both parties. Conservative Republicans were furious with Bush's capitulation on taxes and clung to the mythology that budgets could be balanced without tax increases. Liberal Democrats, meanwhile, objected to the Medicare and Medicaid cuts — some $60 billion worth — and clung with equal vigor to the fiction that budgets could be balanced without drastic spending cuts (particularly in mandatory spending such as Social Security, Medicare, and Medicaid).

Common sense suggests that the bipartisan nature of this agreement should have paved the way for success. But Bush and congressional leaders knew ideologues in both parties could rip the compromise to shreds.

For the first time in his presidency, Bush went on national television to rally the nation behind a domestic policy initiative. For his part, Senate Majority Leader George Mitchell of Maine pleaded with Democrats to support the president.

It was a huge gamble for Bush and a rare display of even-handedness on Mitchell's part. For one of the few times in more than a decade of partisan blood-letting over the deficit, the leaders of the Republican and Democratic parties were united. They were leaders in search of followers.

Bush spoke first:

> To all the people who disagree and all the people on the sidelines that are rushing out and having their press conferences and the critics, let me say this: "You can pick the package apart, but you cannot realistically put a better package together." Now is the time for you, the American people, to have a real impact. Your senators and congressmen need to know that you want this deficit brought down, that the time for posturing and politics is over and the time to come together is now.

During his televised appeal, Mitchell tried to put the delicate agreement into a broader historical perspective. He quoted Founding Father Benjamin Franklin as he rose to vote in favor of the Constitution of the United States:

> "I confess, there are several parts of this Constitution which I do not approve, but I doubt whether any other convention may be able to make a better Constitution. For when you assemble men to have the advantage of their joint wisdom, you inevitably assemble all their prejudices, their passions, their errors of opinion, their local interests, their selfish views. From such an assembly can a perfect product be expected? I consent to this Constitution because I expect no better and because I am not sure it is not the best."

Mitchell's and Bush's words failed to inspire voters or members of Congress. Sadly, they foreshadowed what happened next. Lawmakers tried to pick apart the deal. In doing so, they revealed to Bush and Mitchell all of the "prejudices," "errors of opinion," "local interests," and "selfish views" that Franklin knew so well.

Democratic leaders tried to calm unruly liberals by assuring them the Medicare cuts weren't etched in stone. This is only a blueprint, the leaders kept saying. Only a blueprint.

That wasn't good enough. Liberal Democrats were furious that Bush had prevented raising income tax rates on the wealthy. The liberals had been waging a rhetorical war against the "unfairness" of the Reagan tax cuts and wanted higher tax rates on the rich. They had no use for gasoline and liquor taxes the middle class would have to pay in order to meet Bush's demand that tax rates for the wealthy remain unchanged.

Conservative Republicans refused to accept any tax increases. They also disliked the defense cuts and domestic spending increases (some $20 billion's worth) Bush had accepted. They were convinced a cunning Democratic leadership had bullied the White House into caving in on these bedrock Republican issues (less spending and no new taxes).

The towering irony was that the extremists did not see each other's revolt as a sign that the deal was, in fact, balanced. If both sides disliked it, the deal must have distributed (and, in fact, did distribute) the pain with rough equality. This point was obvious to those trying to hold the agreement together.

Both parties had to share the immediate political pain and, eventually, the credit for lowering the deficit. It was the only road to compromise, and everybody knew it. Bush and congressional leaders hoped to use the bonds of mutual adversity to their advantage. Instead, the ideologues used the adversity to their advantage.

The process began on October 1, when Gingrich, the No. 2 ranking Republican in the House and a participant in the budget talks, opposed the agreement. "It is my conclusion that it will kill jobs," he said.

According to some press accounts, Gingrich read magazines and pulp novels during much of the six-month negotiations. He evidently never intended to support an agreement he was assigned to help broker. Gingrich was the Whip, the lawmaker in charge of counting Republican votes for bills the Bush White House supported. Gingrich's defection deprived the White House of an essential political ally. White House officials had to scramble to assemble an ad hoc group of vote counters while Gingrich used the resources of his office to scuttle the budget compromise.

The White House tried frantically to keep Republicans in line. At first, White House Chief of Staff John Sununu dismissed Gingrich's revolt. He soon learned that Gingrich was the fulcrum for more than half of the House Republican votes and a masterful political strategist. With Gingrich calling the signals for the House Republican conservatives, the Bush

White House could rely on the support of only a few dozen moderate Republicans.

"When people wouldn't return your calls, you knew you were shot out of the saddle," recalled Frenzel, who was the top Republican on the House Budget Committee and a key Bush ally.

At a morning meeting with Republicans the day of the vote, White House Chief of Staff John Sununu threatened that Bush would travel to the districts of Republicans who voted against him. Don't be surprised, Sununu warned House Republicans, if Bush stands on stage, points his finger at one of you, looks you in the eye and tells the audience you deserted him. Instead of intimidating Republicans, it only deepened their hostility toward the White House.

After the meeting, House Republicans began calling the White House economic team — Sununu, Budget Director Richard Darman, and Treasury Secretary Nicholas Brady — "The Three Stooges." Some had another nickname for Sununu and Darman: Haldeman and Ehrlichman, an allusion to Nixon-era hatchet men and Watergate conspirators H. R. Haldeman and John D. Ehrlichman.

Meanwhile, among Democrats the feelings were only slightly less hostile. Despite leadership warnings, liberal Democrats were convinced they could get a better deal if they killed the compromise. The liberals wanted desperately to score political points on the "tax fairness" issue. The compromise prevented that because Democratic leaders had agreed not to fiddle with income tax rates on the wealthy. Undaunted, Democratic leaders pressed ahead. At a caucus of all House Democrats, Foley was asked if the vote on the compromise was a "leadership" vote, that is, a test of party loyalty. Foley said it was.

"Everybody wants to see this pass," Rep. Wayne Owens, Utah Democrat, told the *Wall Street Journal*. "But nobody wants to vote for it."

The vote was held October 4.

That morning, Bush summoned a dozen House Republicans to the White House for breakfast and pleaded for their support. He presented a far more stirring argument than he had four days earlier on national television. The nation's economy and international prestige hung in the balance, Bush said. Two months earlier, Bush had deployed U.S. combat forces to challenge Saddam Hussein's invasion of Kuwait. With troops girding for war, Bush said, the nation and the world were looking for a sign of American political courage at home. The speech proved persuasive to some but not all of the Republicans.

At the same time, Foley convened two meetings of all House Democrats. He warned that if Democrats didn't support the agreement and Republicans did, Bush could fairly and credibly blame Democrats for increasing the deficit and hobbling the economy. To mollify liberals, Foley said the budget blueprint could be changed by the committees who actually wrote the laws. Nothing was sacrosanct, he said. Rostenkowski said he would take another look at the tax increases and Medicare cuts.

Bush needed 94 votes, one more than half of the 186 House Republicans. Foley needed 129 Democrats, one more than half of the 257 House Democrats. Both were far behind when the House debate began, but both sides hoped that if the ideologues of one party could be brought into the fold, ideologues of the other party would follow suit.

Debate on the compromise dragged on for hours. If anyone had picked up a newspaper during the debate and flipped to the movie section, he or she would have found a few feature films with titles that summed up the situation in emotional, political, and economic terms: *Desperate Hours,* starring Mickey Rourke and Anthony Hopkins; *Marked for Death,* starring Steven Seagal; and *Fantasia.*

Shortly after 1 A.M. on October 5, the House began to vote.

Moderates in both parties voted first, attempting to create some momentum. The ideologues held back, eyeing each other suspiciously from opposite sides of the House floor. Many lawmakers huddled around the back of the House, peering into computer screens that tally the votes of individual lawmakers. Ten minutes into the fifteen-minute vote, the tide began to shift as conservative House Republicans began to vote no. That was all the liberals needed to see. If the Republicans weren't going to stand with Bush, liberals weren't going to stand with Foley.

When the vote ended, Bush was dealt a humiliating setback. The final tally against the compromise was 254–179. Bush needed 218 votes to pass it and fell 39 short. Only 71 of 186 Republicans supported the plan. And only 108 of the 257 Democrats were on board.

When the White House and congressional leaders asked lawmakers to stand together, ideologues in both parties skulked away. They took with them all hope of passing a marginally credible plan to reduce the deficit.

"We drummed up enough votes to be highly irresponsible," said Rep. Jerry Lewis, who as the No. 3 House Republican leader tried to help Bush win. "That was the beginning point of George Bush's defeat at the next election. Republicans did that to their own President. I have been seething about that ever since. It was from our own leadership that we put the shive in the back of the president. [Gingrich] knew there would be taxes in that package. You're going to go in the room with the Democrats and not get taxes? Give me a break. [Gingrich] absolutely knew. Absolutely knew."

On the Democratic side, Majority Leader Gephardt persuaded only one of five other Missouri Democrats to vote for the plan; Panetta could not persuade even one of his three roommates (Reps. George Miller of California, Marty Russo of Illinois, and Charles Shumer of New York) to vote yes; Democrats on Ways and Means voted 13–10 against it; and Jamie Whitten, chairman of the House Appropriations Committee, and six other committee Democrats voted against the pact.

"I knew it was going down from day one," said former Rep. Bill Gray of Pennsylvania. At the time, Gray was the Majority Whip, or top party vote counter. "I knew where the votes were, and I said to myself, 'This is not going anywhere.' I knew we were going to be back [to negotiate another deal]."

Later that morning, October 6, the Labor Department reported that unemployment had risen for the third consecutive month to 5.7 percent. This harbinger of a deepening recession, unfortunately, only stiffened the resolve of liberals and conservatives to dismantle as much of the budget compromise as they could. Conservatives said higher taxes would deepen the recession. Liberals said the coming recession demanded even more social spending for the poor.

Massachusetts Rep. Silvio Conte, the senior Republican on the Appropriations Committee, wore a hat that day with two visors pointing in opposite directions and a sign that read "I'm their leader. Which way did they go?"

What followed was nothing short of a disorganized political circus. In a fit of pique, Bush vetoed a short-term spending bill to keep the government running over the first weekend in October. All nonessential government offices and services were closed, including the Statue of Liberty, all National Parks, the Smithsonian museums, the National Zoo, and the White House tours.

Voters threw up their hands in disbelief at the sight of partisan finger-pointing occurring everywhere they looked. Even the White House operator was excused for the weekend and replaced with this partisan recording: "We regret that we're unable to say when the communication lines will reopen, due to Congress's failure to pass the budget resolution."

"That week I know I dropped fifteen points in the tracking polls," said Rep. Tom Tauke, a moderate Iowa Republican who that fall was challenging incumbent Sen. Tom Harkin. "All Republican Senate candidates in the Midwest dropped fifteen points in the polls. And I never recovered from it."

In an episode of high political comedy, conservative House Republicans introduced a new "alternative budget" they said could balance the budget without raising taxes. Incredibly, they said their plan would jump-start the moribund negotiations.

"You had this fairly ridiculous performance of House Republicans thinking they were in charge," Bill Frenzel, Republican from Minnesota, said. "It's like the deposed Mexican general talking to his mule and saying, 'We're going to take Mexico City tomorrow.'"

Negotiations on a budget compromise dragged on for two more weeks before Congress passed a feeble imitation of the original bill. Taxes on the wealthy replaced more reliable taxes on gasoline, beer, wine, and tobacco. Savings in Medicare were reduced, and other social spending was added, further weakening the promise of realistic deficit reduction.

The budget deal, of course, turned out to be an utter failure. The economy slumped throughout 1991, and its sluggish growth in 1992 didn't meet the 1990 budget plan's rosy economic projections. As a consequence, tax revenue fell off sharply and deficits widened. Projections for a federal deficit of $86 billion by 1995 gave way to deficits in excess of $200 billion. Public outrage and cynicism deepened.

Ironically, conservative Republicans and liberal Democrats to this day wear the vote against the 1990 budget deal as a badge of honor. They should be ashamed.

"The first vote [killing the original package] involved the pattern over the last decade and a half of more and more polarization in the House [where both parties are] appealing to the extremes of your own extreme," Lewis said. "It wasn't good for the government or good for the public. The good of the country wasn't involved. It was the worst. There was more energy spent fighting each other to see who can be king of the molehill rather than fighting the battles that lead to policy that helps the country."

TWO PARTIES, ONE PAY RAISE

Republicans and Democrats did come together in 1989. They put partisan differences aside to raise their salaries.

In December of 1989, an independent federal commission proposed raising congressional salaries by 50 percent, from $89,500 to $135,000. President Reagan endorsed the proposal. Some saw it as Reagan's final dig at the Democrats. He knew they wanted a raise and he assumed the commission would suggest a sizable increase. Reagan forced congressional Democrats to publicly endorse a hefty raise. Which they did. Sort of.

Senior House Democrats — then Majority Whip Tony Coelho and Vic Fazio, both of California — decided they would use a special procedure to dodge a floor vote on the raise. The law governing pay raises allowed the raise to take affect automatically unless the House *and* Senate voted to reject the raise.

Congress used this procedural side step in 1987 to raise congressional salaries from $77,400 to $89,500.

The climate was different this time, however.

Radio talk show hosts and editorial writers remembered the 1987 pay raise. They pounced on the House's plan to dodge the vote and take the raise. Anger flared. Within days, thousands of tea bags — reminiscent of the Boston Tea Party — arrived in congressional offices. Voters left nasty phone messages. Venom spilled from fax machines.

A *Washington Post/ABC News* poll showed 85 percent of the public opposed the pay raise.

The reaction spooked Speaker Jim Wright, a man who didn't spook easily. Wright's favorite sport was boxing, and he relished the partisan trench warfare that marked so much of his reign.

John M. Barry's enthralling portrait of Wright's speakership *The Ambition and the Power,* revealed that public opposition led Wright to back away from the raise. Barry quotes Wright in a private meeting with senior Democrats: "It's one thing to vote that sentiment [85 percent of the nation opposed to the pay raise] as a matter of conscience. It's another to line your own pockets."

Wright wanted to shrink the raise by 20 percent in exchange for a permanent ban on honoraria — money lawmakers received for giving speeches. At the time, House members could accept 30 percent of their salary in honoraria. Wright wanted to vote for a 30 percent pay raise and an end to honoraria. That way, House members could accept the raise as part of an effort to clean up government ethics.

Senior House Democrats — then Majority Leader Tom Foley, Coelho, and Fazio — said no. They wanted all of the raise. And they wanted it without a vote.

Wright was alone. His instincts told him there should be a vote. If members wanted a raise, they should have the courage to vote for it and defend it. If they didn't have the courage to vote for it or defend it, then, he thought, they didn't deserve it.

Wright decided to poll all House members. He asked two questions: Do you want a floor vote on the raise? and Is the 51 percent raise too high?

Half said the raise was too high, and half said they didn't want to vote. These mushy results did nothing to resolve the issue.

But the poll drove members crazy. It forced Democrats and Republicans publicly to denounce a raise that many privately favored. The lawmakers' public denunciations only deepened public opposition and made support for the raise politically untenable.

Days later, the House rejected the pay raise on a vote of 238–88.

The seeds of Wright's eventual downfall as House Speaker were sown in his refusal to protect the pay raise. After that, many House Democrats no longer trusted Wright.

In late 1989, the House passed the 51 percent pay raise as part of a larger package of "ethics reforms" very similar to the ones Wright originally proposed. By this time, though, Wright had resigned under the cloud of alleged ethics violations.

This time, however, both parties called a truce. Democrats and Republicans worked together to pass the pay raise. For the first time in his speakership, Speaker Thomas Foley addressed a closed-door meeting of House Republicans, and Newt Gingrich addressed a similarly secret meeting of House Democrats. Foley promised Republicans that Democrats wouldn't use the pay raise vote against Republicans in the next election. Gingrich made the same promise to Democrats.

What's more, both parties ordered their campaign committees to cut off financial support for any challenger who used the pay raise against an incumbent of the other party.

The raise passed.

Quickly.

Quietly.

It happened so quickly and so quietly that the public was caught flatfooted. No campaign against the raise surfaced in large part because efforts to pass it remained underground as well.

"I can really see why the public would look at that deal on the big pay increase and just be livid about it," said former Rep. Vin Weber, Minnesota Republican. "The Congress that can't manage to come together on any of these other problems, but manages to get Newt Gingrich speaking to House Democrats and Tom Foley coming over to talk to House Republicans — assuring each other there's not going to be political retribution. We've never done that on anything of dire importance to the future of the country — just congressional salaries."

THE WARPATH IGNORED

After U.S. and coalition forces routed Saddam Hussein and forced him to withdraw from Kuwait, Bush scored the highest popularity ratings of any President since the advent of public polling.

Some Republicans tried to exploit the war's surprisingly lopsided outcome for partisan gain. House Republican Whip Gingrich and others attacked Democrats for voting against the resolution authorizing U.S. involvement in the war. Gingrich said he hoped the war vote would prove decisive in the upcoming House elections and tried to recruit veterans of the Gulf War as candidates against incumbent Democrats.

"You know, if [U.S. Army Gen.] Norm Schwarzkopf had to report to the Democratic Congress, we'd still be unloading the first five tanks and debating over which way they should point," Gingrich said on March 6, 1991.

The following day Texas Republican Sen. Phil Gramm said the war vote showed that "Democrats cannot be trusted to define the destiny of America, that Democrats cannot be trusted to make America a world leader."

Finally, Senate Minority Leader Dole wrote an op-ed piece published March 13, 1991, in the *Wall Street Journal* entitled "No Amnesty for Senate Democrats."

It began,

> As a proud America welcomes home its Desert Storm heroes, it is sobering to remember that a shift of only three votes in the Senate nine weeks ago could have turned this smashing victory into a catastrophe.
>
> Despite all the new talk these days about "unity," we should not forget that the Senate, after being AWOL for more than two crucial months, backed the president by a timid 52–47 vote.

Dole's piece then listed quotes from Democrats who voted against the war authorization.

Soon thereafter, the *Journal* published "See You in '92: A Quiz." In it, the *Journal* listed the names of sixteen Democratic senators and the quotes that appeared in Dole's earlier piece.

Dole, Gingrich, and Gramm ridiculed Democrats for celebrating the triumph of the U.S. forces, as if defeating Hussein were not a cause for celebration for *all* Americans . . . not just Republicans.

This partisan sniping ignored the deep-seated anxiety that gripped America and the Congress as the nation moved toward war with Iraq. Polls showed most Americans were ambivalent. They wanted to turn back aggression but they didn't know if Kuwait was the place, as Bush put it, to "draw the line in the sand." Many in Congress shared these feelings.

I voted against the war resolution after returning to the United States from a trip to Moscow. During a stopover at the U.S. Air Force base in Frankfurt, Germany, I was led on a tour of the medical facilities awaiting war casualties. I was taken inside an airplane hangar and shown tidy row after tidy row of triage stretchers. I noticed each had crisp white bedding and metal tripods holding intravenous bottles and sterile plastic tubes. I saw the tall metal stands with surgical equipment next to each stretcher. I noticed the emergency electrical generators hunched in the corner. It looked as if the hangar could handle hundreds of casualties each day.

I shuddered.

I was undecided but leaning in favor of the war vote until then. I understood Iraq's invasion of Kuwait was grounds for war and that the United States had to play a leading role in Kuwait's liberation. The sight of that triage unit, however, showed me how many casualties the military thought it might have to absorb in a war with Iraq. I doubted if Americans were prepared for a costly and prolonged conflict with the thousands of casualties the military was preparing to receive. I recalled the service of my two brothers during the Vietnam era and how fear for their safety wrenched my family every day until they returned.

I decided I simply could not vote to prosecute a war with Iraq until I was certain that all other means — economic sanctions and diplomatic pressure — had been exhausted. Nonetheless, once the decision was made, I wanted our military personnel to know that America supported their efforts. I believe that most Americans did not want another generation of soldiers to confront the hostility many Vietnam veterans met when they returned from battle.

The Republicans' attempt to exploit the war vote politically ignored the fact that Democratic leaders exerted no pressure whatsoever. It was not a party vote. It was a vote of conscience. In fact, top Democrats such as House Armed Services Chairman Les Aspin of Wisconsin and Foreign Affairs Committee Chairman Dante Fascell of Florida helped sponsor and strongly supported the war resolution.

The public saw through the Republicans' seamy strategy. Americans were relieved that the war was over quickly and that U.S. casualties were far smaller than had been expected. They knew there were good arguments on both sides of the war vote. They sensed that Republicans were trying to exploit a policy they themselves had endorsed with some misgivings. Fortunately, they found the Republican partisanship distressing and ignored it.

It was particularly galling that Gingrich and Gramm were among those most vocal on the matter, since they avoided military service during Vietnam. (Dole served heroically in World War II and suffered a horrendous wound that nearly killed him and left his right arm immobilized for life.) A colleague of mine, Rep. Andy Jacobs, Indiana Democrat, has labeled Republican "war hawks" who never actually served in the military "war wimps." Jacobs served in the U.S. Marine Corps in Korea even though his father was a congressman at the time and it would have been easy for him to sidestep military service. Jacobs knew most Americans objected to seeing the war politicized, especially by the likes of Gingrich and Gramm.

INVEST-I-GATE

Whatever becomes of the Whitewater investigation (at this writing it remains an open question), the episode exposed the worst partisan instincts of congressional Democrats and Republicans.

Despite serious allegations of wrongdoing by the Clinton administration, congressional leaders refused to convene investigative hearings until the first independent counsel, Robert Fiske, completed his probe into the so-called "Washington phase" of Whitewater.

The putative reason was that Democratic leaders did not want to interfere with Fiske's investigation. Please. The fact is Democratic leaders delayed hearings because they did not want to embarrass the Clinton administration.

When Democrats finally convened hearings, the House proceedings uncovered little more than the depth to which senior Democrats will go to shield an imperiled Democratic administration. The rules prevented cross-examination of witnesses, and aggressive Republican questioners were routinely shouted down by the hyperprotective Henry Gonzalez, chairman of the Banking Committee, which conducted the House hearings. The Senate hearings were far more revealing and much less partisan. (A three-judge federal panel replaced Fiske in July of 1994 and appointed former Bush administration solicitor general Kenneth Starr to assume responsibility for the Whitewater investigation. As this book goes to press, Starr's work continues.)

Nevertheless, the public learned far less from the congressional Whitewater hearings than it would have if Whitewater had been a scandal plaguing a Republican White House. That's because Democrats were rarely reluctant to hold investigative hearings when Republicans were in the White House.

Congress conducted twenty-five separate investigations into allegations of wrongdoing during the Reagan-Bush years. Four of the investigations of the Reagan administration were ordered by Senate Republicans. Democrats in charge of congressional committees conducted the other twenty-one investigations. In each instance, Democrats said hearings were necessary to protect the public from White House abuses of power and were a crucial component of Congress's oversight authority.

That high-minded rhetoric and public spiritedness vanished when the Clinton White House found itself embroiled in Whitewater. Democrats hid behind Fiske's investigation as an excuse to ignore the same obligations they so lustily exercised during the Reagan-Bush years. Congressional Democrats and the Clinton White House opposed naming an independent counsel to investigate Whitewater; when the clamor grew too loud to ignore, they relented and immediately used Fiske as a weapon to fend off a wider public probe.

Starr's obligation is to investigate potential criminal wrongdoing as it relates to Clinton's investment in Whitewater and his relationship with sympathetic financiers his administration regulated while he was governor. Starr is also obliged to investigate potential criminal acts within the White House to submerge information about Whitewater. These are matters of criminal law and Starr's mandate ends there.

Other issues are also involved, however. The Whitewater development is intertwined with the downfall of Madison Guaranty, a Little Rock savings and loan, which was operated by the Clintons' Whitewater partner, James MacDougal. The downfall of that financial institution and a history of lax regulation raise serious questions about the influence politics may have had in creating a $60 million taxpayer liability (the cost of the taxpayer bailout for Madison Guaranty). There are other public policy questions relating to the unauthorized White House searches immediately after his suicide of the office of Vince Foster, the Clintons' chief legal adviser. Foster possessed most of the relevant documents pertaining to Whitewater.

These are topics suitable for congressional hearings. There is no doubt in my mind that a Republican White House beset by the same questions would have been subject to congressional inquiry almost immediately. The Democrats' unwillingness to hold the Clinton White House to the same standard exposes their own partisan favoritism and undermines our party's ability to rebuild public trust in government.

Republicans have shown no less partisanship in Whitewater. After arguing for most of the 1980s that the Constitution prohibited appointment of an independent counsel to investigate the White House, Republicans immediately sought one to probe Clinton. Republican opposition allowed the independent counsel law to expire in 1992. Congress and Clinton revived it in 1993 over strong Republican objections.

Democrats consistently supported extending the independent counsel law and have done so throughout the Whitewater saga. Throughout the 1980s Republicans said special prosecutors shattered the constitutionally rigid boundaries between congressional oversight and executive privilege. Those concerns vanished when a Democrat occupied the White House.

In both cases, the wolf of partisanship was cloaked in the sheep's clothing of public spirit. And not very well, I might add.

If protecting the public from government malfeasance is the goal, which it should be, common sense tells us that both political parties are obliged to give and take their lumps with fairness and a minimum of partisan grandstanding. The public knows no government is perfect. The public also knows that human frailty knows no party label and that politicians will sometimes break the law or commit unethical acts. What the public expects from government is a seriousness of purpose. The public expects and deserves a full and honest accounting — not partisan witch hunts or partisan snow jobs.

Partisanship in pursuit — or cover-up — of political wrongdoing diverts attention from the larger goal, which is to punish the malefactor and deter future misconduct. Partisanship creates a poisonous climate for all future inquiries. It breeds mistrust. New allegations are judged not on their merits, but on the partisan gains that might accrue to the accuser. It also unleashes wasteful counterstrategies to fend off what might be legitimate allegations. And it quickens the appetite for partisan retribution.

Unfortunately, all of these needless partisan ploys were visible in the congressional reaction to Whitewater.

Partisanship of the kind I'm decrying does not and should not have to be a part of daily life within Congress. That it has been is one of the many reasons life in Congress is so unpleasant. For years Congress operated under agreed-upon standards of civility and collegiality.

Those days, I'm afraid, may be gone forever.

THE BLOODY EIGHTH

No single event in my career deepened partisan animosity in the House more than a disputed House election in Indiana's Eighth Congressional District in 1984. Most people in the House now just refer to it as the "Bloody Eighth."

Freshman Democrat Frank McCloskey at first appeared to have won a razor-thin reelection victory over Republican challenger Richard McIntyre. The first vote count showed McCloskey garnered 72 more votes than McIntyre out of 234,055 cast. It was the closest House race in the twentieth century.

At the time, Democrats outnumbered Republicans in the House 253–182.

Republican Secretary of State Edwin J. Simcox refused to certify McCloskey's apparent victory and ordered a recount of two precincts where votes had been counted twice. McCloskey sued to block the recount, but his suit was dismissed. In early December, the recount gave McIntyre a thirty-four vote margin of victory, and Simcox declared McIntyre the winner.

On January 3, 1985, the House voted 238–177 on party lines to declare the election returns null and void and ordered the seat open until a separate House investigation could decide the winner. This action was predicated on the constitutional provision that reserves to the Congress final authority over the conduct of all House elections. On January 22, the state completed a recount of all ballots, and McIntyre was again declared the winner. This time his margin of victory was 418 votes. Officials threw out 4,808 ballots because of irregularities.

In early February, the House Administration Committee appointed a three-person task force — two Democrats and one Republican — to recount the ballots. Leon Panetta, now Clinton's chief of staff, was named chairman. In late March the task force hired auditors from the General Accounting Office to count many of the ballots Indiana officials threw out. The task force agreed to accept ballots that had only minor irregularities, such as lacking a poll worker's initials or the proper precinct number.

The most divisive issue in the task force's recount dealt with absentee ballots. Indiana law required that all legal absentee ballots had to be signed and notarized. In early April, the task force found sixty-two absentee ballots that did not meet this legal standard but that poll workers had nevertheless sent to the precincts for counting. Fifty-two of those ballots had been opened and counted. Ten were returned uncounted to the county clerks. The task force decided to count all sixty-two ballots. There was another set of thirty-two absentee ballots that hadn't been signed or notarized that were never sent to the precincts for counting.

The lone task force Republican, Bill Thomas, said the thirty-two ballots should be counted. The two Democrats, Panetta and William Clay of Missouri, disagreed and defeated his motion 2–1. Thomas then asked the task force to count eleven absentee ballots from military personnel that had been postmarked before the election but arrived after the polls closed. This request, too, was denied.

Thomas complained that Democrats had arbitrarily decided which ballots to count and which to reject. To bolster his argument he asked the Arizona election official whom the task force had hired to supervise the recount, James Shumway, if all of the absentee ballots should have been counted. Shumway said they should all have been counted. Enraged, Thomas called for a new election to settle the matter. Ironically, by this time Republicans had already attempted on three occasions to pass resolutions declaring McIntyre the winner. Democrats defeated these resolutions on party-line votes. The task force rejected Thomas's motion as well, and the House Administration Committee declared McCloskey the winner by four votes.

As the full committee prepared to vote, Republican Pat Roberts, a moderate known for his willingness to compromise and deal fairly with Democrats, warned that this election could poison relations for years to come. "You're going to win here," Roberts told the committee. "But you're losing by tearing the fabric of this place. If you worry folks like me, we're in serious trouble."

Democratic leaders moved to seat McCloskey and made the House vote for McCloskey and against a Republican motion to hold another election a test of party loyalty.

Panetta justified the recount this way:

> Yes there were judgments made here. Let us make no question about that. Some of the ballots were counted, some were not, based on those judgments. The question you have to ask as members of this House is: Were those judgments justified, reasonable and supported by House precedent? The decisions were justified. They were supported, and they were right.

The committee action infuriated Republicans, who began tying up legislative business in protest.

"Every House Republican who was in the House at that time believed that election was stolen," Weber recalled recently. "There isn't a single one that thought this was a legitimate process and that we just lost. Every single one thought it was a raw, naked exercise of power."

Enter Ron Mazzoli, the Kentucky Democrat I spoke of in chapter 6.

Throughout his years in Congress, Ron has resisted the seemingly incessant tug of Democratic leaders toward strident partisanship.

Mazzoli hails from Louisville and won his election to Congress by 211 votes in 1970. His district borders Indiana's Eighth District, which made it easy for him to monitor the controversy and get a feel for the fairness of the House recount.

Like many members, Mazzoli rose through the ranks quietly. Unlike most members, moderate Democrats especially, he did so by serving on the Judiciary Committee. Moderates generally shy away from Judiciary because it deals with abortion, crime, immigration, and censorship. Democratic leaders demand liberal positions on all of these issues. That means Democrats who come from moderate districts, like Mazzoli, either have to take risky positions or displease the leadership. In most cases, Mazzoli bucked the leadership, justified his votes to the folks back home, and won reelection handily.

When it came time to vote on the McCloskey-McIntyre report, Mazzoli and I and seventeen other Democrats defied the party leaders. We thought the issue was too clouded and feared the leadership's gambit would poison all that we hoped to accomplish during that year's legislative session.

Of the defectors, only Mazzoli had the courage to give a floor speech opposing the Democratic leadership's motion to seat McCloskey.

Mazzoli shook as he approached the dais and looked into a standing room–only audience of House leaders, rank-and-file lawmakers, senior leadership aides, and other curious staff. Mazzoli knew his speech would irritate Democratic leaders and lead to some internal criticism and, perhaps, party sanction. But after looking at the recount and many of the details closely, Mazzoli felt he had to speak out against the leadership's maneuver.

"I was very nervous," Mazzoli said recently. "My legs were weak. It was probably one of the more nerve-wracking moments that I've had to say anything on the floor. It was a real impassioned moment."

Mazzoli told the House:

> I rise with my heart in my throat, more nervous than I have ever been in this House to say that I have to rise in behalf of the proposition which I consider to be fair and correct, which is that the Indiana seat be declared vacant and there be a special election. I rise to tell my friends on [the Democratic] side of the aisle that the race appears to be tainted, it does appear to have a cloud hanging over it, which I think can only be dispelled if there were a special election.

Mazzoli encountered glares and muttered denunciations from fellow Democrats as he left the chamber.

"Leon Panetta is one of the most estimable people I've ever known, so he's not going to have a hand in anything that's questionable," Mazzoli said recently. "It was just the whole process led people to think this was a fix. It led people to think that the fix was in and that this guy was going to be elected regardless of what the vote for him was."

To Republicans, however, Mazzoli's speech confirmed their darkest suspicions and deepened their sense of outrage.

"When Ron Mazzoli came out on our side of it from across the district line in Kentucky, it validated everything," Weber said. "Of course, we thought, 'You've got one honest man in the Democratic party who is now telling the truth,' which is that they were just blatantly stealing from us. It was a highly radicalizing event."

After the vote, Democrats gathered in the well for McCloskey's swearing-in ceremony. As O'Neill was about to give McCloskey the oath of office — a solemn occasion customarily witnessed in silence by Republicans and Democrats — Republicans rose in unison, marched out of the House chamber and down the Capitol steps to denounce the outcome to waiting reporters. It was the first time a party had staged a formal walkout since 1890, when Democrats protested a contested election in South Carolina's 7th Congressional District.

Mazzoli's courage made him a marked man in some Democratic circles for years.

"It took from 1985 until well into the early 1990s for some guys who were involved with that to even talk to me," Mazzoli said. "Because they thought it was an act of apostasy that I would not support the party in that setting. I think what I was doing, more than an act of apostasy was an act of renewal. I think it was to try to make my party better, to give it a better reputation than it has."

The McCloskey-McIntyre episode contributed mightily to the rise of gratuitous Republican partisanship. Georgia Republican Newt Gingrich had already been pressuring Republicans to confront Democrats and create loud, visible disagreements over politics and policies. He lectured Republicans on the "sucker deal" of compromising with Democrats who held all the power. He told Republicans they would never dislodge Democrats by working with them but only by questioning their motives, attacking their policies, and provoking them into public confrontations.

"It perfectly underscored Gingrich's point," Weber recalled, "which was, How can you possibly do business as usual with these people unless you are a political cuckold? They've just said they are not even going to let you win when you win."

So began a vicious cycle of partisanship. Democrats resented the attacks of Gingrich and other like-minded Republicans and responded with tougher partisan actions and rhetoric of their own. Now, ten years later, the battle continues to rage, while many issues suffer from lack of attention. It astonishes me how neither side sees the folly of its ways. Republicans must know by now how their constant negativity turns off the average voter. And Democrats must see how their power grabs provoke Republicans in ever more acidic partisanship, which only strengthens the hand of their number one nemesis — Newt Gingrich.

"The Democrats didn't make Newt Gingrich a possibility for us," Rep. Dick Armey, Texas Republican, said recently. "They made him an imperative for us."

The Democrats' No. 1 nemesis now goes by a different title: Speaker of the House.

AGAINST THE GRAIN

At the time of the McCloskey-McIntyre conflict, Mazzoli was leading efforts to reform immigration laws (an issue that meant little to his constituents). But after the McCloskey vote, party leaders quietly forced him to cede his leadership role to Peter Rodino, then chairman of the Judiciary Committee.

Later, after Mazzoli sided with Republicans on other votes and his insistence on a bipartisan approach, Democratic leaders stripped Mazzoli of his chairmanship of a Judiciary subcommittee. It was clear that Democratic leaders would not tolerate a renegade like Mazzoli — even though he'd supported the leadership on gun control and crime and given the party a strong immigration policy. The sanction was designed to whip him into line and discourage other Democrats from pursuing a similarly independent course. This independent streak also made Mazzoli unpopular among some of the Democratic activist groups in Kentucky. State party insiders have run tough challengers against Mazzoli every year since 1988.

Mazzoli also defied the prevalent customs by taking on entrenched interests back home. He voted against a protectionist trade bill in 1988 that his labor supporters favored and voted for a ban on smoking on domestic airline flights in 1990 that tobacco interests in his home state opposed. He also declined to scrape for pork barrel projects even though Rep. William Natcher, a fellow Kentuckian, was influential on the appropriations committee that distributed most pork barrel spending and could have been most helpful to Mazzoli.

In another unorthodox move, Mazzoli decided to give up PAC money and survive on individual contributions alone. Only twenty-one members of Congress did not accept PAC contributions in their 1992 campaigns. Yet Mazzoli won in 1990 even after being outspent by his challenger. He had an even tougher opponent in 1992 but won even though he ran no television commercials and spent only $216,638. This time his opponent spent $364,659.

Mazzoli cut his campaign expenses by more than $155,000 from 1988 to 1992, the very time he was facing the toughest primary and general election challenges of his career. He forswore all PAC money and raised what money he did use from individuals. Meanwhile, the typical incumbent seeking reelection allowed his campaign expenses to rise from $378,000 in 1988 to $594,000 in 1992. Statistics reveal that the better financed candidates win. In 360 of 404 races in 1992, the candidates who outspent their opponents won.

Clearly, Mazzoli is a rare politician. He's been intellectually flexible, politically fair, and willing to take risks in a hostile political environment. He has fought for what he believes in, put the nation first, and refused to buckle when party leaders in Washington or back home tried to break his spirit. He will be missed. Mazzoli retired in 1994 and happily returned to Kentucky.

SEARCHING FOR SOLUTIONS

Just as Ron Mazzoli has forged a bipartisan record within Congress, two Republicans have as well. One is a veteran who is about to retire. Another arrived here in 1993.

Steve Gunderson of Wisconsin was elected in 1980 at the age of twenty-nine. He represents southwestern Wisconsin, a district that leans Democrat and expects moderation from its representative. An able legislator on the Agriculture and Education and Labor committees — committees I also served on — Gunderson and I have worked together on many issues.

Gunderson rose to the position of chief deputy whip in the House Republican Conference in 1989 (that made him part of the party "leadership"). The Republicans' moves toward social conservatism, however, cut short his rise to power. In January of 1993, Gunderson voluntarily resigned his leadership post.

"You can't govern a diverse nation or a diverse party if you don't have diversity at the top," Gunderson said. "Our leadership today has eight white male conservatives. That is not reflective of either the Republican Party in Congress, the Republican Party in the nation, or the population of this country."

Gunderson said the party's "growing image of intolerance," which manifested itself at the Republican National Convention in 1992, had left him disillusioned with the direction of Republican politics. He said hard-core Republican activists were less concerned about the building blocks of GOP success in the 1980s: economic growth, smaller government, a strong defense, and the nurturing of freedom and democracy abroad.

"We have put those elements on the shelf and allowed a narrow ideological test on the social and domestic issues to become the party's foundation, and that has to stop," Gunderson said after announcing his resignation.

Gunderson later announced he would not seek reelection in 1996 and pledged to make bipartisan cooperation the hallmark of his last two years in office.

The newcomer is Mike Castle, the former governor of Delaware. In 1988 Castle worked with another small state governor to forge a compromise on welfare reform legislation then pending in Congress. The other governor was Bill Clinton.

State law prevented Castle from seeking a third term, so he opted for a career in the House. He swapped places with Democratic Rep. Tom Carper, an ally of mine on many budget-cutting efforts. Carper is now governor of Delaware.

Based on his previous working relationship with Clinton, Castle hoped he and other moderate Republicans could have worked with the administration to pass bipartisan initiatives to reduce the deficit, provide universal health insurance, and further reform the welfare system.

Castle governed for two terms as a bipartisan consensus builder. He encouraged a private foundation to open clinics across the state to provide universal health care to the state's children. It's this kind of ingenuity Castle hoped Clinton's health care reform proposals would foster. Sadly, the Clinton administration did not reach out to Castle and other moderate Republicans who are prepared to work for bipartisan solutions.

Castle arrived in Washington hoping to serve as an emissary for moderate Republicans and the White House. In addition to his work with Clinton on welfare reform, Castle and Clinton co-chaired two other task forces while members of the National Governors Association.

Before the 103rd Congress began, Castle was optimistic about dealings with the White House. Clinton's reluctance, and at times, hostility, to working with moderate Republicans has surprised and disappointed Castle.

As the only former governor in the House, Castle believes federal regulations discourage ingenuity. He has sought to halt Congress's maddening tendency to pass new laws without providing the money necessary for states to enforce them.

Congress's own bureaucracy baffles him as well. He didn't understand, for example, why he found a bucket of ice in his office every morning. His staff couldn't figure it out, either. Then some Capitol Hill veterans told them it was for their soft drinks and that they could have more hand delivered throughout the day. Then Castle tried to replace some burned out light bulbs. His chief aide had to call one office for the light bulb and another office to have it installed. He had to call the offices on the same day or the job wouldn't get done.

Castle has questioned these customs and has tried to abolish other perks that cost taxpayers money and undermine confidence in government.

He has sponsored legislation to immediately reduce allowances for free congressional mailings by 50 percent. Castle would cut allowances by another 75 percent in two years. He projects these cuts would save $35 million annually.

In his first year in office, Castle spent only $5,489 of his yearly $200,827 allowance for "free" congressional mailings. Castle refuses to send "newsletters" to constituents. He dips into his mailing allowance only when sending letters in reply to constituent correspondence. When Castle does send "newsletters," he pays for them with campaign donations.

"I do not believe we should be using taxpayer money for what amounts to a reelection effort," Castle said when he introduced the legislation.

My only hope is that in the years ahead, Republicans like Castle and Gunderson can steer House Republicans away from partisanship. By reaching out to moderate Republicans, the current Democrat in the White House could go a long way toward ending the partisan strife that grips Washington and irks the electorate.

I believe all of us who come to serve in Congress would do well to remember the note of reconciliation Thomas Jefferson sounded to his arch rivals, the Federalists, in his first inaugural address:

> But every difference of opinion is not a difference of principle. We have called by different names brethren of the same principle. We are all Republicans — we are all Federalists.

Nine

Agents of Change

I hold it, that a little rebellion, now and then, is a good thing, and as necessary in the political world as storms in the physical.

—Thomas Jefferson

BY NOW, you might be feeling a bit glum about the future of your Congress and your country.

You shouldn't be.

Help is on the way.

Many of the freshmen elected in 1992 and 1994 are committed to changing the cultures I've described. Not all of them approach reform with the same dedication or the same definition. After all, political agendas differ from state to state and district to district. But all of these new lawmakers have been exposed to voters who share the same goals for the Congress of the 1990s and the twenty-first century: rid Washington of old congressional customs, obsolete programs, and wasteful spending.

Voters want a government devoted to bipartisan solutions—not partisan squabbles. They want a government that sets priorities and concentrates its resources on getting the job done. They want lawmakers willing to tell them the truth and face the heat of unpopular decisions. They want leaders who will take a fresh look at problems and risk the ire of party heavyweights. They want leaders willing to risk their careers to make this a better country.

There are some new members of Congress you've probably never heard of who meet some of these standards. In their own ways they are trying to undo or at least reshape some of the irksome cultures of Congress. They are trying to cut spending. They are trying to eliminate duplication. They are trying to bring Congress under the same laws it applies to the private sector. They are trying to make congressional campaigns more competitive. They are trying to build bridges between the political parties.

A NEW ATTITUDE

The most noticeable difference between the newer members and their elders is the newcomers' willingness to cut spending. While some freshmen favor new spending programs, virtually all of them are prepared to eliminate antiquated programs to pay for the new ones.

A National Taxpayers Union study of voting patterns in 1993 showed that nearly half of the freshmen in Congress supported more bills to cut spending than bills to increase it. Two-thirds of the senior members of Congress supported bills that spent significantly more than they saved.

"The data . . . demonstrates beyond any reasonable doubt that many members elected since 1990 have established their own subculture within the Congress," said James Dale, the chairman of the National Taxpayers Union Foundation. "Major relief could be in store for the taxpayer if this becomes the dominant culture."

Freshmen from both parties provided big majorities for the most important votes to cut spending in 1993 and 1994.

- More than 70 percent of the freshmen supported killing the Superconducting Super Collider, saving at least $11 billion.
- More than 80 percent of all freshmen voted to terminate the Advanced Solid Rocket Motor program—a piece of aerospace pork. The one-year savings exceeded $157 million.
- More than 60 percent of the freshmen Democrats and nearly 40 percent of the freshmen Republicans supported an unsuccessful effort to kill Space Station Freedom, a project first proposed by President Reagan. Riddled with cost overruns and beset by constant design changes ordered by Congress, the project could cost as much as $30 billion.
- Ninety percent of the House Republican freshmen and more than 30 percent of the House Democrat freshmen supported the Penny-Kasich effort to reduce the deficit by $90 billion over five years. Although the percentage of Democrats might appear small, it was twice the support Penny-Kasich got from senior Democrats. The freshmen Democrats had to withstand intense White House and special interest group pressure to vote for Penny-Kasich. That they did proves they are true agents of change.

I don't believe voters expect perfection from Congress. I believe they expect honesty, hard work, and leadership. Many new members of Congress are trying to live up to these commonsense standards.

OUT WITH THE OLD, IN WITH THE NEW

The mighty Mississippi is nothing more than a humble stream as it rises from Lake Itasca in northern Minnesota. By the time it unites with the Missouri and Ohio rivers in Cairo, Illinois, the Mississippi stretches more than a mile from bank to bank. At the end of its 2,348-mile journey, the river disgorges more than six hundred thousand square feet of water per second into the Gulf of Mexico.

The point is that all powerful forces, be they natural or man-made, start small and grow.

Such is the case of the reform movement in Congress.

It began on September 22, 1989, when, as a consequence of special elections, two young Democrats were sworn in to replace two of the most powerful, ambitious, and hidebound leaders of the Democratic Party.

The press and public could be forgiven for overlooking the ceremony. They had little inkling how different Pete Geren of Texas and Gary Condit of California were going to be from their predecessors, Jim Wright and Tony Coelho, respectively.

Coelho, the Majority Whip and No. 3 in the Democratic leadership, announced his resignation from Congress in late May of 1989. That was the same month that Speaker Wright, under the pall cast by an Ethics Committee report accusing him of accepting favors from a friend who lobbied Congress and skirting limits on outside income, was forced to resign. Coelho left under the cloud of an investment deal hatched by a friend at junk bond dealer Drexel Burnham Lambert Inc. The friend bought $100,000 in bonds for Coelho but did not demand payment up front and let the debt languish without interest payments. While it wasn't clear Coelho broke any laws or violated ethics rules, he resigned to save the party from a repeat of the ugly Wright spectacle.

Coelho succeeded congressman Bernie Sisk in 1978, for whom he had been a top aide. While working for Sisk, Coelho soon learned the best way to curry favor with fellow members: raise money and do them favors. After his victory, Coelho secured a seat on the House Administration Committee, which oversees budgets for congressional offices, doles out money for taxpayer subsidized mail (known as franked mail), and decides who parks where.

As a legislator, Coelho's liberalism and appetite for partisan clashes helped him rise swiftly through the ranks and into the House leadership. There was one issue, however, in which Coelho abandoned partisanship. That was the Americans with Disabilities Act (or ADA), a sweeping civil rights law for the nation's handicapped citizens. An epileptic, Coelho passionately fought for the ADA. The bill passed after Coelho had left Congress, but his advocacy was important in keeping the issue on Washington's radar screen.

Coelho caught the eye of Democratic leaders in his first term by selling more tickets than any other freshman to a fund-raising dinner for all House Democratic candidates. Coelho became the chairman of the Democratic Congressional Campaign Committee in 1982. His job was to raise money for incumbents and challengers running for the House. The committee had raised $2 million while Jimmy Carter was President. With Reagan in office and the nation turning against Democrats, Coelho raised $6 million by reminding big business that Democrats still controlled the House—where all tax and spending bills originate. In 1984 Coelho raised $11 million; in 1986 he raised $16 million. Record-breaking numbers for Democrats.

Coelho understood the cultures of Congress. He didn't try to change them. He tried to use them.

His successor, Gary Condit, couldn't be more different.

Instead of appeasing his party leaders, Condit has spent most of his political career aggravating them.

Elected to the California state assembly in 1983, Condit quickly established a record for fiscal conservatism that pleased wealthy farmers in the Central Valley but proved irksome to the liberal Assembly Speaker, Willie Brown. For years, necessity forced Brown to tolerate Condit. He needed his vote and those of other contrary moderate Democrats to maintain his sometimes tenuous grip on the speakership. Then in 1988, Condit joined four other moderate Democrats in a revolt against Brown. They were known as the "Gang of Five" and their grievances were political and procedural. They resented Brown's autocratic ways and disagreed with his undiluted liberalism. They failed to oust Brown. In response, Brown had Condit's Sacramento office moved every Friday. He also removed Condit's top aide from the payroll for five months and stripped Condit of his chairmanship of the Government Organization Committee and his leadership slot of assembly majority leader. Condit's career appeared stalled.

Then Coelho resigned.

Condit won the race easily. His constituents admired his courage in standing up to the entrenched powers at the state capitol.

When he arrived in Washington, Condit started bothering party leaders all over again. He got an early start by quietly aligning himself with efforts to cut waste from all thirteen annual spending bills. Condit didn't sponsor these amendments, but he voted for all of them. He also helped persuade other newcomers to join a rebellion against the spending culture.

Condit voted against Clinton's 1993 "economic stimulus" bill—something I wish I had done. The bill was full of make-work government projects financed by deficit spending. A lot of Democrats voted for it out of deference to Clinton; we didn't want to see him suffer a defeat so early in his administration. We were wrong. Condit was right.

Later in 1993, Condit was one of only thirty Democrats to vote for an amendment that axed $58 million in agricultural research projects that government watchdogs decried as pork barrel waste. This sounds easy. It wasn't. Condit represents one of the most productive agriculture districts in the nation. He sits on the Agriculture Committee, where votes against research pork are decidedly frowned upon.

Condit has also joined the effort to require the EPA to calculate the costs of future environmental regulations. And he supports halting Congress's common practice of imposing new rules on state and local governments without providing the funds to enforce them. These two commonsense reforms would force the federal government to weigh the costs of future policies on the private sector and local and state governments.

Most Washington "experts" chuckle condescendingly at Condit's independence. They are sure the leadership will freeze him out. They underestimate Condit. He is emerging as a leader of the new breed of Democrats. As voters send more lawmakers like Condit to Congress, maybe, just maybe, the fiscally conscious rebels someday will outnumber their big spending elders. Then House leaders won't be chuckling anymore.

Geren succeeded Jim Wright in the House. Wright represented Fort Worth for thirty-five years, rising through the ranks to become Speaker in 1987. Voters kept Wright because of his clout. His successor had to win on policy. Geren campaigned as a moderate Democrat and has followed that path in Washington.

Wright established a respectable record during his lengthy tenure in Congress, particularly on the issue of civil rights. Wright won his seat to Congress by defeating an anti-labor Democrat (of which there were plenty in Texas in 1954). He arrived as a Roosevelt Democrat and throughout the 1950s and 1960s was among the most liberal Democrats in the Texas delegation. He supported civil rights, more government spending—especially on public works projects—and an interventionist foreign policy. This irked southern conservatives that dominated Congress at the time. When he ran for Majority Leader in 1976, his opponents reminded conservative Democrats of Wright's refusal to sign the "Southern Manifesto," a document denouncing the 1954 Supreme Court decision to outlaw segregation and his support for the 1957 Civil Rights Act.

Wright won that race and set his sights on the speakership. He maintained a mostly liberal voting record but feigned enough conservative positions, particularly on defense issues, to placate his constituents.

To his credit, Wright set an ambitious agenda as House Speaker and met more deadlines than his predecessor, Tip O'Neill, or his successor, Tom Foley. Under his leadership, the House passed a major highway construction bill, farm credit legislation, education reforms, and a clean water bill. During his first year as speaker, the House also passed every spending bill in time to meet legal budget deadlines. It was the first time that had occurred in nearly forty years.

There was a dark side to Wright as well. As a part of the House leadership and later as a speaker, Wright pursued a relentlessly partisan agenda. As a product of the Great Depression, Wright harbored a deep mistrust of and dislike for Republicans. He acted on these feelings as speaker and used every lever of power to foist his agenda on the House, which meant stepping on the toes of Republicans and many moderate Democrats.

"He was driven to a certain extent by an intensely partisan streak that I don't have," Geren said. "He saw [victory on] a party line Democratic vote . . . as a triumph over evil. I take my greatest satisfaction out of bipartisan victories like NAFTA, where I think dispassionate and nonpartisan action prevails. This sounds crazy, but I believe that party labels should be checked at the door of the House, that they are an election tool, not a tool of government."

Unlike Wright, Geren is not a partisan street fighter. He seeks out Republicans on issues of mutual interest and isn't afraid to cross the Democratic leadership.

Pressures from the Texas delegation have at times caused Geren to compromise his budget-cutting instincts. He supported the Superconducting Super Collider, which was under construction near his district, and the Space Station.

Overall, however, Geren has been a serious advocate for fiscal sanity, economic growth, and congressional reform. He organized the freshmen "Gang of Six." This band of Democrats led the charge to approve a balanced budget amendment to the Constitution. Geren was one of the few Democrats to oppose the Family and Medical Leave Act in 1993 because he thought it imposed too many burdens on business. He also voted against the 1989 congressional pay raise.

"[Wright] spent his entire life in politics," Geren said recently. "Mayor, state representative, then Congress. I grew up in a family that was cynical about politics and politicians, particularly career politicians. I never thought of politics as something you do forever—never have seen it as my life. And I don't fear or dread life without it."

The differences between these newcomers and the barons they replaced are most apparent when you compare their voting records.

Interest groups rate members of Congress based on how often they agree with them. The higher the score, the more frequently a lawmaker sided with that particular interest group. In 1988, Coelho's last full year in Congress, he scored a 90 percent voting record from Americans for Democratic Action (ADA), a liberal political organization. Coelho scored a

12 percent rating from the American Conservative Union (ACU), a Republican organization.

In 1992, Condit registered a 55 percent rating from ADA and a 48 percent score from ACU.

In 1986, Jim Wright's last year as a regular voting House member (the Speaker rarely votes), he scored 90 percent with ADA and 14 percent with ACU.

Geren scored 45 percent with ADA and 60 percent with ACU in 1992.

These scores vividly illustrate that Wright's and Coelho's successors are moderate Democrats who are willing to compromise with Republicans. The election of Condit and Geren to replace Coelho and Wright represents a dramatic shift within the Democratic party toward the center of the political spectrum.

Condit and Geren confronted the congressional orthodoxy their predecessors not only embraced but helped institutionalize and are at the leading edge of the reform movement.

ROADBLOCKS TO REFORM

Voters across the country hoped the 110-member freshman class of 1992 —nearly one-fourth of the entire House—would deliver the reforms many of them campaigned for on their way to Washington.

As is clear now, many of these attempts failed. That doesn't mean the freshman class was a failure. It simply means change comes slowly to Washington.

Some of that is due to the obstructionism of imperious legislative leaders who built bases of power atop the old system. Some of it is due to the natural flow of events within Congress; many freshmen thought it more important to help the President pass a new economic plan than wage a bloody internal battle over the seniority system or the jurisdiction of certain committees. Lastly, the 1992 freshman class arrived with built-in limitations that they themselves did not understand until well into their first year in Congress.

In most cases, the will of a handful of congressional barons ran roughshod over the reformers in the 103rd Congress. These barons do more to frustrate the agenda of the American electorate than most voters realize. Unfortunately, in 1992 they were aided by a sympathetic leadership and a pliant portion of the freshman class. Together, these forces conspired to thwart many of the changes voters hoped would come by sending 110 new members to Congress.

I'm ashamed to admit that this was largely a problem within my own party. For forty years, Democrats controlled the House and established the rules. Many of the logical changes freshmen sought would make the House run more smoothly and eliminate some of the perks that have contributed to the deepening estrangement between lawmakers and their constituents. The lack of progress on institutional reform was due in large part to the obduracy of my party's leaders and those chairmen whose power would be jeopardized by reform.

Worse still, many promising Democratic members of Congress lost in 1994 because voters blamed them for failing to bring necessary reforms to Congress. If they had been given the chance to change Congress, I strongly believe many of these Democrats would have created a better Congress while improving their image and the image of the President. But congressional leaders in my party wouldn't allow it. Party elders talked Clinton out of a reform agenda and bullied the freshmen into submission. In the process, fifteen of the most promising new Democrats lost in 1994 — not because they didn't fight for change, but because powerbrokers wouldn't let them make changes. And what did they get? A Republican House for the first time in forty years.

The desire of the Democratic leadership to quash reform was evident in late 1992 when they fanned out across the country just after the 1992 election to meet the sixty-three newly elected freshmen Democrats. In late November, the leaders conducted mini-orientation meetings in Chicago, Los Angeles, and Atlanta in what was obviously a preemptive strike against the "reform" movement.

THE *60 MINUTES* MAN

Rep. Luis Gutierrez, elected in a newly created and largely Hispanic district in Chicago, remembers the leadership's divide-and-conquer strategy. From the moment the leadership arrived, Gutierrez said it was clear their intention was to distract freshmen from the reform movement by enticing them with prized positions on powerful House committees and stressing that Democrats must avoid internal disputes in deference to the President's agenda.

At the freshman meeting in Chicago, all the top House leaders were deployed to dampen the reform agenda. Who was there?

Well, Speaker Foley, Majority Leader Richard Gephardt, Majority Whip David Bonior, Caucus Chairman Steny Hoyer, and chief deputy whips Barbara Kennelly, Bill Richardson, John Lewis, and Butler Derrick. For good measure, Ways and Means Chairman Rostenkowski showed up. Never known as a reformer of House procedures, Rostenkowski was there to size up the freshmen. Because there were so many vacancies in Congress, he knew he might be called upon to appoint at least one freshman to his committee. He didn't want a loose cannon.

That gives you an idea of the mentality the freshmen were up against at the Chicago meeting.

At first, it looked as if the Democratic leaders were trying to strike an egalitarian pose with the freshmen in Chicago. Instead of lining chairs in regimented rows and lecturing the freshmen from behind a podium, they sat everyone at an enormous circular table.

This setting looked inclusive, but was really part of a deft divide-and-conquer strategy. A top leadership official was positioned next to each freshman. No two freshmen sat next to one another and each freshman had a leadership official on his or her elbow. In this configuration, the freshmen couldn't even swap whispers or notes with one another if they happened to disagree with the leadership's pitch. Psychologically, it was a masterful strategy. Each freshman was alone, and the only people on either side were the potentates of the status quo.

But before the meeting concluded, Gutierrez made a pitch for radical House reforms because, as he said, "Congress is held in such low esteem."

He wanted to freeze congressional pay, limit perks such as free and unobstructed parking at National Airport, and dramatically lower campaign spending limits.

With Hoyer, the No. 4 man in the House, running the meeting, Gutierrez asked what role the freshmen could play in bringing visible change to Congress. "I said, 'Let us be the agents of change. Help us to restore this institution's image. Who better than us?'"

The leadership attempted to steer the discussion to other topics. Gutierrez, the son of a cab driver and factory worker, persisted. Perhaps the leadership expected him to play the "go along to get along game" because he was known as a cagey operator on the Chicago City Council, where he served for ten years. They were wrong. This time, Gutierrez was going to press for change, even if it cost him a shot at a top committee.

"Before the meeting broke up I asked the leaders, 'When do we [the freshmen] get a chance to develop our own agenda so we can leave an imprint on the 103rd Congress?'"

This time the leaders glowered at Gutierrez. Their taut lips and furrowed foreheads communicated what they would not say: Forget it!

"I might as well have been throwing a pie in their face," Gutierrez recalled recently. "It was obviously a mistake to expect the leadership to concur in the reform agenda."

Obviously, the meetings were about the leadership's agenda, not the freshmen's agenda. Believe me and Luis Gutierrez, when it comes to reform, the top leaders in Congress just didn't get it.

You may remember Gutierrez's celebrated appearance last year on *60 Minutes*. In an interview with Morley Safer, he explained that the House leadership had thwarted many reforms pushed by certain freshmen and that powerful committee chairmen had tried to intimidate him from pursuing his renegade agenda. I also appeared in that episode. Perhaps due to my impending retirement I was spared the kind of ribbing—some good-natured, some mean-spirited—that was directed toward Gutierrez in the aftermath of that broadcast.

House Democrats were furious with Gutierrez, and many let him know it face to face. Others told reporters they thought Gutierrez was acting like a show-off and some derisively called him "the Great Reformer." In Washington, if you challenge the status quo, the power structure immediately assumes you're posturing for political gain. It never occurs to the power brokers that you might actually believe in what you're doing.

Many Democrats assumed Gutierrez had gratuitously criticized the congressional leadership for his own political gain.

They weren't upset because they thought he lied, mind you. They were upset because he had violated a sacred but unspoken custom in Democratic circles: Never criticize internal House operations. The way Democrats look at it, there are more than enough Republicans attacking Congress. If no Democrats join them, they can be dismissed as partisan snipers frustrated with being out of power for so long. If Democrats join the criticism, however, voters might actually conclude something is wrong. That could be dangerous!

Months after the *60 Minutes* piece aired, Gutierrez was still deflecting attacks from prominent Democrats. When fellow Chicagoan Dan Rostenkowski was running for reelection in last March's Illinois primary and he appeared at a campaign event in Gutierrez's district, reporters asked the chairman why Gutierrez was absent.

"I don't know. Maybe he is busy doing another interview with *60 Minutes,*" Rostenkowski replied.

Rostenkowski purposely excluded Gutierrez from the event. That fed the criticism leveled by Gutierrez's primary opponent, namely, that the freshman was in such disfavor with the leadership that he wouldn't be able to bring any new federal dollars to Chicago. That same opponent filed a complaint with the Federal Election Commission alleging that the *60 Minutes* piece was so popular with voters in Gutierrez's district that it amounted to a campaign commercial and that he should be given equal broadcast time. Gutierrez handily won his primary with 63 percent of the vote.

Gutierrez's experience illustrates the gulf between what Washington demands and what voters at home want. Voters admired Gutierrez's spunk and candor. It's that kind of voice they wanted to send to Washington. Gutierrez's colleagues in Congress, on the other hand, despised his spunk and candor. They did everything in their power to discourage him from speaking out again.

The rewards and penalties in Washington simply don't make sense. Just ask Luis Gutierrez.

THE OTHER WASHINGTON

In 1993, Jay Inslee was a freshman from Washington. His district borders that of Speaker Thomas S. Foley. He possesses the kind of handsome earnestness of a young Jimmy Stewart. This forty-three-year-old newcomer to politics campaigned to cut congressional salaries and halve the deficit in five years. He ran a low-budget campaign to replace a Republican who'd held the seat for twelve years. Inslee spent hours on street corners waving at motorists and shaking hands. He promised to give out his home phone number if he got elected.

Inslee beat his well-financed Republican opponent by 2 percentage points, meaning he had to make good on promises to cut spending and reform the House or face the ire of the folks back home.

Inslee stood up at the first full meeting of freshmen Democrats and asked a question that would define the limitations of the freshman class for the remainder of the 103rd Congress.

"We were talking about the idea of a balanced budget amendment, and I said, 'Broadly speaking, how many believe Congress should spend less money?' About forty percent of the hands went up. I then asked, 'Broadly speaking, how many believe Congress should spend more money?' Another forty percent of the hands went up. About twenty percent were undecided."

Inslee and all others present then realized how divided freshmen Democrats were on the subject of spending. Inslee and other like-minded reformers knew that if all the Democrats were opposed to higher spending, they could link arms with the 47 freshmen Republicans and wield a terrifying 110-vote bloc against those who wanted to ignore the ravages of deficit spending. No one in Washington, not even the President, could ignore a bloc that large.

But it wasn't to be.

"If all one hundred and ten freshmen thought the deficit was the biggest issue and were willing to stake their political careers on it, we could have changed things," Inslee said. "Fundamentally, not all Democratic freshmen share that belief about the deficit."

Washington state sent another Democratic reformer to Congress when it elected Maria Cantwell, who represented suburban Seattle. Cantwell broke the Republicans' forty-year hold on the 1st District and immediately spearheaded efforts of freshmen Democrats to win important committee positions and adopt a reform agenda.

Many of the nation's future economic and political trends intersect in Cantwell's district. It's home to Microsoft, Nintendo, Eddie Bauer, and high-tech firms such as SpaceLabs and Sundstrand Data Control. It's also home to lush evergreen vistas and the breathtakingly clear Lake Washington and Puget Sound. The suburbs are carved into niches in the woods, and the residents seem intent to harness the dynamism of an entrepreneurial economy so as not to trample upon the natural beauty that envelops it.

Cantwell translated these demands into a hybridized Democratic platform. She campaigned as a Paul Tsongas Democrat and opposed the Clinton stimulus plan until the administration made a stronger effort to advance its deficit-reduction agenda. Early in her first year, Cantwell and other freshmen Democrats, after hearing the class was likely to receive low-grade committee assignments, drafted a letter to House leaders demanding representation on *all* high octane committees. The letter meant Cantwell was instantly crossing swords with Foley, who had enthusiastically backed her campaign. This display of independence won Cantwell praise among freshmen and, more important, helped nine freshmen land seats on the House's three power committees: Appropriations (three), Ways and Means (one), and Energy and Commerce (five).

Cantwell also was a leader in shaping the Democratic freshman reform package. While internal disputes prevented it from being as aggressive as she would have preferred, the Democrats did call for significant changes: term limits for committee chairmen, a 25 percent cut in the congressional budget, and rules disclosing where lobbyists funnel their campaign contributions.

Cantwell also led by example. She hired 25 percent fewer staff members than current rules allow and saved more than $240,000 in her first year in Congress. She also voted to kill the Superconducting Super Collider, the Space Station, $140 million in agricultural subsidies, $1.5 billion in ballistic missile defense, and $2.1 billion for the Advanced Solid Rocket Motor program.

Cantwell and Inslee were part of the new wave of Democrats willing to bridge the political chasm between business and labor interests or development and environmental concerns. They were also willing to chart an independent course that at times puts them at odds with Foley and other party leaders. I have always admired Foley's personal integrity and felt that his thoughtful and collegial manner was just the balm the House needed in the aftermath of the forced resignation of Speaker Wright in 1989. However, after thirty years in Congress Foley was an institution man invested in the status quo and leery of change.

"I have avoided laying out a political career plan," Inslee said. "If you do, you make stupid decisions. It's more important to be dynamic and lose a few than to stay here forever."

It seems to me that Foley could have learned from youthful lawmakers such as Inslee and Cantwell. Both demonstrate how Democrats can win in Republican districts with a moderate, reform-oriented agenda.

Foley was the most powerful Democrat in the House and a towering figure in Washington state politics. He may have been irked by these two young upstarts, but they represented the future of the Democratic party in Washington state and Washington, D.C. Ironically, all three of them lost in 1994. Foley became the first sitting House Speaker to lose a bid for re-election since 1860. Inslee and Cantwell lost in the Republican sweep of 1994. Voters in this predominantly Democratic state blamed all three for failing to deliver on basic congressional reform. Two of these victims had the foresight to at least try to reform Congress. One of them—the most powerful of them all—couldn't see it. His blindness condemned him and several others to defeat.

REBELS WITH A CAUSE

Eric Fingerhut is a Democrat from Cleveland, Ohio, and in many ways he resembles Inslee from Washington. He's a bit younger, thirty-five, and not as tall and muscular. He has a thin, angular physique and prominent wire-rim glasses that belie his intensity, intellect, and political sophistication. Someone in the House gallery could easily mistake him for a college intern, but members of the House know better.

Like Inslee, Fingerhut came from a competitive congressional district, and he arrived in Washington eager to prove his "reformist" bona fides. He wanted to break the stranglehold powerful committee chairmen put on legislation by limiting their terms in power and allowing merit-based elections—instead of seniority—to determine who chairs all committees. Fingerhut favored streamlining the process of referring bills so time isn't wasted on frivolous turf battles. He also wanted to cut spending before raising taxes.

Fingerhut made an abortive attempt at becoming president of the Democratic freshmen class, but discovered that his intense desire to push reform irritated freshmen from "safe" congressional districts.

"About half of the freshmen Democrats are members for life. They come from one-party districts. People who are 'Members for Life' have no stake in changing the system. They have no interest in reform. They are not alarmed by the deficit."

Fingerhut lost his bid for class presidency to Eva Clayton, a black woman from North Carolina's 1st District, which meanders through parts of twenty-eight counties in the eastern part of the state and was drawn to maximize the black vote.

The differences between Clayton's and Fingerhut's politics typified the ideological strains among freshmen Democrats in the 103rd Congress.

Clayton's district is rural and largely poor. Michael Dukakis carried 61 percent to 39 percent for George Bush there in 1988. Bill Clinton pulled in the same 61 percent in 1992, while Bush took 29 percent and Perot settled for 10 percent. Clayton's a former social worker who co-founded an anti-poverty group that turned abandoned schoolhouses and churches into day care centers. Her politics are liberal, and her major concern is using the government to relieve poverty.

Fingerhut's district melds the politically muddled urban and suburban neighborhoods in Cleveland and the heavily Republican Western Reserve in the northeast part of the state. Bush carried this district with 57 percent in 1988 and lost to Clinton 40 percent to 37 percent. Perot won 23 percent, among the highest totals in Ohio.

These are very different Democrats, and each brought separate agendas to Washington. For now, Clayton's agenda has prevailed because it better matches that of the Democratic leadership.

Foley once told Fingerhut why reforms had to be put on the back burner.

"He said, 'If we take up something like committee jurisdiction, it will be the only thing we'll do all session,'" Fingerhut recalls. "He told me there were members who hadn't spoken to each other for twenty years over the last attempt to touch jurisdiction."

Sadly, Foley was probably right.

And that's the problem. The Culture in Congress has become so devoted to the expansion and maintenance of power that members would waste an entire year feuding over committee jurisdiction instead of debating and passing legislation vital to the national interest.

Fingerhut said that congressional leaders devised a shrewd argument against reform in the early days of the administration.

"They said the worst mistake Clinton and the Democrats in Congress could make would be to repeat the Carter years [which were fraught with intra-party antagonisms and gridlock]. The biggest mistake Democrats could make, they said, would be for us to fail to produce. They sold that line partially in the House and totally to the White House."

In Clinton's first year, virtually every one of their initiatives became a test of party loyalty. Congressional leaders measured the Democratic freshmen for their party loyalty, not their loyalty to the voters back home. Worse yet, on some of the toughest votes of the year in 1993, the Democratic leaders demanded more from the freshmen than they did of established Democrats with safer districts and firmer political footing. Democratic freshmen had little desire to be disloyal, and many fell in line out of a genuine desire to help the President.

As they did, they discovered, however, that loyalty meant different things to different people. More senior members with safe seats and big campaign war chests were sometimes allowed to vote against the President, while freshmen like Fingerhut and Inslee and others were told to toe the line or pay the price—political exile.

"They are inconsistent in the application of power," Fingerhut said of the leadership. "Different rules apply to different people."

In response, another freshman Democrat, Leslie Byrne of Virginia, led her own revolt against this double standard during debate on the Clinton budget in May of 1992. The President's budget was perilously close to losing, and several Democratic subcommittee chairmen, many of them with safe seats, were voting no. The bill barely passed.

Byrne led a petition drive among Democrats to convene a special meeting to strip these chairmen of their positions of power if they defected. More than eighty members signed, including nine full committee chairmen (who have lots of power over subcommittee chairmen). A special caucus meeting was held, but no action was taken. The episode brought the double standard to light and made a difference, albeit a small one, in the way more senior members abuse junior members.

Why the double standard?

Tragically, when campaign season rolls around, both parties tend to give free passes to congressional barons. Frequently, each political party funnels campaign contributions into efforts to defeat the freshmen legislators of the opposing party simply because they are considered the most vulnerable targets. Each party seems more willing to sacrifice the fresh new faces rather than challenge power brokers who might strike back after the election.

This is why most members of Congress are reelected. Even in anti-incumbent years like 1992 and 1994, roughly 88 percent and 90 percent of all House members seeking reelection won. True, those were among the lowest reelection percentages since 1974, when the legacy of Watergate led to a massive purge of Republicans. But 88 percent and 90 percent are depressingly low numbers and a reflection of the "free pass" approach both parties give to lawmakers with seniority and hefty campaign war chests.

As for congressional reform, Fingerhut did team up with Utah Democrat Karen Shepherd to co-chair the Democratic Freshmen Task Force of Reform. Republicans Peter Torkildsen of Massachusetts and Tillie Fowler of Florida led the Freshman Republican Reform Caucus.

As a Democrat, I'm sorry to say the Republicans' reform agenda outshone that put forward by the freshmen Democrats. Shepherd and Fingerhut had a harder time persuading new Democrats to back reforms that stepped on the toes of party leaders and committee chairmen.

That didn't stop Shepherd from pushing for reforms on her own. She supported term limits and a balanced budget amendment to the Constitution, which put her at odds with Democratic leaders. She also introduced legislation to prevent retiring members from buying their old office furniture at drastically reduced prices. Senior Democrats contemplating their own retirement really disliked this idea.

Shepherd did not mind standing out and is a bit of a political anomaly. She was only the second woman to represent Utah in Congress and the first who is non-Mormon and pro-choice. She's a former English teacher and the founder of *network*, the state's first magazine dedicated to working mothers. Shepherd built a children's play area at her campaign headquarters and stressed issues such as full funding for Head Start and tougher enforcement of child support obligations.

Despite their failure to organize all freshmen Democrats behind a tough reform agenda, Fingerhut and Shepherd applied constant pressure on Democratic leaders to hold floor votes on reforms many moderate Democrats and Republicans support. Sadly, both of them lost in 1994 — again as a result of having no solid reforms to deliver to the folks back home.

Fowler and Torkildsen come from very different parts of the country but share the same goals.

Fowler came to Congress after serving on the Jacksonville City Council for seven years and was the first Republican woman elected Council president. When she campaigned for Congress, Fowler promised to leave after eight years in office. That stood in stark contrast to the man Fowler replaced, Democrat Charles Bennett, who served in Congress for forty-four years. Fowler's self-imposed term limit gave her the credibility to press for term limits for all members of Congress.

Fowler's district is caught in the cross-currents of southern politics; historically Democratic but trending Republican. Jacksonville is the state's most populous city and equally dependent on white-collar, blue-collar, and military jobs. Cargo haulers and ship builders ply the St. John's River, a rare northerly flowing river, which has become the nation's top port of entry for foreign-made automobiles; insurance, telecommunications, banking, and health care firms provide the white-collar employment; and Mayport Naval Air Station and the Naval Aviation Depot support a strong military constituency.

Torkildsen defeated Democratic Rep. Nicholas Mavroules, who was indicted in August of 1992 on bribery, extortion, and tax evasion charges. His district is one of the few in Massachusetts to lean Republican recently, and Torkildsen, who served as Republican Gov. William Weld's labor commissioner, has tried to consolidate his base by pushing a wide array of congressional reforms.

The 6th District, north of Boston, is home to a hodgepodge of traditional northeastern political voting blocs: liberal Yankee Republicans and blue-collar Irish. Historically Democratic, the district has leaned Republican through the 1980s in presidential elections. But it took a scandal to rock Mavroules, who was elected in 1978, from power.

Torkildsen built on his reputation as a giant slayer—in his first campaign for state office he upset state House majority leader John Murphy Jr. in 1984 —and adopted a pro-business, pro-choice agenda that mirrored Weld's. He ran few negative campaign advertisements and generally ignored the scandal that threatened Mavroules's career. He did criticize Mavroules for accepting PAC contributions and refused to accept them in his own campaign.

Fowler and Torkildsen led Republican freshmen to adopt a nineteen-point agenda of long-overdue changes. Among them are reducing the amount of political action committee (PAC) donations from $5,000 to $1,000 per year; requiring candidates to raise at least 51 percent of all campaign contributions from within their state or district; requiring lobbyists to disclose how much money they donate to congressional candidates; limiting to five years the previously unlimited government funding for office space and two secretaries for each former House Speaker; and, lastly, placing Congress under the same health, safety, labor, and anti-discrimination standards it imposes on the private sector.

The freshmen Republicans also endorsed limiting the terms of committee chairmen and requiring any Republican with No. 1 committee seniority to step down if he or she is charged with a criminal indictment. Previously, Republican rules allowed indicted members to retain their seniority.

Fowler and Torkildsen deserve most of the credit for advocating these changes and applying constant pressure to see some of them enacted.

The House passed the limitation on office and secretarial assistance for former speakers in 1993 and also passed another key GOP reform: public disclosure of those who sign discharge petitions. Previously, lawmakers could cosponsor a bill but refuse to sign a discharge petition that would pry it loose from a hostile committee and bring it to a floor vote. By keeping discharge petitions secret, the House made it easy for members to say they supported a controversial bill while refusing to help bring it to the floor.

Both of these reforms pitted Torkildsen against powerful lawmakers back home.

Former Speaker Tip O'Neill opposed Torkildsen's amendment to limit subsidies that maintain office space and secretaries for former speakers. He saw it as an insult to former speakers and one that wouldn't save much money anyway. (It costs about $600,000 per year for each former speaker's office.) According to press accounts in Boston, O'Neill chewed out Democrat Rep. Joseph P. Kennedy II for voting to trim his perks. Kennedy replaced O'Neill in Congress in 1986 (just as O'Neill had followed in the footsteps of Joe's uncle, John F. Kennedy, some thirty years earlier), and the former speaker's eleventh-hour endorsement had put Kennedy over the top. O'Neill monitored the votes of all ten Massachusetts congressmen, and Kennedy was the only Democrat to back the subsidy cut. Kennedy apologized the next day and said he mistakenly voted for Torkildsen's amendment, which passed 383–26.

The attempt to publicize discharge petitions threatened the power of all committee chairmen and especially Democrat Joseph Moakley, the dean of the Massachusetts delegation. Elected in 1972, Moakley had, with the help of O'Neill, risen through the ranks to become chairman of the Rules Committee. Moakley's committee sets the terms of debate for all bills that reach the House floor. Discharge petitions circumvent this process. Moakley saw the move as a threat to his turf and lobbied aggressively against it.

If the struggle had been left to internal House politics, the discharge petition reform would probably have failed. But media coverage and steady attention devoted to the issue by talk shows galvanized public support behind the effort. The House passed an amendment to disclose the names of all lawmakers who sign discharge petitions in the summer of 1993. This reform has already forced some committee chairmen to act on bills they had ignored for years.

In all of these cases, freshmen shook up some part of the system in Washington. They didn't always win, but they did rouse the power structure out of hibernation.

Tragically, Fingerhut and Shepherd were narrowly defeated in 1994. However, Torkildsen and Fowler were returned to office and they are in position to implement the reforms they championed.

Ten

Ten Real Reforms

The care of human life and happiness, and not their destruction, is the first and only legitimate object of good government.

—Thomas Jefferson

CONGRESS IS REPLETE with reform movements these days. Some are sincere. Some are smoke screens.

There are ideas circulating in Washington that I believe would turn the cultures I've described upside down. There are other ideas that sound particularly appealing to voters, but in the end, would do nothing to alter the cultures of Congress or deliver better government.

Reform is coming to Congress. Public hostility is leading new lawmakers to propose serious changes to the status quo. The old guard is trying to hold the reformers back. To preserve their bases of power, congressional power brokers have been trying to water down the most important reform proposals.

That's one danger.

Another is that Congress will pass new rules that sound good, but do not change what's fundamentally wrong with government. This chapter is dedicated to separating real reforms from fake reforms. A few ideas that have captured voters' attention would do little to change the status quo.

One idea is that lawmakers shouldn't move their families to Washington so they can maintain their "official" home in their district or state. More than a dozen House challengers in 1992 promised they would not move their family to Washington if elected. In many instances, the voters applauded the idea.

After twelve years in Congress, one thing is clear to me. Your family is one of the few humanizing aspects of your life, and you need to have them with you in Washington. Barb and I moved to Washington with our three children after I was elected to my first term. Being able to see my wife and children every day helped me live a life outside politics. My children's activities made it necessary to skip some fund-raisers, party confabs, and society functions in Washington.

If a lawmaker lives alone in Washington, he or she is much more likely to get caught up in the city's twenty-four-hour-a-day political climate. There's a greater chance lawmakers will "go Washington" if they live alone than if they have their family with them.

But I *do* recommend keeping a residence in the district. Doing so allows lawmakers to remain property taxpayers and retain community connections. My wife, Barb, and I and the kids have spent the school years in D.C. and the summers in Minnesota.

Another popular idea is to prohibit lawmakers from using a special parking lot close to National and Dulles airports in Washington. I know this perk irritates voters.

But it doesn't matter.

More accurately, it doesn't matter as much as you think.

Imagine that you woke up tomorrow to discover that henceforth members of Congress would have to park in lots farthest from the National and Dulles terminals.

That would satisfy your populist hunger for revenge against political elite.

Would it improve your government? Would it reduce the millions wasted on franked mail or office expenses? Would it stop budgetary chicanery? Would it break the stranglehold those in power hold over the institution? Would it make Congress live under the laws it forces you to obey?

No.

Forget the parking. Stick with the big stuff.

Another popular idea is banning gifts for members of Congress. That's fine by me. I'm all for eliminating junkets lawmakers take when lobbyists pick up the tab. A speaking engagement is one thing, but some trips, especially those to vacation hideaways, are another. But it's ludicrous to think a lawmaker's vote can be bought for a Caesar salad for lunch or a filet mignon dinner. It doesn't happen.

I'm afraid Congress will pass a tough ban on gifts but go much lighter on reforming the way campaigns are financed, which is the real culprit in swaying votes with money.

If voters want to reduce the influence of money in politics, they should forget the gift ban and focus their attention and ire on campaign finance reform (see real reform No. 10, below).

TEN REAL REFORMS

No reform package is perfect. This one is no different. These reforms, however, can break down some of the cultures I've talked about. And that's a good place to start.

I know that today's reforms are tomorrow's antiques. Congress probably needs to overhaul its rules every ten or twenty years to keep pace with the real world. The last reform crusade occurred in the mid 1970s. It helped. Those reforms, like all institutional changes, have been overtaken by events their authors could never have anticipated. If Congress passes these reforms, the time will come when they will have outlived their usefulness and it will be time for a new crusade.

These ten reforms won't solve all of Congress's problems, but they will reduce bureaucracy, provide for a broader competition of ideas, and empower those who want to follow through on the voters' desire to "cut spending first."

These reforms are meant to bring new choices to voters. They will jettison silly budget procedures that propel so many pet projects into the budget. They will dismantle much of the budgetary double-talk and let voters know what Congress is really doing with their money. They will improve the flow of ideas and legislation by rotating powerful lawmakers onto different committees.

These reforms are radical in their simplicity, and radically simple changes are just what Congress needs. My twelve years in Congress have taught me that incremental change is all about nuance; incremental change typically creates new language to describe old behaviors. What sounds new is really quite old. What Congress needs is radical reform simply done and simply worded.

1. PLACE CONGRESS UNDER ALL HEALTH, SAFETY, LABOR, AND DISCRIMINATION LAWS THAT GOVERN THE PRIVATE SECTOR.

Nothing would do more to elevate Congress's standing with the public than for it to bring itself under the laws it has imposed on the rest of the nation. Doing so would force Congress to confront the costs and difficulties of complying with these often cumbersome and ambiguous laws. The experience might deter lawmakers from imposing more workplace regulations. At the very least, lawmakers might learn how to draft laws that deal more specifically with the problems they are trying to solve. As it is now, Congress aggravates problems with red tape and regulation.

House Speaker Tom Foley gave the idea a lukewarm endorsement in 1994 but declined to put the weight of the speakership behind it. A number of senior Democrats filled the vacuum and stalled the movement to pass this reform. Nonetheless, the House passed it (with only four dissenting votes) late in the 103rd Congress. But like so many other reforms, it died in the Senate. Even so, public support is so high for this reform that it seems unlikely congressional heavyweights will be able to stand in the way much longer.

By the way, of the four Democrats who opposed this reform two would have lost power under the new system. They were Bill Clay of Missouri and William Ford of Michigan. The other two opponents were Kika De La Garza of Texas and Eva Clayton of North Carolina.

Republicans have pledged to pass this in the first hundred days of the 104th Congress. If they do, I hope President Clinton signs it and administrations of both parties punish congressional violations with the same vigor as would be visited upon a private citizen. The executive branch should not flinch when it comes to punishing Congress for violations of any of these laws.

2. REDUCE THE NUMBER OF CONGRESSIONAL COMMITTEES AND THE NUMBER OF STAFF EMPLOYEES IN CONGRESS.

There were 252 congressional committees in January 1993. That's about twice what we need. As I mentioned in chapter 3, the rise in committees has spawned an increase in federal spending and an entrenched hostility to cut spending.

Congress could function quite well with half the number of committees it has now. The best way to eliminate committees is to abolish the three-step process of drafting the federal budget. Please. If you care about the deficit and how Congress spends your tax dollars, indulge me for just a moment. I promise not to bore.

The process works like this.

One committee, called the Budget Committee, drafts a blueprint for all federal spending.

Another set of committees, called authorizing committees, writes laws deciding how much Congress can spend on each program. These laws regulate the maximum amount Congress can spend on a program each year. It's not uncommon for authorizing committees to write bills that call for spending that the Congress simply can't afford. This does not bother them. Under current budget rules, they are allowed to recommend how much to spend on a certain program without having to worry about where the money comes from.

Another set of committees, called appropriations committees, writes laws deciding how much Congress *will actually* spend on each program. These committees can spend as much or as little as they choose, as long as they don't spend more than the authorizing committees have recommended. On occasion, the appropriating committees spend money an authorization committee has not approved. The Steamtown railroad museum is a perfect example of this phenomenon.

Congress's multistep process increases the incentive to concoct new programs and spend more money. No one wants to be on a committee that spends less money. Spending less means giving up a part of the federal budget. Doing that means giving up a portion of power. Each committee becomes a fiefdom, a hothouse of specialization where lawmakers toil feverishly over one minuscule part of the federal budget. In this environment, no problem appears more pressing than the one they are trying to solve. This narrow focus proves the popularity of the old adage "When your only tool is a hammer, all problems look like nails." Often, no solution appears more reasonable than spending more money.

Committees are the foundation upon which many of the most insidious cultures of Congress rest.

The best way to eliminate committees and reduce the incentive to spend is to combine the chores of the authorizing and appropriating committees. That way the same people make all the spending decisions.

Various House committees fight over the right to study, debate, and vote on a bill. The public never sees these jurisdictional disputes, but they account for much of the difficulty in bringing bills to the floor in a coherent and efficient manner. The Founding Fathers never intended to have three, four, and sometimes half a dozen committees fighting over the same bill. They foresaw what many frustrated members of Congress now must endure: a system bogged down by petty and meaningless power grabs by committee chairmen whose desire to occupy center stage politically overwhelms their desire to serve the national interest.

"Bills are assigned to several committees by the parliamentarian," Rep. Dan Glickman, Kansas Democrat, recently told a committee on congressional reform. "Too often, once important bills are introduced they simply get lost in the morass of committee jurisdictions. Good ideas are tossed aside without discussion because overlapping jurisdictions make progress on a bill too difficult."

Just look at the health care debate as a recent example of the waste of time and talent caused by turf wars. Five major committees in the House and Senate fought for jurisdiction, and a dozen other committees fought for their turf. All this did was slow progress on this important piece of legislation.

Common sense suggests that reducing the number of committees would reduce these needless committee cat fights.

Numerous vested interests oppose this essential reform. Voters can help increase the odds by asking their own lawmaker to support cutting committees—even if means giving up "power" that in some way benefits their district or state. Cutting committees would also allow a dramatic reduction in congressional committee staff.

In 1991, there were more than twenty-seven thousand people working for Congress. More people work for Congress than for any legislative body in the world. That's because Congress operates as its own vacuum-sealed village. It has its own police and mail careers; its own carpenters and plumbers; its own electricians and carpet layers; its own barbers and hairdressers; its own parking attendants and elevator operators.

Congress cost the taxpayers $2.2 billion in 1994.

Since 1946, the cost of operating Congress has risen 4,165 percent. That's right. Four-thousand-one-hundred-and-sixty-five percent! The consumer price index for that period rose 618 percent. Congressional budgets have increased at nearly seven times the rate of inflation since the end of World War II. During this time the staff sizes swelled by twelve times in the House and fourteen times in the Senate. Congressional apologists like to point out that costs reached a plateau in the mid 1970s. From 1976 to 1992, the cost of Congress rose by *only* 143 percent while the consumer price index rose 146 percent.

That's still unacceptable.

Taxpayers are paying nearly twice as much now for Congress than they were in the 1970s. Yet the Congress—need I say it?—is not twice as efficient, productive, or competent.

The federal government is the only remaining institution in American life to ignore the need to downsize and become more efficient. All commercial enterprises and many state and local governments have had to slash their operating budgets to adapt to foreign competition or dwindling tax bases. But not the federal government. It's time the Congress joined the real world by taking on the tough task of downsizing.

Republicans have pledged to eliminate as many as four full House Committees and cut House staff by one-third. The Senate Republicans are expected to make more modest cuts. Voters should demand still deeper staff cuts in the future and a further consolidation of committees. And voters must keep a watchful eye on both parties in the future because the temptation to create a bigger and more power-hungry Congress will never be far away—no matter which party is in control.

3. LIMIT TERMS FOR COMMITTEE CHAIRMEN.

I referred to this recommendation in chapter 5. In 1994, more than 50 percent of all House Democrats were chairmen of full committees or subcommittees. A Democratic colleague of mine, Jim Traficant of Ohio, addressed every member he saw as "Mr. Chairman."

On a more serious note, committee chairmen can and sometimes do abuse their power. There are many more examples than the ones I gave in chapter 5 of chairmen bottling up legislation simply because they opposed it. Few legislatures in the world adhere so slavishly to seniority as we do.

If Congress rotated chairmen out of their positions of power, there would be less incentive to block legislation or to protect programs that have outlived their usefulness.

Voters could improve the odds of Congress enacting this reform by asking their own lawmaker to support limiting the terms of chairmanships. If successful, this reform could do more to improve the quality of legislation than imposing term limits on all members of Congress. First, it could happen much more quickly because there are no constitutional questions involved. A constitutional amendment requires a two-thirds vote in each house of Congress and ratification by three-fourths of the states, whereas a single majority in Congress can limit terms for committee chairmen. In fact, all each party has to do is change its own rules of procedure. Congress doesn't even have to pass a law. Second, rotating committee chairmanships would allow qualified legislators to stay in Congress while encouraging them to apply their skills to a broader range of issues.

While we're at it, it might be beneficial to rotate committee memberships. Moving lawmakers to different committees would also reduce hyperspecialization in Congress. Able lawmakers with proven legislative skills could take their talents to new committees and apply their talents in a new area of public policy. For example, too often farm state legislators secure a slot on the Agriculture Committee and remain there strictly to defend agricultural interests. The same is true of lawmakers from different regions of the nation. They all seek membership on the one committee most apt to protect their interests, such as military bases, oil and gas industries, high tech research, or public lands. That's a logical impulse but one that tends to overshadow national interests. If lawmakers were required to change committees on a somewhat regular basis, they would, I believe, develop a better sense of what programs are truly necessary and which remain simply to satisfy a core group of lawmakers wedded to a particular industry or constituency. Republicans plan to pass this reform. My guess is that once this occurs it will be difficult to resurrect the seniority system.

4. ABOLISH BUDGETARY DECEPTION.

There are three things Congress does with its budget that could not pass what I call the "coffee shop test." If it doesn't make sense to people at your neighborhood coffee shop, it doesn't pass the test.

First, Congress uses a baseline to write each budget. I talked about this process in chapter 3. The baseline assumes spending for every program in the federal government increases each year by the rate of inflation. Instead of investigating if the program deserves what it got last year, Congress assumes spending will rise *every year on every program.*

We should stick the baseline in the basement and start each year with last year's budget and build from there. In this way, Congress would honestly freeze spending on each program unless it found justification for an increase and voted for it. There would be no more automatic increases. In other words, a freeze would be a freeze.

Second, budget rules prevent lawmakers from cutting spending and using the savings to lower the deficit. If the House or Senate approves a spending cut, the committee in charge of the bill just cut spends the savings somewhere else. If Congress approves a spending cut, lawmakers who sponsored the cut should have the right to use the savings to cut the deficit. In other words, a cut would be a cut.

Third, Congress tacks all sorts of pork barrel spending onto emergency relief bills. When Congress drafted a bill to provide $8 billion in aid to victims of the Los Angeles earthquake, it added another $3.2 billion for programs that had nothing to do with that emergency. Congress added pork barrel spending to bills providing relief for the Midwest floods, the Los Angeles riots, Hurricane Andrew, Hurricane Hugo, and the San Francisco earthquake. It's sickening and wasteful. It ought to stop. All emergency spending bills ought to deal specifically with the emergency at hand.

The House passed two of these reforms (numbers 1 and 3) in 1994 but they died in the Senate. The House votes represented good progress on the road to reform. The incoming chairman of the House Budget Committee, John Kasich of Ohio, has predicted these reforms will pass easily in the 104th Congress. I hope he's right.

5. ALLOW LAWMAKERS TO RETURN UNSPENT OFFICE ALLOWANCES TO THE TREASURY.

House members receive $557,400 to pay for staff and $174,000 for expenses. If lawmakers spend less than this amount, the difference is diverted to a catchall spending account where it's spent by other legislators. There is no incentive to economize. If lawmakers could direct their savings to the Treasury to reduce the deficit, they would have a strong political incentive to economize.

This would change the cultures of Congress in two ways.

First, it would acquaint lawmakers with the discipline of establishing and living within a budget. Currently, many lawmakers don't need all the funds they receive but find ways to spend them anyway. If they could achieve some political credit for keeping costs down, they would. Creating a culture of personal frugality in Congress could change many lawmakers' attitudes toward the national budget. It could cause lawmakers to budget their offices the way they would budget their family or business finances.

Second, reducing office budgets would lead many lawmakers to hire fewer employees (House members are allowed to hire eighteen full-time and four part-time employees). Reducing the number of staff would require lawmakers to do more work themselves. Overworked lawmakers might have to scale back their legislative efforts. Right now, the average House member serves on six committees. If the lawmaker had to do the work that three staff members were doing, he or she might cut back to three committees. If members served on fewer committees there would be more support for elimination and consolidation of committees. Fewer committees would reduce the incentive to spend, and, well, you can see what wonders this tiny reform might unleash.

6. ALLOW LAWMAKERS TO EARN OUTSIDE INCOME.

Abolishing outside income was supposed to clean up Washington. The idea was to eliminate potential conflicts for lawmakers by making their life in Congress their only livelihood.

What did we get?

Career politicians, people with no financial support other than their job in Congress. In an ironic twist, the very wealthy were exempted from this restriction. Current rules allow lawmakers to collect "unearned" income from investments. That means those in Congress with hefty investment portfolios can sit back and collect interest from their investments, but the lawmaker who came to Congress with an average job has no other avenue to pursue financial independence. Eliminating outside income forced most lawmakers to become financially dependent on their careers in Congress. By prohibiting them from keeping a hand in a law practice, real estate business, small family business, or other occupation, the law has made financial hostages of most members of Congress.

What could be wrong with allowing a lawmaker to maintain a job on the side as long as he or she reports the income annually? Voters and the media could scrutinize the records for any signs of conflict of interest. If there was a conflict of interest, it would be a potent issue for any challenger. I am not suggesting lawmakers should receive fees for giving speeches. That income has properly been banned. Lawmakers are supposed to use their talents to inform voters and deepen public understanding of complex issues. They should not collect fees for public speaking—an essential part of public service. There are, however, countless other legitimate ways to earn income.

Denying lawmakers an outside income gives them an even greater incentive to stay in Washington. This is one of the reasons that congressional sessions last almost the entire year. Why go home? If members had a real job to go home to, I believe they would find ways to move legislation more rapidly and forgo so many of the mindless delaying tactics and partisan tussles that gum up the works.

Lastly, lawmakers who have real jobs have a new, nonpolitical attachment to their community. Interacting with customers and clients is different from interacting with constituents—most of whom demand more from government.

The public distrusts undoing a reform that's already on the books. That's shortsighted. The problem with outside income in the old days was that it wasn't publicly disclosed. With public disclosure, only the foolhardy would grant favors under the table. The public, however, would benefit greatly by allowing politicians to earn a living at home and in Washington. It would encourage the politician to sink even deeper roots in the community and discourage him or her from "going Washington."

Most other nations, by the way, allow their national legislators to earn outside income. In most instances, state legislators are allowed to earn outside income.

In a related reform, we should also eliminate the congressional pension program. A pension suggests a career. Elected office should not be viewed as a life-long career. It ought to be viewed as public service. If there is no pension, then personal financial gain is no longer a factor in a lawmaker's decision to build a career out of a life in Congress. Furthermore, the current pension plan is far more generous than any pension available to the private sector, or, for that matter, federal civil servants.

7. END THE CONGRESSIONAL SESSION ON OR BEFORE JULY FOURTH.

Congress stays in session too long.

Most of the work it needs to do could be done by the Fourth of July weekend. Accelerating the schedule on Capitol Hill would put a premium on work and penalize posturing. It's just the opposite now.

Most lawmakers know serious legislative work is left to the last minute. That's because power brokers are able to secure more concessions the longer they hold out. Why should anyone want to compromise any earlier than necessary?

Currently, the federal fiscal year begins October 1.

If Congress moved the beginning of the fiscal year to July 1, it would have to draft and pass its budget by June 30. That would accelerate matters greatly on Capitol Hill. Lawmakers would have less incentive to stay in Washington beyond July 1 because all of the spending decisions would have already been made.

It would also discourage Congress from meeting only three days a week. That's right. Congress ordinarily meets Tuesday, Wednesday, and Thursday. Members fly home to their districts or states on Friday and return to Washington on Monday. Congress would work more effectively if lawmakers stayed in Washington for six months and worked five days a week. After finishing their work, lawmakers could return home for six months.

The lawmakers could return to their districts and states to work at other jobs—if they have them—or simply rotate among their offices in the district. Voters would see more of their lawmakers and vice versa. The pulse of each lawmaker's district or state would become as familiar to him or her as the pulse of Washington. That, I believe, would do wonders for each lawmaker's perspective on the nation's needs.

Lastly, on a purely symbolic note, wouldn't it be great to end each congressional session on Independence Day? Instead of celebrating another three-day weekend and reveling in history, the nation and the Congress could use the Fourth of July as a time to take stock of its overall performance and compare it to the dreams and aspirations of our Founding Fathers.

I can't imagine a better way to bring voters and Congress together in a celebration of the laws of this land.

8. LOWER THE AMOUNT OF MONEY LAWMAKERS CAN SPEND ON FREE MAIL, OTHERWISE KNOWN AS FRANKED MAIL.

During my first nine years in Washington, Congress spent $835 million on free mailings. That's more than $92 million per year.

That's absurd.

We spend much of this money on propaganda disguised as newsletters. A close reading of these "newsletters" reveals they are little more than taxpayer-financed advertisements for the sitting incumbent. I should know. I mailed plenty of them myself during my first few years in Congress.

Thankfully, Congress barred lawmakers a few years ago from carpet bombing their districts with "newsletters" just before Election Day. The new rules prohibit mailing "newsletters" fewer than sixty days before a primary or general election.

Nevertheless, Congress should limit free congressional mail to responses to constituent letters and press releases. If lawmakers want to send out newsletters, let them pay for them out of their campaign account. That's what freshman Rep. Mike Castle, Delaware Republican, has done. His is an example we should all follow.

9. REQUIRE LAWMAKERS TO RAISE MORE THAN 50 PERCENT OF THEIR CAMPAIGN CONTRIBUTIONS FROM HOME.

As I mentioned in chapter 9, too many lawmakers raise too much money from outside their district or state. As long as there are no restrictions on the source of contributions, politicians will have less incentive to search for money at home when it's easier to collect from wealthy out-of-state contributors. Voters should look for candidates who apply this standard voluntarily, but Congress, by passing meaningful campaign reform, should impose this standard on all candidates. This would help challengers by reducing the advantage incumbents have in securing contributions from special interest groups.

Listen to what Rep. Ron Mazzoli, a Kentucky Democrat, has to say about the virtue of rejecting big contributions and running a less expensive campaign. Mazzoli refused to accept PAC contributions in 1990 and 1992 and won reelection even though he was outspent by a challenger who accepted PAC contributions.

"It was liberating," Mazzoli said. "It was so wonderful because I knew I was doing it [campaigning] right. And the people around me knew that I was doing it right. And they kept energized and motivated like they've never felt since sixty-seven [Mazzoli's first campaign for state office]. I tell you we had more people come out, more contributions, more volunteers, more enthusiasm than we have had except in those very early years. All because they knew I was at risk. It was the most wonderful [experience]. It was liberating. We were like we were when we were young people; in the basement and people were kind of bustling around and we didn't have the big shots telling us what to do and all the polling and such. But I've told every member to a person that they would be astonished if they were to try it. What it does for them and what an increased sense of self-esteem you have."

10. SET AN INFLEXIBLE LIMIT ON THE AMOUNT CANDIDATES CAN SPEND ON HOUSE AND SENATE RACES.

This is the essence of campaign finance reform.

Campaigns will become more competitive when more challengers can effectively compete in campaigns for the House or Senate.

The only way to do that is to establish a campaign spending limit that's lower than what incumbents now spend to win seats in Congress.

In 1992, all incumbents running for the House spent an average of $595,000. On average, challengers spent only $167,900.

Congress must lower the costs of campaigning. The only way to do that is by adopting a legal limit on expenses.

I suggest $335,000 for House races. I do not have a suggested figure for Senate races, although I favor a limit on their expenses as well.

This amount is twice what the average challenger raised in their campaigns for the House in 1992. Surely, a member of Congress can mount a credible campaign with roughly twice the money the average challenger raised in 1992.

Under this system, challengers will attract more contributions because potential donors will know there is a limit to what the incumbent can spend. If an incumbent can spend $1 million, why would a donor give to a challenger with less than $200,000? In most cases, the donors wouldn't because the odds run too strongly against a challenger in such circumstances. That's the problem.

With these limits, more challengers would be encouraged to run for

Congress. As it is now, incumbents stockpile contributions from special interests to discourage potential opponents. If subjected to strict spending limits, incumbents and challengers would have to abandon costly TV and radio advertisements that do more to distort important national issues than inform voters. Without the crutch of media campaigns, candidates would have to develop grassroots campaigns with committed volunteers and small contributions. These are the kinds of campaigns that would reinvigorate the public's interest and trust in Congress.

If voters were to focus their attention on this aspect of campaign finance reform, Congress would have to respond. As it is now, Congress is tied in knots over secondary issues such as the size of PAC or individual contributions and whether public funds should be used to subsidize campaigns. (Believe it or not, one so-called reform circulating on Capitol Hill would offer challengers the use of "franking," or free mail, privileges now available to incumbents.)

The only way to increase competitiveness is to limit the cost of congressional campaigns. That's the only worthwhile goal of campaign finance reform. Everything else is secondary.

Eleven

Ten Common Cents Tips to Elect a Better Congress

I know no safe depository of the ultimate powers of the society but the people themselves; and if we think them not enlightened enough to exercise their control with a wholesome discretion, the remedy is not to take it from them, but to inform their discretion.

—Thomas Jefferson

THE MOST IMPORTANT contribution you can make to reforming Congress is to seek out and support candidates who bring a new perspective to old problems. No approach is fool-proof, but based on my experience I believe these ten guidelines will help you choose a Congress more willing to dismantle the barriers to new ideas.

This list will prove useless, however, unless you exercise your obligation to vote. Notice I didn't say your "right" to vote. Of course it's a right, one enshrined in our Constitution. I want to focus on the obligation you have as a citizen to participate in this government. Although voter participation rose slightly in the 1992 presidential election (from 50.1 percent in 1988 to 55.2 percent), voter participation in off-year congressional elections remains pitifully small.

In 1960, the election I stayed up past my bedtime to follow, 62.6 percent of the eligible voters cast ballots for President, and 58.5 percent voted in congressional elections. In 1994, the last non-presidential election, only 38 percent of eligible voters cast ballots in congressional elections.

Let me suggest that the rise in public dissatisfaction with Congress is at least partly related to the staggering decline in voter participation. So much of the behavior of Congress seems out of touch with the concerns of the average taxpayer. With fewer people casting ballots in congressional elections, the outcome is more easily controlled by special interest constituencies. The majority of voters who turn out for congressional elections in non-presidential years are special interest activists. Their voice becomes even more powerful because there are fewer general interest voters competing with them.

Few things empower the special interest more than a passive electorate. Special interests are never passive. They are always agitating, always pushing for the advantage. Their vigilance is partly responsible for many of the enervating cultures I've already discussed.

There's a rule lobbyists on Capitol Hill know as well as they know their own name: If a politician has a choice between 5,000 votes and $5,000, he or she will take the votes every time. Lobbyists in touch with a reliable voting constituency always have more influence in Congress than those who simply cut checks. That's because it takes more than $5,000 to create support from 5,000 voters. Politicians are not stupid. Nothing counts more than votes. Nothing.

When less than 65 percent of eligible voters cast ballots in nonpresidential congressional elections, they are ceding all political terrain to the special interests. They are muzzling their own voice while amplifying the special interests' voice.

If you want to make a difference in Congress, there are many things you can do. None is more important than voting. Once you've decided to do that, here are ten guidelines to follow as you size up candidates in your next congressional race.

1. DON'T VOTE FOR LAWYERS.

If you have a choice and it doesn't mean voting for someone with whom you fundamentally disagree on the issues, trust someone who is not a lawyer.

There were 181 lawyers (42 percent) in the House in 1993. There were 58 lawyers (58 percent) in the Senate. The next closest profession was the combined pursuits of business and banking. This broadly defined group was represented by 131 members (30 percent) of the House and 27 members (27 percent) of the Senate. My sense is that this ratio may have been changed for the better by the 1994 election.

Frankly, we have too many lawyers in Congress. Even though I like most of my colleagues who are lawyers, I believe they are overrepresented. Only .07 (seven-tenths of 1 percent) of the American workforce are practicing attorneys. I think the track record of lawyers dominating the legislative output of Congress is clear. The problem with lawyers is that law school trains people to be legalistic, prosecutorial, and argumentative. As is the case in the courtroom, lawyers in the Congress tend to compile a mountain of facts to defend their preexisting political beliefs; it's all about winning the argument, not revealing the truth.

It may surprise you to learn how many professions have almost no voice or representation in Congress.

In the 103rd Congress:

Only nineteen members of the House and nine senators have any background in agriculture.

Only five members of the House have experience in engineering. There are no senators with an engineering background.

Only two members of the House and one senator have any experience in aeronautics.

Only ten members of the House have a law enforcement background. No senators have a law enforcement background.

Only two members of the House were officials in a labor union. No senators were.

There are only six members of the House with a background in medicine. No senators have a background in medicine.

Only one senator and no member of the House was a military professional before coming to Congress.

Sending men and women from different professions to Congress is crucial to improving the quality of our laws. Books and conversations influence a person's judgment, but their strongest beliefs—their principles—are often forged by personal experiences. I believe our legislation would improve if we had a better balance of occupations in Congress. At the very least, all of us would have to reexamine our laws from the bracing, real-life perspective of professionals from medicine, telecommunications, law enforcement, aeronautics, or agriculture.

As it is now, our perspective is commonly influenced by arid legalese. The result is technically precise laws that prove unworkable in real life. It would be great to have more people in Congress who could spot these errors earlier and save us from ourselves.

I'm not the first to pine for fewer lawyers in Congress.

In 1964, William L. Hungate, a Missouri Democrat, learned that to carry one particular county, he needed the endorsement of an elderly newspaper editor. It was Hungate's first campaign, and he left nothing to chance.

After an hour with the old-timer, Hungate felt he'd made a good impression.

"Son," the editor said. "I like you, and I think we're going to endorse you, but one thing first. I hope you're not one of those goddamned lawyers!"

Hungate gulped.

"Well, sir, yes, I am. But if it helps, I'm not much of one."

2. KEEP A GRAIN OF SALT HANDY FOR POLITICIANS WHO OBTAIN PERFECT SCORES FROM SPECIAL INTEREST GROUPS.

Members of Congress routinely tout their perfect or near-perfect scores from special interest groups when they're running for reelection.

Republicans will tub thump about 100 percent scores from the Chamber of Commerce, the American Conservative Union, the Tax Foundation, or the Christian Coalition.

Similarly, Democrats will pound their chests about 100 percent scores from the AFL-CIO, Americans for Democratic Action, the Sierra Club, or the National Education Association.

Politicians hope these perfect scores will illustrate their principles, their unbending support of this or that special interest group's agenda. They wear them as a badge of honor, mostly because they know a 100 percent record means a steady flow of campaign contributions and the loyalty of the voters represented by a particular special interest group.

These scores should alarm any voter interested in lawmakers capable of weighing national interests against parochial ones and acting independently of special interest pressure.

Many of the votes that appear on these scorecards are on issues the special interests forced onto the congressional agenda. In some cases, they are legitimate issues. In other cases, they are simply test votes to see which members are still toeing the special interest's line.

More often than not, these test votes are far more important to politicians and special interests than they are to the average voter. The tug of special interest support, either through votes or campaign contributions, is something lawmakers today don't dare ignore.

Even if you are a member of one of these special interest groups, you should logically wonder whether a lawmaker with a perfect score has a mind of his or her own. It's harmful to our legislative process to reward members with voting records in the 80 percent to 100 percent range with one special interest group or another. You should also wonder about the independent judgment of those with 0 to 20 percent ratings with other special interest groups. Such voting patterns reveal a certain rigidity to public policy generally reflecting that a legislator is out on the extreme, not in the mainstream. This ideological rigidity makes genuine compromise more difficult.

Polarization along ideological lines usually leads Congress into legislative battles that produce plenty of speeches and "test votes" but precious little constructive public policy-making.

I strongly disagree with Jim Hightower, the liberal Democrat and former Agriculture Commissioner of Texas. Of moderates, Hightower once said: "The only thing you'll find in the middle of the road is dead skunks and yellow stripes."

In truth, the vast majority of American people can be found in the middle of the road. It takes a lot more courage in today's Congress to seek a middle ground between ideological rivals than it does to camp out with the liberal or conservative extremists.

The polarization of Congress fomented by special interests and reflected in their annual vote scorecards makes it more difficult for lawmakers to summon the courage to reach out to search for consensus.

It's safe to assume that lawmakers who score between 20 percent and 80 percent on special interest scorecards have sought a more reflective and independent path on national issues. It's also safer to conclude they've made a conscious decision to resist special interest pressure on some votes and instead applied their own independent judgment.

Minnesota Senator Hubert H. Humphrey once had to defend himself against charges that he was too liberal. He was running for reelection in 1954 when his opponent criticized him for belonging to the Americans for Democratic Action, or ADA, a liberal organization. Later, a reporter asked him what farmers in his state thought of his ADA membership.

"I simply declared to them in answer that things had come to a sad pass when a man could be so abused for belonging to that fine old American institution, the American Dairyman's Association!" Whether it is one ADA or another, voters should view skeptically a legislator's perfect fidelity to any interest group.

3. ALL ELSE BEING EQUAL, GIVE THE BENEFIT OF THE DOUBT TO THE FEMALE CANDIDATE SEEKING A SEAT IN CONGRESS.

Even after the overhyped "Year of the Woman," the number of women in Congress remains embarrassingly low. There were forty-eight women in the House after the 1992 elections, or 10 percent of the 535 total members. And 1992 was a breakthrough year. The number of women increased 71 percent over 1990, when only twenty-eight women were in the House. Only seven women are in the Senate, or 7 percent of the total (that is a 250 percent increase over the two who served there in 1990).

Women represent 51 percent of the U.S. population. We need a national legislature more reflective of the voices and experiences of the nation's population. Women from both parties bring a unique perspective to the issues that come before Congress.

In my years in politics, I have noticed that there is a distinct difference in the way male and female lawmakers approach the issues. In my judgment, women are better lawmakers than men. Too many men treat politics like sports. They bring a competitive "us versus them" approach to policy-making. Ego trips and gratuitous displays of machismo sometimes overwhelm better judgment. Privately, men often resort to locker-room jargon to describe legislative or political maneuvers: "scoring political points" on the opposition, "hitting home runs" with a speech, "blindsiding" a political opponent, "moving the ball forward" in a political skirmish, "moving the goal posts" in a legislative negotiation, seeking a "level playing field" before debate begins. Sports metaphors are everywhere when men play politics. The mentality of winning overrules the better instincts of many male lawmakers. I've seen numerous instances where the desire to "win" has overtaken the desire to settle an issue equitably.

It's been my experience that women are far more willing to seek consensus and compromise than are men. They seem more eager to solve problems and move on. They don't seem the least bit concerned about "home runs," "goal posts," or "blindsiding." They are more willing to clean up a mess, even if they weren't around at its creation. The first instinct of many male lawmakers is to blame someone else for the mess.

Voters who want to shake up the system and break up the "Old Boys Club" in Congress would do well to send a lot more women to Washington. I'm not saying women alone would solve all the nettlesome problems Congress faces, but it's my belief that the election of more women would increase the likelihood of Congress's seeking and finding consensus solutions to these problems. More women in Congress would also force men to look at issues differently than they have in the past.

4. ALL ELSE BEING EQUAL, VOTE FOR A MINORITY CANDIDATE.

Amendments passed in 1982 to the Voting Rights Act of 1965 helped create nearly two dozen minority districts after the 1990 census. This contributed to the election of thirteen new blacks and eight new Hispanics to the House in 1992. There are now forty blacks in the House (thirty-eight Democrats and two Republicans) and one black in the Senate; there are nineteen Hispanics (sixteen Democrats and three Republicans) in the House and no Hispanics in the Senate. In 1990, there were twenty-five blacks and eleven Hispanics in the House and none of either race in the Senate.

Obviously, this is an improvement, but it still falls far short of a fair representation of the nation's minorities. Blacks make up 7.5 percent of the Congress and 12 percent of the nation's population. Hispanics represent 3.5 percent of the Congress and 9 percent of the nation's population.

While creating so-called "black" and "Hispanic" districts to increase the number of blacks and Hispanics has succeeded, the exercise has not been without costs. The state legislatures that drew the lines for these new districts were forced by the wishes of white incumbents in the Congress to stitch together minority populations from vastly different parts of the state. Many of the new districts violate the Founding Fathers' intention of bringing "regional" representation to Congress. One of the basic principles of the House is that each member represents a region that, despite party differences, is influenced by the same geography. Republicans and Democrats in a given district, say, are both affected by the oil refinery in their district; or the auto plant; or the national forest; or the wheat farms.

The concept of a "community of interest" was created to see to it that congressional districts were defined and, to a certain degree, unified, by the common geography.

The new strictly minority districts ramble over hill and dale in search of enough black or Hispanic voters to constitute a majority of the voting population. This geographic wandering creates absurdities, such as the 12th District in North Carolina, which connects black voters inside a 120-mile hairline district with boundaries often no wider than Interstate 85. The lines are so narrow that in one county northbound drivers on the interstate are in the 12th District but southbound drivers are in the 6th District. What's worse, North Carolina legislators could have created a more compact black-majority district. Doing so, however, would have encroached on the well-tended political terrain of Rep. Charlie Rose, North Carolina Democrat. Instead, the courtiers in the state legislature accommodated Rose and drew the absurdly shaped 12th District.

Republicans have cheered this process. They have done so for selfish political reasons. Republicans hope that white Democrats who lose black voters to majority black districts will be more vulnerable to challenge from a white Republican. They are correct. In Georgia, for example, the 1990 reapportionment increased the number of safe black districts from one to three. At the same time, the number of white Democrats has fallen from eight to one, while Republican representation has risen from one to seven. This is not an ideological or political makeup that bodes well for black voters.

This entire process is now being reviewed by the courts.

While that is being sorted out, I want to point out that there is a better way to bring more minority representation to Congress. Vote for more minorities. The black-majority and Hispanic-majority districts do enlarge the number of minorities in Congress, and I applaud that. But they do not address the more important issue of creating more trust among all ethnic and racial groups. Creating precise pockets of black or Hispanic representation tends to separate ethnic groups from one another, even though they share the same geographic interests I spoke of before. In North Carolina's 12th District, for example, white voters in Durham do not share political representation with blacks in Durham. Whites in Greensboro are prohibited from sharing political representation with blacks in Greensboro. Instead, the whites of these two cities have their own white congressman while blacks in Durham and Greensboro (two very different cities—one a college town, the other an emerging urban jewel of the South) have the same congressman, Mel Watt.

Our Founding Fathers made it possible for the Congress to evolve into a melting pot, where regional, ethnic, racial, and ideological perspectives could compete on a roughly equal footing. It would be foolish to suggest the founders had in mind the kind of representation we have today, since they did not allow women or blacks to vote (in fact, they didn't even resolve the central issue of slavery). The founders established principles of representation that resonated long after they died and provided the moral impetus and political latitude for this nation to amend the Constitution and expand political rights to women and minorities.

We can further these noble principles by opening our minds to the idea of voting for representatives from different cultural backgrounds. Yet, there are only three blacks in the House, Democrat Alan Wheat of Missouri and Republicans Gary Franks of Connecticut and J. C. Watts of Oklahoma, who are from white majority districts (the black voting population in these districts are 21 percent, 5 percent, and 6 percent, respectively). Sadly, the Congressional Black Caucus frequently bars Franks from its meetings. Nevertheless, Franks enlightens the debate and strengthens our legislative work by voicing the opinions of black conservatives.

Voters who bring a flexible outlook to the polls will greatly enhance the prospects of electing minorities to Congress. When Republicans and Democrats stop playing games with congressional districts (either to protect themselves or punish the other party) and voters open their minds to the merits of minority candidates, Congress will be well on its way to fulfilling the standard the Rev. Martin Luther King, Jr. established on August 28, 1963, while standing before the Lincoln Memorial:

> I have a dream that one day this nation will rise up and live out the true meaning of the creed: "We hold these truths self evident; that all men are created equal." . . . I have a dream that my four little children will one day live in a nation where they will be judged not by the color of their skin but by the content of their character.

5. GIVE THE EDGE TO A CANDIDATE COMMITTED TO RAISING MOST OF THEIR CONTRIBUTIONS FROM INDIVIDUALS WITHIN THEIR STATE OR DISTRICT.

Voters are, as usual, way ahead on this question. A survey released in April of 1994 showed that 70 percent of registered voters favored requiring members of Congress to raise at least 50 percent of their contributions locally.

While campaign contributions from organizations outside your state or community are not always evil, they may affect a lawmaker's ability to bring independent judgment to his or her job. Special interests, such as bankers, oil interests, the Hollywood set, or environmentalists, that do not have specific interests in a certain district or state give money to encourage or reward political allegiance. Again, this isn't a corruption of democracy or representative government. *But it can be taken to extremes.* While absolutes are tough to come by in politics, it's safe to assume that lawmakers who raise at least *half* of their campaign funds at home will find it easier to resist pressure from outside special interest groups.

As a general rule, contributions from political action committees come from outside the candidate's district. A good way to judge a candidate's fund-raising approach is to examine the ratio of PAC contributions to individual contributions. This isn't a fail-safe approach, however, because some individual contributors will also live outside of the candidate's district or state.

In 1994, for example, all 383 incumbents raised an average of $263,282, or 46 percent of their expenditures. Challengers raised far less overall and received almost no assistance from PACs. The 347 challengers raised an average of $32,320 from PACs.

Overall in 1994, incumbents raised eight times as much PAC money as their challengers: $126,741,604 to $16,095,463.

This sizable fund-raising advantage paid off handsomely for incumbents. Three hundred and forty-seven of the 382 incumbents running won reelection. Their reliance on PACs made it less likely that they will ignore the pleadings of special interest outside their district. To monitor the PAC receipts of your congressman, senator, or any other member of Congress, call or write the Federal Election Commission at: 999 E. Street, N.W., Washington, DC 20463. Toll-free: 1-800-424-9530.

6. DON'T ACCEPT GENERALITIES WHEN CANDIDATES TALK ABOUT THE FEDERAL BUDGET.

There are few issues in which rhetoric and reality have so little to do with one another. Lawmakers and challengers from both parties distort, fudge, and lie about the realities of the federal budget more than they do on any other issue.

Republicans say they support a balanced budget amendment to the Constitution, but rarely explain what such a thing would mean. Let me tell you what it would mean: higher taxes and controversial changes in middle class entitlement programs such as Social Security, Medicare, federal pensions, farm subsidies, and college loans.

The next time a politician tells you he or she supports a Balanced Budget Amendment, you should ask the following questions: (1) Does that mean you are willing to raise taxes, at least as a last resort? and (2) Does that mean you are willing to reduce the so-called entitlements such as Social Security, Medicare benefits, federal pensions, or farm subsidies?

If he or she answers no to either of these questions, he or she is a phony. You can count on it. Here, there is an absolute. Any politician who tells you Congress can balance the budget without a combination of these elements is lying. There is no other word for it. The Republican Contract

With America is brimming with generalities about how to reduce the deficit. I fear their numbers will never add up.

The same is true of that glittering generality—the line-item veto. While I support it, the line-item veto would affect only a fraction of federal spending. Here's the truth. Congress almost never spends more than the President asks for from one year to the next. For example, from 1983 to 1992, Congress spent *$59.5 billion less* than was sought by Presidents Reagan and Bush.

The most egregious congressional waste is found inside supplemental spending bills. Here's the trick: During much of the 1980s, Congress intentionally underfunded politically popular programs, and months later, when the money was about to run out, legislators passed a "supplemental" bill to provide the needed funds . . . but that's not all. Congress usually took the opportunity to tack on pork barrel items left out of the last budget. In recent years, this practice has been less evident; but emergency spending bills for natural disasters, such as Hurricane Andrew, the Midwest floods, and the Los Angeles earthquake, have also served as vehicles for billions in pork barrel waste.

It's this type of bill that the line-item veto would scale back the most. From 1983 to 1992, Congress passed twenty-one supplemental or emergency spending bills, appropriating more than $138 billion. That *is* a lot of money. It's nearly $14 billion per year. Even so, it's a mere fraction of total federal spending. Over those ten years, total federal spending was nearly $11 trillion. In other words, the money spent in the supplemental bills was 1 percent of all federal spending from 1983 to 1992. Only a portion of this amount could be categorized as pork barrel spending.

In other words, had the President had the line-item veto, he likely would veto only a small portion of the total congressional spending. Don't misunderstand me. I support the line-item veto. At the margins, I think it could reduce wasteful congressional spending. You must understand, however, that the line-item veto is insufficient to dramatically reduce rampant federal deficits. Symbolically, it would be important to inhibit Congress from piling on the pork barrel spending. But that's about all it will accomplish.

If a politician implies it can do more, he or she is a phony. As they say, numbers do not lie. Unfortunately, when it comes to the budget, many politicians do.

7. VIEW WARILY CANDIDATES OR INCUMBENTS WHO PROMISE TO BRING MORE FEDERAL MONEY OR PORK BARREL SPENDING TO YOUR DISTRICT.

You can't be half pregnant on this issue. You are either part of the solution or part of the problem. If your highest criterion for a candidate or incumbent is his or her willingness to funnel tax dollars to your district, you can't be a champion of balanced budgets. These roles are mutually exclusive.

If you care about reducing the deficit, you must be willing to give up projects in your region that are not national priorities. That doesn't necessarily mean giving up disaster aid. It doesn't necessarily mean giving up necessary improvements to flood plains, highways, bridges, airports, or military bases. But it definitely means doing without federal goodies such as research grants to your local university or hospital and federal funding for local tourist projects and mass transit operating subsidies, and it could mean forgoing construction of an extra post office or federal courthouse.

In order to secure funding for a local project, lawmakers are often obligated to support dozens of other projects around the country. Yet, to a legislator's constituent the attitude runs something like this: Except for our pork barrel spending, all pork barrel spending is evil. Voters have to ask themselves: "What is the proper role of the federal government, and what am I willing to pay to support it?"

Should the federal government pay for daily transit operating subsidies in big eastern cities? Should the government subsidize crops such as peanuts and sugar, even though doing so forces consumers to pay more for products made with these crops? Should the government provide subsidized water to corporate farmers in California who are wealthy enough to pay market rates for it? Should it pay for museums and parks that states and local governments could just as easily pay for and maintain?

Why should the federal government take tax dollars out of your pocket to pay for a project a distant state or local government could and should finance? Well, that's what happens with pork barrel spending.

Viewed in that light, all pork barrel spending is evil. It wastes money the national government needs to pursue national interests. Put more bluntly, in an era of tight budgets and deficits, pork barrel spending steals directly from programs to immunize America's children, fully fund Head Start, retrain displaced workers, or—Need I say it again?—reduce the federal deficit.

8. SUPPORT THE CANDIDATE WILLING TO IMPOSE HIS OR HER OWN TERM LIMIT.

I'm not sure if term limits would be good public policy. I know voters strongly favor them, but that is not enough for me to endorse them. I see strengths and weaknesses in a Congress composed of members elected under constitutional term limits.

What I'm far more comfortable with is creating a dialogue between voters and lawmakers about the time someone should spend in Congress. I think it's important for voters to ask candidates and current office holders just how long they intend to stay in Congress.

Instead, voters are expressing support for term-limit initiatives (fourteen states passed term limits referenda in 1992 while at the same time reelecting legislators who have served longer than the term limit referenda suggested; seven more states and the District of Columbia approved them in 1994). While many of these term-limit initiatives would theoretically affect lawmakers in some distant time, they would do little to reform campaigns and Congress *now.*

One way to do that is by making the topic of a self-imposed term limit an integral part of any congressional campaign. A few years ago most politicians refused to discuss their personal finances, but it's now a common practice. Voters forced this change because they wanted to know more about their candidates' ethics.

I find it amusing that South Carolina Sen. Strom Thurmond, at ninety-two years of age and after thirty-nine years in Congress, is among those who support term limits.

While in Congress, I tried to lead by example, and now, by retiring after twelve years, I'm trying to leave by example. As I said in my speech the day I announced my retirement, "Too many politicians stay for too long." On the whole, I believe it would be better for politicians to arrive in Congress having at least considered the question of how long they ought to stay. I think it would be helpful for all politicians to think seriously about what their life will be like after leaving Congress. In general, those who are willing to impose their own term limit are more likely to treat their job as public service instead of a career.

9. AVOID THOSE CANDIDATES WITH PARTISAN TENDENCIES.

As with most of our society, civility has become harder and harder to find in national politics. It's illogical to think a government can function without it. Think about your drive to work each day, or about standing in line at a grocery store or walking down a crowded street. Aren't all of these encounters improved by a dose of common decency?

The same is true of politics. It's common sense. Politics is about the fusing of different priorities into a coherent whole. The legislative process depends on people who can disagree without being disagreeable. It's no easier for a lawmaker to sympathize with a legislative opponent who's just attacked him than it is for you to sympathize with the guy who has just stepped in front of you at the checkout counter.

Let me explain what I mean about partisanship. I don't mean to suggest that you should shy away from people who strongly disagree with their political opponent. Definite opinions strongly held are a tonic for political debate. By themselves, they cause no problems and contribute immensely to the public's understanding of the issues at hand.

What I'm talking about is the "my party right or wrong" approach to politics. You find it in lawmakers who vote with their party or President 90 percent or 100 percent of the time. This reflects a monochromatic view of political life: my party wears white hats, and your party wears black hats; we're the heroes, and you're the villains. Lawmakers blinded by partisanship cannot see that compromise lubricates the legislative machinery. Knee-jerk partisanship gums the gears.

The real damage wrought by this mentality is not found in what Congress does but in what it *doesn't* do. Many members of Congress dismiss new proposals simply because they've come from someone in the opposing party. As a result, new ideas shrivel before they've been given a chance to take root. While partisanship pleases the party hierarchy, it rarely paves the way for a melding of the best ideas Congress can muster. Frequently, it leads to ideological standoffs where both parties assail the other's ideas while the problem they are supposedly addressing festers. Steer clear of partisan candidates. They tend to be blame-layers and problem-makers. That's not what we need in Congress.

10. REJECT NEGATIVE POLITICAL CAMPAIGNS.

This is a corollary to rule number 9.

Negative campaigns tell you that the politician is willing to win at all costs. *We don't need any more of that attitude in Congress!*

Treat any charge leveled in the heat of a campaign with great skepticism. Increase your level of skepticism as the election approaches. One of the most successful tactics in negative campaigns is to unleash a sensational charge in the final days in hopes the other candidate will not have the time or the money to respond adequately.

These tactics were in full and humorous display in the 1950 campaign that pitted Republican challenger George Smathers against Florida Rep. Claude Pepper. Smathers tried to scandalize incumbent Democrat Claude Pepper with misleading attacks that left rural audiences gasping.

"Are you aware," Smathers intoned darkly, "that Claude Pepper is known all over Washington as a shameless extrovert? Not only that, but this man is reliably reported to practice nepotism with his sister-in-law, and he has a sister who was once a thespian in wicked New York. Worst of all, it is an established fact that Mr. Pepper, before his marriage, habitually practiced celibacy."

The Common Cents rule to filtering negative campaign attacks is to disbelieve everything you hear that cannot be independently verified. Fortunately, most newspapers in America now attempt to do just that. You can often find stories that examine the charges leveled in all campaign advertisements and an analysis of how truthful the candidates are being with the public. This is an excellent resource for voters leery of campaign lies or distortions.

This is slippery territory for a politician because most of the pollsters and consultants tell us that negative campaigns "work." By "work" they mean they attract the attention of undecided voters and help to move voters previously inclined to vote for a candidate to reconsider their choice.

Negative campaigns usually appeal to voter passions by trying to make them focus on one particular issue or flaw.

A typical advertisement might sound like this: "Candidate X voted to cut your Social Security benefits while using a free airport parking space and drinking free bottled water . . . perks ordinary people have to pay for. It's time for a change. Vote for Candidate Y."

Well, here's the game at work, folks. First, pollsters and consultants will try to find an issue a majority of voters in a district or state support. Then they scour the opponent's record to see if he or she ever voted against that issue. Generally, it doesn't matter what kind of vote it was, just as long as it can be said it was a vote against that issue. This threat terrifies lawmakers in Washington. It's one reason they are so skittish about debating and voting on tough issues.

I think it's a good idea to reject a candidate whose speeches are laced with acidic criticism of their opponent's motives. Candidates who resort to harsh personal attacks rarely have anything constructive to say about the issues. And character assassination is often used to shift attention away from their own shortcomings. Some may have a paper-thin legislative record, for example. Others might be trying to divert voters from ethical lapses or from an embarrassing reversal on a once strongly held position.

Here is a good rule of thumb: Negative campaigning tactics generally say more about the character of the attacking candidate than the quality of the candidate being attacked.

Twelve

The Common Cents Guide to Empowering Yourself as a Citizen

If a nation expects to be ignorant and free, in a state of civilization, it expects what never was and never will be.

—Thomas Jefferson

IF YOU WANT to change your government, you should understand its basic structure. This is an attempt to help you. Voters who understand their government will make better decisions about the policies that are best for the nation and the lawmakers most likely to support them. Armed with this basic knowledge you are prepared to create the change you believe the government needs. To exercise nominal influence with your government, you must know the answers to the following ten questions. If you don't know, find out.

COMMON CENTS TEST OF GOVERNMENT KNOWLEDGE

1. Who is your congressman?______________________________
2. Who are your state's two senators?______________________________
____
3. To which parties do your congressmen and senators belong?__________
____
4. Where do you go to register to vote?______________________________
5. Where do you vote in your neighborhood?________________________
6. Which party currently controls each house of Congress?____________

7. On which committees do your congressmen and your state's two senators serve?______________________________

8. What are the phone number and address of your local congressional office?______________________________

9. What are the phone number and address of the nearest senatorial field office?______________________________

10. What is the address and telephone number of the Federal Election Commission?______________________________

COMMON CENTS GUIDE TO CITIZEN EMPOWERMENT

1. GET TO KNOW YOUR ELECTED OFFICIALS PERSONALLY.

A politician's value system is more important than his or her view on a given issue because it can give you an idea about how he or she goes about making decisions. You can best measure a politician's value system—or character—if you meet him or her one-on-one. What you observe in a meeting will tell you more about a candidate's value system than a hundred television or radio campaign commercials will.

How can you meet a member of Congress?

It's easy.

(a) Attend a town hall meeting, fund-raiser, local civic club meeting, or any of the public functions members of Congress attend on their frequent trips to their district or state. (You can easily obtain a list of the lawmaker's public schedule by calling your local lawmaker's office or the regional office of either one of your state's senators.) Most local newspapers are aware of a politician's scheduled appearances.

(b) Introduce yourself to the lawmaker and be prepared to discuss the issue you're concerned about. Bring with you a written summary of your concerns that includes your name, address, and home or business phone number.

Believe me, you will get a response, either on the spot or by mail shortly thereafter. More important, from your first-person encounter you'll have your own impression of the politician as a person and not simply as a name in the news.

2. CONTRIBUTE FINANCIALLY TO A POLITICAL CAMPAIGN.

The best way to check the power of special interest money is to support candidates of your choice financially. The size of your contribution does not matter; renewing your involvement in and commitment to the political process does. Voters will never eliminate money from politics. But they can dilute the special interests' influence by letting candidates know they have supporters who want them to pursue the nation's best interests. Also, the special interests will be less important to a candidate's success if individual supporters contribute enough to finance a credible campaign. In addition, analyze your congressmen's or senators' FEC report to determine their reliance on PACs as opposed to individual contributors.

3. REGISTER TO VOTE AND ENCOURAGE OTHERS TO REGISTER.

"Bad officials," said George Jean Nathan, a twentieth-century American author, editor, and drama critic, "are elected by good citizens who do not vote."

Except for a small upward spike in 1992, voter participation in elections has been declining steadily since 1960. (The 55.2 percent turnout in 1992 was 5.1 percent higher than the 1988 presidential election. Most experts believe Ross Perot's third-party candidacy led to higher voter turnout.)

Don't be caught by surprise on Election Day. If you have recently moved, make a note to change your voter registration. See to it that your son or daughter registers on his or her eighteenth birthday. Help coworkers or new neighbors register to vote. Voting is not simply a right, it is your responsibility. It's a cliché, I know, but if you don't vote, you really have no right to complain about Congress. Nonvoters are part of the problem, not part of the solution.

4. QUESTION YOUR OWN INTEREST GROUP.

As I mentioned earlier, 70 percent of all adults belong to at least one special interest group, and 25 percent belong to four or more. The national interest is not the sum of all its special interests. Congress has responded to special interest pleadings for years, and the result is an overextended government that does many things but few of them very well.

If you belong to a special interest group, you're likely to receive biased information to persuade you that a policy you favor is in jeopardy (whether it is or not). Typically, the special interest group will present only one side of the argument and ask you for money. Collect more objective sources of information before you respond. If you detect a pattern of willful distortion from your special interest group, demand that they change their tactics or consider withdrawing your support.

5. BECOME BETTER INFORMED.

This will help you sift through information from your special interest group should you belong to one. It will also help you shape better opinions about all issues before Congress. Don't rely simply on television news or talk radio. Supplement these sources with on-line computer networks, C-SPAN, newspapers, news magazines, opinion journals, and books.

Thomas Jefferson once warned of the consequences of an ill-informed public. In a letter to James Madison on December 20, 1787, Jefferson said,

> Educate and inform the whole mass of the people. Enable them to see that it is their interest to preserve peace and order, and they will preserve them. They are the only sure reliance for the preservation of our liberty.

There is no excuse today for being ill-informed. There are more sources of information available than ever before. Take time to educate yourself and your children about the issues before Congress. Doing so will make you a better voter and better citizen.

6. IGNORE POLITICAL POLLS.

According to the *National Journal* magazine, the number of presidential popularity polls released each month has increased 100 percent since 1989. It's safe to assume that polling for other purposes has increased by at least that much.

Polling is a ubiquitous part of political life in America. But polls tell us very little about the nation's most important issues. News organizations trumpet the results of their own polls for publicity reasons—not necessarily because they are newsworthy.

Too often, polls discourage voters from considering an underdog candidate. Voters mistakenly assume a candidate's lagging poll numbers mean he or she lacks solid ideas or qualifications. In the early stages of a campaign, poor poll numbers usually mean a candidate can't afford the commercials necessary to introduce his or her name or ideas to a sizable number of voters.

Polls sometimes discourage voters from supporting candidates they are afraid will lose. But most Americans don't believe they wasted their vote for Ross Perot, even though it was clear he would lose. Perot's 19 percent popular vote sent a strong message to the leaders of both political parties. There are some notable examples where polls were patently wrong. Before his upset victory in 1948, President Harry Truman ridiculed polls predicting his defeat. He called them "sleeping polls" and warned voters to guard against being lulled to sleep by such polls. Truman scored a stunning upset of Republican Thomas Dewey. Ignore polls. Make up your own mind.

7. VOTE BOLDLY.

This tip is a corollary to tip number 6. Even if you support a losing candidate, your vote can send a message. Voting for a third-party candidate allows you to signal a strong interest in a particular philosophy (libertarian, socialist, nativist) or issue (environment, term limits, education, tax cuts, military preparedness). Your vote is your best weapon. Use it as you wish and send the message you want reflected in public policy.

8. PARTICIPATE IN COMMUNITY SERVICE.

It does not matter what route you choose. Just find a way to give something to your community. Join a civic club, the League of Women Voters, or a church project; volunteer for a local government task force; join a volunteer rescue squad or fire department; lead a youth activity or a Boy Scout or Girl Scout troop.

Your involvement will heighten your interest in politics and government. More important, it will demonstrate that the government can't work as effectively as motivated individuals in their own community. You will see that not all problems need to be dumped on the doorstep of the government. There are problems the government can't or shouldn't try to solve. Community service will also inspire your children and neighbors. You, too, can lead by example.

9. WRITE LETTERS TO THE EDITOR AND YOUR ELECTED OFFICIALS.

Make your views known not only to your elected leaders but also to your friends and neighbors. Letters to the editor will help stimulate a healthy debate on the important issues facing your community and nation. Besides, an elected official is less likely to listen to your views if you cannot even persuade your friends and neighbors to agree with you.

10. READ THE DECLARATION OF INDEPENDENCE AND CONSTITUTION.

Most Americans believe passionately in the virtue of our democratic system of government. We extol the value of our hard-earned freedoms, yet few Americans take the time to read our country's most precious documents. When you read these powerful words, you will sense some of the inspiration that motivated our Founding Fathers more than two hundred years ago.

I am going to make it easy for you. Just turn to the appendixes.

CONCLUSION

Today's public distemper toward Congress is neither fleeting nor benign. I fear it could destroy the cohesive bonds of civility, respect, and trust that have historically animated the relationship between the governing and the governed.

In America, when the voters begin to hate their government they must look at themselves and ask why. After all, our Constitution says that "We the people" are in charge of this government. In the final analysis, we are responsible for the good our government does and the mistakes it makes.

Voters and politicians must take a fresh look at each other and themselves. Both the governing and the governed have failed to honor the noble principles and permanent truths upon which the Founding Fathers built this nation.

We must resurrect our first principles: that laws will be created to serve the needs of society as a whole; that one generation should not mortgage the future of another through the accumulation of needless debt; that political integrity fosters respect and allegiance for our governmental institutions.

Courageous ideas cannot grow in the grit of public cynicism. Rational thought will shrivel under the heat of partisan rage. To the degree possible, we must expel both from our political process.

In the final analysis, the success or failure of this government reflects upon all of us, politicians and voters alike.

If you don't commit yourself to changing the system, you have no one to blame but yourself for outcomes you oppose. If you want to change the Congress you have to change your approach to politics. I hope this book has shown you some new ways to think about politics and how your involvement can change Congress.

Common sense can return to government if the voters demand it.

Of course, your voice can't change national policy overnight. And we wouldn't want it to. The Founding Fathers, as Thomas Jefferson said, intentionally built a cautious legislature prone more to plod than to gallop:

> Democracy is cumbersome slow and inefficient, but, in due time, the voice of the people will be heard and their latent wisdom will prevail.

The latent wisdom of the people does prevail. But only when that wisdom is given a voice. Those who idly complain about government but refuse to vote inhibit the people's wisdom from exerting its vital influence on Congress.

Within Congress, a single vote can change the course of history.

Clinton's tax bill and the extension of the draft in 1941 (just four months before the Japanese bombed Pearl Harbor) each passed by one vote. President Thomas Jefferson's attempt to abolish slavery in all new U.S. territories lost by just one vote, setting the stage for continued North-South hostility over slavery that culminated in the Civil War.

Our government will not allow a solitary voice to change its laws. It will not allow a minority to impose its will on the majority. But it will allow every solitary voice to be heard. Each American has the right and the obligation to help chart this nation's course. Congress has never abolished your right to lend your solitary voice to discussion of this nation's future. And it never will.

It is my hope this book has helped you see Congress as it really is—better than you thought in some ways, perhaps worse in others. But redeemable. The Congress can change. It is changing. It's changing because voters are demanding it. The system is working. Maybe it's not working as quickly or on as many fronts as you would prefer, but it is working. New lawmakers with new ideas are beginning to alter the cultures of Congress I've described. This is no time for cynicism. It's time for determination. Cynicism encourages people to give up. That only protects the status quo. Determination encourages people to join. That creates new centers of power. These forces reshape the status quo.

There has never been an idea more radical than a government that derives its powers from the consent of the people. This book is about rekindling in you this most revolutionary idea. If you are unhappy with your government, you must do something about it. I've given you some basic suggestions that *I know* make a difference. You can come up with plenty more. Your consent is the key to this democracy. No one in Congress has power unless you give it to him or her. If you want a better government, you must first become a better citizen.

It's only Common Cents.

Appendix One

The Declaration of Independence

THE DECLARATION OF INDEPENDENCE was adopted by the Continental Congress in Philadelphia, on July 4, 1776. John Hancock was president of the Congress and Charles Thomson was secretary. A copy of the Declaration, engrossed on parchment, was signed by members of Congress on and after Aug. 2, 1776. On Jan. 18, 1777, Congress ordered that "an authenticated copy, with the names of the members of Congress subscribing the same, be sent to each of the United States, and that they be desired to have the same put upon record."

IN CONGRESS, July 4, 1776
A DECLARATION
By the REPRESENTATIVES of the
UNITED STATES OF AMERICA,
In GENERAL CONGRESS assembled

When in the Course of human Events, it becomes necessary for one People to dissolve the Political Bands which have connected them with another, and to assume among the Powers of the Earth, the separate and equal Station to which the Laws of Nature and of Nature's God entitle them, a decent Respect to the Opinions of Mankind requires that they should declare the causes which impel them to the Separation.

We hold these Truths to be self-evident, that all Men are created equal, that they are endowed by their Creator with certain unalienable Rights, that among these are Life, Liberty, and the Pursuit of Happiness—That to secure these Rights,

Governments are instituted among Men, deriving their just Powers from the Consent of the Governed, that whenever any Form of Government becomes destructive of these Ends, it is the Right of the People to alter or to abolish it, and to institute new Government, laying its Foundation on such Principles, and organizing its Powers in such Form, as to them shall seem most likely to effect their Safety and Happiness. Prudence, indeed, will dictate that Governments long established should not be changed for light and transient Causes; and accordingly all Experience hath shewn, that Mankind are more disposed to suffer, while Evils are sufferable, than to right themselves by abolishing the Forms to which they are accustomed. But when a long Train of Abuses and Usurpations, pursuing invariably the same Object, evinces a Design to reduce them under absolute Despotism, it is their Right, it is their Duty, to throw off such Government, and to provide new Guards for their future Security. Such has been the patient Sufferance of these Colonies; and such is now the Necessity which constrains them to alter their former Systems of Government. The History of the present King of Great-Britain is a History of repeated Injuries and Usurpations, all having in direct Object the Establishment of an absolute Tyranny over these States. To prove this, let Facts be submitted to a candid World.

He has refused his Assent to Laws, the most wholesome and necessary for the public Good.

He has forbidden his Governors to pass Laws of immediate and pressing Importance, unless suspended in their Operation till his Assent should be obtained; and when so suspended, he has utterly neglected to attend to them.

He has refused to pass other Laws for the Accommodation of large Districts of People, unless those People would relinquish the Right of Representation in the Legislature, a Right inestimable to them, and formidable to Tyrants only.

He has called together Legislative Bodies at Places unusual, uncomfortable, and distant from the Depository of their Public Records, for the sole Purpose of fatiguing them into Compliance with his Measures.

He has dissolved Representative Houses repeatedly, for opposing with manly Firmness his Invasions on the Rights of the People.

He has refused for a long Time, after such Dissolutions, to cause others to be elected; whereby the Legislative Powers, incapable of Annihilation, have returned to the People at large for their exercise; the State remaining in the mean time exposed to all the Dangers of Invasion from without, and Convulsions within.

He has endeavoured to prevent the Population of these States; for that Purpose obstructing the Laws for Naturalization of Foreigners; refusing to pass others to encourage their Migrations hither, and raising the Conditions of new Appropriations of Lands.

He has obstructed the Administration of Justice, by refusing his Assent to Laws for establishing Judiciary Powers.

He has made Judges dependent on his Will alone, for the Tenure of their Offices, and the Amount and payment of their Salaries.

He has erected a Multitude of new Offices, and sent hither Swarms of Officers to harrass our People, and eat out their Substance.

He has kept among us, in Times of Peace, Standing Armies, without the consent of our Legislatures.

He has affected to render the Military independent of, and superior to the Civil Power.

He has combined with others to subject us to a Jurisdiction foreign to our Constitution, and unacknowledged by our Laws; giving his Assent to their Acts of pretended Legislation:

For quartering large Bodies of Armed Troops among us:

For protecting them, by a mock Trial, from Punishment for any Murders which they should commit on the Inhabitants of these States:

For cutting off our Trade with all Parts of the World:

For imposing Taxes on us without our Consent:

For depriving us, in many Cases, of the Benefits of Trial by Jury:

For transporting us beyond Seas to be tried for pretended Offences:

For abolishing the free System of English Laws in a neighbouring Province, establishing therein an arbitrary Government, and enlarging its Boundaries, so as to render it at once an Example and fit Instrument for introducing the same absolute Rule into these Colonies:

For taking away our Charters, abolishing our most valuable Laws, and altering fundamentally the Forms of our Governments:

For suspending our own Legislatures, and declaring themselves invested with Power to legislate for us in all Cases whatsoever.

He has abdicated Government here, by declaring us out of his Protection and waging War against us.

He has plundered our Seas, ravaged our Coasts, burnt our towns, and destroyed the Lives of our People.

He is, at this Time, transporting large Armies of foreign Mercenaries to complete the works of Death, Desolation, and Tyranny, already begun with circumstances of Cruelty and Perfidy, scarcely paralleled in the most barbarous Ages, and totally unworthy the Head of a civilized Nation.

He has constrained our fellow Citizens taken Captive on the high Seas to bear Arms against their Country, to become the Executioners of their Friends and Brethren, or to fall themselves by their Hands.

He has excited domestic Insurrections amongst us, and has endeavoured to bring on the Inhabitants of our Frontiers, the merciless Indian Savages, whose known Rule of Warfare, is an undistinguished Destruction, of all Ages, Sexes and Conditions.

In every stage of these Oppressions we have Petitioned for Redress in the most humble Terms: Our repeated Petitions have been answered only by repeated Injury. A Prince, whose Character is thus marked by every act which may define a Tyrant, is unfit to be the Ruler of a free People.

Nor have we been wanting in Attentions to our British Brethren. We have warned them from Time to Time of Attempts by their Legislature to extend an unwarrantable Jurisdiction over us. We have reminded them of the Circumstances of our Emigration and Settlement here. We have appealed to their native Justice and Magnanimity, and we have conjured them by the Ties of our common Kindred to disavow these Usurpations, which, would inevitably interrupt our Connections and Correspondence. They too have been deaf to the Voice of Justice and of Consanguinity. We must, therefore, acquiesce in the Necessity, which denounces our Separation, and hold them, as we hold the rest of Mankind, Enemies in War, in Peace, Friends.

We, therefore, the Representatives of the UNITED STATES OF AMERICA, in General Congress, Assembled, appealing to the Supreme Judge of the World for the Rectitude of our Intentions, do, in the Name, and by Authority of the good People of these Colonies, solemnly Publish and Declare, That these United Colonies are, and of Right ought to be, Free and Independent States; that they are absolved from all Allegiance to the British Crown, and that all political Connection between them and the State of Great-Britain, is and ought to be totally dissolved; and that as Free and Independent States, they have full Power to levy War, conclude Peace, contract Alliances, establish Commerce, and to do all other Acts and Things which Independent States may of right do. And for the support of this declaration, with a firm Reliance on the Protection of divine Providence, we mutually pledge to each other our lives, our Fortunes, and our sacred Honor.

JOHN HANCOCK, President
Attest.
CHARLES THOMSON, Secretary.

Appendix Two

The Constitution of the United States

PREAMBLE

We, the people of the United States, in order to form a more perfect Union, establish justice, insure domestic tranquility, provide for the common defense, promote the general welfare, and secure the blessings of liberty to ourselves and our posterity do ordain and establish this Constitution for the United States of America.

ARTICLE I.

Section 1

Legislative powers; in whom vested:

All legislative powers herein granted shall be vested in a Congress of the United States, which shall consist of a Senate and House of Representatives.

Section 2

House of Representatives, how and by whom chosen. Qualifications of a Representative. Representatives and direct taxes, how apportioned. Enumeration. Vacancies to be filled. Power of choosing officers, and of impeachment.

1. The House of Representatives shall be composed of members chosen every second year by the people of the several States, and the electors in each State shall have the qualifications requisite for electors of the most numerous branch of the State Legislature.
2. No person shall be a Representative who shall not have attained to the age of twenty-five years, and been seven years a citizen of the United States, and who shall not, when elected, be an inhabitant of that State in which he shall be chosen.
3. (Representatives and direct taxes shall be apportioned among the several States which may be included within this Union, according to their respec-

tive numbers, which shall be determined by adding to the whole number of free persons, including those bound to service for a term of years, and excluding Indians not taxed, three-fifths of all other persons.) (The previous sentence was superseded by Amendment XIV, section 2.) The actual enumeration shall be made within three years after the first meeting of the Congress of the United States, and within every subsequent term of ten years, in such manner as they shall by law direct. The number of Representatives shall not exceed one for every thirty thousand, but each State shall have at least one Representative; and until such enumeration shall be made, the State of New Hampshire shall be entitled to choose three, Massachusetts eight, Rhode Island and Providence Plantations one, Connecticut five, New York six, New Jersey four, Pennsylvania eight, Delaware one, Maryland six, Virginia ten, North Carolina five, South Carolina five, and Georgia three.

4. When vacancies happen in the representation from any State, the Executive Authority thereof shall issue writs of election to fill such vacancies.
5. The House of Representatives shall choose their Speaker and other officers; and shall have the sole power of impeachment.

Section 3

Senators, how and by whom chosen. How classified. Qualifications of a Senator. President of the Senate, his right to vote. President pro tem., and other officers of the Senate, how chosen. Power to try impeachments. When President is tried, Chief Justice to preside. Sentence.

1. The Senate of the United States shall be composed of two Senators from each State, (chosen by the Legislature thereof), (The preceding five words were superseded by Amendment XVII, section 1.) for six years; and each Senator shall have one vote.
2. Immediately after they shall be assembled in consequence of the first election, they shall be divided as equally as may be into three classes. The seats of the Senators of the first class shall be vacated at the expiration of the second year, of the second class at the expiration of the fourth year, and of the third class at the expiration of the sixth year, so that one-third may be chosen every second year; (and if vacancies happen by resignation, or otherwise, during the recess of the Legislature of any State, the Executive thereof may make temporary appointments until the next meeting of the Legislature, which shall then fill such vacancies.) (The words in parentheses were superseded by Amendment XVII, section 2.)
3. No person shall be a Senator who shall not have attained to the age of thirty years, and been nine years a citizen of the United States, and who shall not, when elected, be an inhabitant of that State for which he shall be chosen.
4. The Vice President of the United States shall be President of the Senate, but shall have no vote, unless they be equally divided.
5. The Senate shall choose their other officers, and also a President pro tempore, in the absence of the Vice President, or when he shall exercise the office of President of the United States.
6. The Senate shall have the sole power to try all impeachments. When sitting for

that purpose, they shall be on oath or affirmation. When the President of the United States is tried, the Chief Justice shall preside: and no person shall be convicted without the concurrence of two-thirds of the members present.

7. Judgment in cases of impeachment shall not extend further than to removal from office, and disqualification to hold and enjoy any office of honor, trust or profit under the United States: but the party convicted shall nevertheless be liable and subject to indictment, trial, judgment and punishment, according to law.

Section 4

Times, etc., of holding elections, how prescribed. One session each year.

1. The times, places and manner of holding elections for Senators and Representatives, shall be prescribed in each State by the Legislature thereof; but the Congress may at any time by law make or alter such regulations, except as to the places of choosing Senators.
2. The Congress shall assemble at least once in every year, and such meeting shall (be on the first Monday in December,) (The words in parentheses were superseded by Amendment XX, section 2.) unless they shall by law appoint a different day.

Section 5

Membership, quorum, adjournments, rules. Power to punish or expel. Journal. Time of adjournments, how limited, etc.

1. Each House shall be the judge of the elections, returns and qualifications of its own members, and a majority of each shall constitute a quorum to do business; but a smaller number may adjourn from day to day, and may be authorized to compel the attendance of absent members, in such manner, and under such penalties as each House may provide.
2. Each House may determine the rules of its proceedings, punish its members for disorderly behavior, and, with the concurrence of two-thirds, expel a member.
3. Each House shall keep a journal of its proceedings, and from time to time publish the same, excepting such parts as may in their judgment require secrecy; and the yeas and nays of the members of either House on any question shall, at the desire of one-fifth of those present, be entered on the journal.
4. Neither House, during the session of Congress, shall, without the consent of the other, adjourn for more than three days, nor to any other place than that in which the two Houses shall be sitting.

Section 6

Compensation, privileges, disqualifications in certain cases.

1. The Senators and Representatives shall receive a compensation for their services, to be ascertained by law, and paid out of the Treasury of the United States. They shall in all cases, except treason, felony and breach of the peace, be privileged from arrest during their attendance at the session of

their respective Houses, and in going to and returning from the same; and for any speech or debate in either House, they shall not be questioned in any other place.

2. No Senator or Representative shall, during the time for which he was elected, be appointed to any civil office under the authority of the United States, which shall have been created, or the emoluments whereof shall have been increased during such time; and no person holding any office under the United States, shall be a member of either House during his continuance in office.

Section 7

House to originate all revenue bills. Veto. Bill may be passed by two-thirds of each House, notwithstanding, etc. Bill, not returned in ten days, to become a law. Provisions as to orders, concurrent resolutions, etc.

1. All bills for raising revenue shall originate in the House of Representatives; but the Senate may propose or concur with amendments as on other bills.
2. Every bill which shall have passed the House of Representatives and the Senate, shall, before it becomes a law, be presented to the President of the United States; if he approves he shall sign it, but if not he shall return it, with his objections to that House in which it shall have originated, who shall enter the objections at large on their journal, and proceed to reconsider it. If after such reconsideration two-thirds of that House shall agree to pass the bill, it shall be sent, together with the objections, to the other House, by which it shall likewise be reconsidered, and if approved by two-thirds of that House, it shall become a law. But in all such cases the votes of both Houses shall be determined by yeas and nays, and the names of the persons voting for and against the bill shall be entered on the journal of each House respectively. If any bill shall not be returned by the President within ten days (Sundays excepted) after it shall have been presented to him, the same shall be a law, in like manner as if he had signed it, unless the Congress by their adjournment prevent its return, in which case it shall not be a law.
3. Every order, resolution, or vote to which the concurrence of the Senate and House of Representatives may be necessary (except on a question of adjournment) shall be presented to the President of the United States; and before the same shall take effect, shall be approved by him, or being disapproved by him, shall be repassed by two-thirds of the Senate and House of Representatives, according to the rules and limitations prescribed in the case of a bill.

Section 8

Powers of Congress.

The Congress shall have power

1. To lay and collect taxes, duties, imposts and excises, to pay the debts and provide for the common defense and general welfare of the United States; but all duties, imposts and excises shall be uniform throughout the United States;

2. To borrow money on the credit of the United States;
3. To regulate commerce with foreign nations, and among the several States, and with the Indian tribes;
4. To establish a uniform rule of naturalization, and uniform laws on the subject of bankruptcies throughout the United States;
5. To coin money, regulate the value thereof, and of foreign coin, and fix the standard of weights and measures;
6. To provide for the punishment of counterfeiting the securities and current coin of the United States;
7. To establish post-offices and post-roads;
8. To promote the progress of science and useful arts, by securing for limited times to authors and inventors the exclusive right to their respective writings and discoveries;
9. To constitute tribunals inferior to the Supreme Court;
10. To define and punish piracies and felonies committed on the high seas, and offenses against the law of nations;
11. To declare war, grant letters of marque and reprisal, and make rules concerning captures on land and water;
12. To raise and support armies, but no appropriation of money to that use shall be for a longer term than two years;
13. To provide and maintain a navy;
14. To make rules for the government and regulation of the land and naval forces;
15. To provide for calling forth the militia to execute the laws of the Union, suppress insurrections and repel invasions;
16. To provide for organizing, arming, and disciplining the militia, and for governing such part of them as may be employed in the service of the United States, reserving to the States respectively, the appointment of the officers, and the authority of training the militia according to the discipline prescribed by Congress;
17. To exercise exclusive legislation in all cases whatsoever, over such district (not exceeding ten miles square) as may, by cession of particular States, and the acceptance of Congress, become the seat of the Government of the United States, and to exercise like authority over all places purchased by the consent of the Legislature of the State in which the same shall be, for the erection of forts, magazines, arsenals, dockyards, and other needful buildings;

And

18. To make all laws which shall be necessary and proper for carrying into execution the foregoing powers, and all other powers vested by this Constitution in the Government of the United States, or in any department or officer thereof.

Section 9

Provision as to migration or importation of certain persons. Habeas corpus, bills of attainder, etc. Taxes, how apportioned. No export duty. No commercial preference. Money, how drawn from Treasury, etc. No titular nobility. Officers not to receive presents, etc.

1. The migration or importation of such persons as any of the States now existing shall think proper to admit, shall not be prohibited by the Congress prior to the year one thousand eight hundred and eight, but a tax or duty may be imposed on such importation, not exceeding ten dollars for each person.
2. The privilege of the writ of habeas corpus shall not be suspended, unless when in cases of rebellion or invasion the public safety may require it.
3. No bill of attainder or ex post facto law shall be passed.
4. No capitation, or other direct, tax shall be laid, unless in proportion to the census or enumeration herein before directed to be taken. (Modified by Amendment XVI.)
5. No tax or duty shall be laid on articles exported from any State.
6. No preference shall be given by any regulation of commerce or revenue to the ports of one State over those of another: nor shall vessels bound to, or from, one State, be obliged to enter, clear, or pay duties in another.
7. No money shall be drawn from the Treasury, but in consequence of appropriations made by law; and a regular statement and account of the receipts and expenditures of all public money shall be published from time to time.
8. No title of nobility shall be granted by the United States: and no person holding any office of profit or trust under them, shall, without the consent of the Congress, accept of any present, emolument, office, or title, of any kind whatever, from any king, prince, or foreign state.

Section 10

States prohibited from the exercise of certain powers.

1. No State shall enter into any treaty, alliance, or confederation; grant letters of marque and reprisal; coin money; emit bills of credit; make anything but gold and silver coin a tender in payment of debts; pass any bill of attainder, ex post facto law, or law impairing the obligation of contracts, or grant any title of nobility.
2. No State shall, without the consent of the Congress, lay any imposts or duties on imports or exports, except what may be absolutely necessary for executing its inspection laws: and the net produce of all duties and imposts, laid by any State on imports or exports, shall be for the use of the Treasury of the United States; and all such laws shall be subject to the revision and control of the Congress.
3. No State shall, without the consent of Congress, lay any duty of tonnage, keep troops, or ships of war in time of peace, enter into any agreement or compact with another State, or with a foreign power, or engage in war, unless actually invaded, or in such imminent danger as will not admit of delay.

ARTICLE II.

Section 1

President: his term of office. Electors of President; number and how appointed. Electors to vote on same day. Qualification of President. On whom his duties devolve in case of his removal, death, etc. President's compensation. His oath of office.

1. The Executive power shall be vested in a President of the United States of

America. He shall hold his office during the term of four years, and together with the Vice President, chosen for the same term, be elected as follows:

2. Each State shall appoint, in such manner as the Legislature thereof may direct, a number of electors, equal to the whole number of Senators and Representatives to which the State may be entitled in the Congress: but no Senator or Representative, or person holding an office of trust or profit under the United States shall be appointed an elector. (The electors shall meet in their respective States, and vote ballot for two persons, of whom one at least shall not be an inhabitant of the same State with themselves. And they shall make a list of all the persons voted for, and of the number of votes for each; which list they shall sign and certify, and transmit sealed to the seat of the Government of the United States, directed to the President of the Senate. The President of the Senate shall, in the presence of the Senate and House of Representatives, open all the certificates, and the votes shall then be counted. The person having the greatest number of votes shall be the President, if such number be a majority of the whole number of electors appointed; and if there be more than one who have such majority, and have an equal number of votes, then the House of Representatives shall immediately choose by ballot one of them for President; and if no person have a majority, then from the five highest on the list the said House shall in like manner choose the President. But in choosing the President, the votes shall be taken by States, the representation from each State having one vote; a quorum for this purpose shall consist of a member or members from two-thirds of the States, and a majority of all the States shall be necessary to a choice. In every case, after the choice of the President, the person having the greatest number of votes of the electors shall be the Vice President. But if there should remain two or more who have equal votes, the Senate shall choose from them by ballot the Vice President.) (This clause was superseded by Amendment XII.)
3. The Congress may determine the time of choosing the electors, and the day on which they shall give their votes; which day shall be the same throughout the United States.
4. No person except a natural born citizen, or a citizen of the United States, at the time of the adoption of this Constitution, shall be eligible to the office of President; neither shall any person be eligible to that office who shall not have attained to the age of thirty-five years, and been fourteen years a resident within the United States. (For qualification of the Vice President, see Amendment XII.)
5. In case of the removal of the President from office, or of his death, resignation, or inability to discharge the powers and duties of the said office, the same shall devolve on the Vice President, and the Congress may by law provide for the case of removal, death, resignation or inability, both of the President and Vice President, declaring what officer shall then act as President, and such officer shall act accordingly, until the disability be removed, or a President shall be elected. (This clause has been modified by Amendments XX and XXV.)
6. The President shall, at stated times, receive for his services, a compensation, which shall neither be increased nor diminished during the period for

which he shall have been elected, and he shall not receive within that period any other emolument from the United States, or any of them.

7. Before he enter on the execution of his office, he shall take the following oath or affirmation: "I do solemnly swear (or affirm) that I will faithfully execute the office of President of the United States, and will to the best of my ability, preserve, protect and defend the Constitution of the United States."

Section 2

President to be Commander-in-Chief. He may require opinions of cabinet officers, etc., may pardon. Treaty-making power. Nomination of certain officers. When President may fill vacancies.

1. The President shall be Commander-in-Chief of the Army and Navy of the United States, and of the militia of the several States, when called into the actual service of the United States; he may require the opinion, in writing, of the principal officer in each of the executive departments, upon any subject relating to the duties of their respective offices, and he shall have power to grant reprieves and pardons for offenses against the United States, except in cases of impeachment.
2. He shall have power, by and with the advice and consent of the Senate, to make treaties, provided two-thirds of the Senators present concur; and he shall nominate, and by and with the advice and consent of the Senate, shall appoint ambassadors, other public ministers and consuls, judges of the Supreme Court, and all other officers of the United States, whose appointments are not herein otherwise provided for, and which shall be established by law: but the Congress may by law vest the appointment of such inferior officers, as they think proper, in the President alone, in the courts of law, or in the heads of departments.
3. The President shall have power to fill up all vacancies that may happen during the recess of the Senate, by granting commissions, which shall expire at the end of their next session.

Section 3

President shall communicate to Congress. He may convene and adjourn Congress, in case of disagreement, etc. Shall receive ambassadors, execute laws, and commission officers.

He shall from time to time give to the Congress information of the state of the Union, and recommend to their consideration such measures as he shall judge necessary and expedient; he may, on extraordinary occasions, convene both Houses, or either of them, and in case of disagreement between them, with respect to the time of adjournment, he may adjourn them to such time as he shall think proper; he shall receive ambassadors and other public ministers; he shall take care that the laws be faithfully executed, and shall commission all the officers of the United States.

Section 4

All civil offices forfeited for certain crimes.

The President, Vice President, and all civil officers of the United States, shall be removed from office on impeachment for, and conviction of, treason, bribery, or other high crimes and misdemeanors.

ARTICLE III.

Section 1

Judicial powers, Tenure. Compensation.
The judicial power of the United States, shall be vested in one Supreme Court, and in such inferior courts as the Congress may from time to time ordain and establish. The judges, both of the Supreme and inferior courts, shall hold their offices during good behavior, and shall at stated times, receive for their services, a compensation, which shall not be diminished during their continuance in office.

Section 2

Judicial power; to what cases it extends. Original jurisdiction of Supreme Court; appellate jurisdiction. Trial by jury, etc. Trial, where.

1. The judicial power shall extend to all cases, in law and equity, arising under this Constitution, the laws of the United States, and treaties made, or which shall be made, under their authority; to all cases affecting ambassadors, other public ministers and consuls; to all cases of admiralty and maritime jurisdiction; to controversies to which the United States shall be a party; to controversies between two or more States; between a State and citizens of another State; between citizens of different States, between citizens of the same State claiming lands under grants of different States, and between a State, or the citizens thereof, and foreign states, citizens or subjects. (This section is modified by Amendment XI.)
2. In all cases affecting ambassadors, other public ministers and consuls, and those in which a State shall be party, the Supreme Court shall have original jurisdiction. In all the other cases before mentioned, the Supreme Court shall have appellate jurisdiction, both as to law and fact, with such exceptions, and under such regulations as the Congress shall make.
3. The trial of all crimes, except in cases of impeachment, shall be by jury; and such trial shall be held in the State where the said crimes shall have been committed; but when not committed within any State, the trial shall be at such place or places as the Congress may by law have directed.

Section 3

Treason Defined, Proof of, Punishment of.

1. Treason against the United States, shall consist only in levying war against them, or in adhering to their enemies, giving them aid and comfort. No person shall be convicted of treason unless on the testimony of two witnesses to the same overt act, or on confession in open court.
2. The Congress shall have power to declare the punishment of treason, but no attainder of treason shall work corruption of blood, or forfeiture except during the life of the person attainted.

ARTICLE IV.

Section 1

Each State to give credit to the public acts, etc., of every other State.
Full faith and credit shall be given in each State to the public acts, records, and judicial proceedings of every other State. And the Congress may by general laws prescribe the manner in which such acts, records and proceedings shall be proved, and the effect thereof.

Section 2

Privileges of citizens of each State. Fugitives from justice to be delivered up. Persons held to service having escaped, to be delivered up.

1. The citizens of each State shall be entitled to all privileges and immunities of citizens in the several States.
2. A person charged in any State with treason, felony, or other crime, who shall flee from justice, and be found in another State, shall on demand of the Executive authority of the State from which he fled, be delivered up, to be removed to the State having jurisdiction of the crime.
3. No person held to service or labor in one State, under the laws thereof, escaping into another, shall in consequence of any law or regulation therein, be discharged from such service or labor, but shall be delivered up on claim of the party to whom such service or labor may be due.) (This clause was superseded by Amendment XIII.)

Section 3

Admission of new States. Power of Congress over territory and other property.

1. New States may be admitted by the Congress into this Union; but no new State shall be formed or erected within the jurisdiction of any other State; nor any State be formed by the junction of two or more States, or parts of States, without the consent of the Legislatures of the States concerned as well as of the Congress.
2. The Congress shall have power to dispose of and make all needful rules and regulations respecting the territory or other property belonging to the United States; and nothing in this Constitution shall be so construed as to prejudice any claims of the United States, or of any particular State.

Section 4

Republican form of government guaranteed. Each state to be protected.
The United States shall guarantee to every State in this Union a Republican form of government, and shall protect each of them against invasion; and on application of the Legislature, or of the Executive (when the Legislature cannot be convened) against domestic violence.

ARTICLE V.

Constitution: how amended; proviso.
The Congress, whenever two-thirds of both Houses shall deem it necessary, shall

propose amendments to this Constitution, or, on the application of the Legislatures of two-thirds of the several States, shall call a convention for proposing amendments, which, in either case, shall be valid to all intents and purposes, as part of this Constitution, when ratified by the Legislatures of three-fourths of the several States, or by conventions in three-fourths thereof, as the one or the other mode of ratification may be proposed by the Congress; provided that no amendment which may be made prior to the year one thousand eight hundred and eight shall in any manner affect the first and fourth clauses in the Ninth Section of the First Article; and that no State, without its consent, shall be deprived of its equal suffrage in the Senate.

ARTICLE VI.

Certain debts, etc., declared valid. Supremacy of Constitution, treaties, and laws of the United States. Oath to support Constitution, by whom taken. No religious test.

1. All debts contracted and engagements entered into, before the adoption of this Constitution, shall be as valid against the United States under this Constitution, as under the Confederation.
2. This Constitution, and the laws of the United States which shall be made in pursuance thereof; and all treaties made, or which shall be made, under the authority of the United States, shall be the supreme law of the land; and the judges in every State shall be bound thereby, any thing in the Constitution or laws of any State to the contrary notwithstanding.
3. The Senators and Representatives before mentioned, and the members of the several State Legislatures, and all executive and judicial officers, both of the United States and of the several States, shall be bound by oath or affirmation, to support this Constitution; but no religious test shall ever be required as a qualification to any office or public trust under the United States.

ARTICLE VII.

What ratification shall establish Constitution.
The ratification of the Conventions of nine States, shall be sufficient for the establishment of this Constitution between the States so ratifying the same.

Done in convention by the unanimous consent of the States present the Seventeenth day of September in the year of our Lord one thousand seven hundred and eighty seven, and of the independence of the United States of America the Twelfth. In witness whereof we have hereunto subscribed our names.
George Washington, President and deputy from Virginia.
New Hampshire—John Langdon, Nicholas Gilman.
Massachusetts—Nathaniel Gorham, Rufus King.
Connecticut—Wm. Saml. Johnson, Roger Sherman.
New York—Alexander Hamilton.
New Jersey—Wil: Livingston, David Brearley, Wm. Paterson, Jona: Dayton.
Pennsylvania—B. Franklin, Thomas Mifflin, Robt. Morris, Geo. Clymer, Thos. FitzSimons, Jared Ingersoll, James Wilson, Gouv. Morris.
Delaware—Geo: Read, Gunning Bedford Jun., John Dickinson, Richard Bassett, Jaco: Broom.

Maryland—James McHenry, Daniel of Saint Thomas' Jenifer, Danl. Carroll.
Virginia—John Blair, James Madison Jr.
North Carolina—Wm. Blount, Rich'd. Dobbs Spaight, Hugh Williamson.
South Carolina—J. Rutledge, Charles Cotesworth Pinckney, Charles Pinckney, Pierce Butler.
Georgia—William Few, Abr. Baldwin.
Attest: William Jackson, Secretary.

TEN ORIGINAL AMENDMENTS: THE BILL OF RIGHTS

In force Dec. 15, 1791

AMENDMENT I.

Religious establishment prohibited. Freedom of speech, of the press, and right to petition.
Congress shall make no law respecting an establishment of religion, or prohibiting the free exercise thereof; or abridging the freedom of speech, or of the press; or the right of the people peaceably to assemble, and to petition the Government for a redress of grievances.

AMENDMENT II.

Right to keep and bear arms.
A well-regulated militia, being necessary to the security of a free State, the right of the people to keep and bear arms, shall not be infringed.

AMENDMENT III.

Conditions for quarters of soldiers.
No soldier shall, in time of peace be quartered in any house, without the consent of the owner, nor in time of war, but in a manner to be prescribed by law.

AMENDMENT IV.

Right of search and seizure regulated.
The right of the people to be secure in their persons, houses, papers, and effects, against unreasonable searches and seizures, shall not be violated, and no warrants shall issue, but upon probable cause, supported by oath or affirmation, and particularly describing the place to be searched, and the persons or things to be seized.

AMENDMENT V.

Provisions concerning prosecution. Trial and punishment—private property not to be taken for public use without compensation.
No person shall be held to answer for a capital, or otherwise infamous crime, unless on a presentment or indictment of a Grand Jury, except in cases arising in the land or naval forces, or in the militia, when in actual service in time of war or public danger; nor shall any person be subject for the same offense to be twice put in jeopardy of life or limb; nor shall be compelled in any criminal case to be a witness

against himself, nor be deprived of life, liberty, or property, without due process of law; nor shall private property be taken for public use without just compensation.

AMENDMENT VI.

Right to speedy trial, witnesses, etc.
In all criminal prosecutions, the accused shall enjoy the right to a speedy and public trial, by an impartial jury of the State and district wherein the crime shall have been committed, which district shall have been previously ascertained by law, and to be informed of the nature and cause of the accusation; to be confronted with the witnesses against him; to have compulsory process for obtaining witnesses in his favor, and to have the assistance of counsel for his defense.

AMENDMENT VII.

Right of trial by jury.
In suits at common law, where the value in controversy shall exceed twenty dollars, the right of trial by jury shall be preserved, and no fact tried by a jury shall be otherwise re-examined in any court of the United States, than according to the rules of common law.

AMENDMENT VIII.

Excessive bail or fines and cruel punishment prohibited.
Excessive bail shall not be required, nor excessive fines imposed, nor cruel and unusual punishments inflicted.

AMENDMENT IX.

Rule of construction of Constitution.
The enumeration in the Constitution, of certain rights, shall not be construed to deny or disparage others retained by the people.

AMENDMENT X.

Rights of States under Constitution.
The powers not delegated to the United States by the Constitution, nor prohibited by it to the States, are reserved to the States respectively, or to the people.

AMENDMENTS SINCE THE BILL OF RIGHTS

AMENDMENT XI.

Judicial powers construed.
The judicial power of the United States shall not be construed to extend to any suit in law or equity, commenced or prosecuted against one of the United States by citizens of another State, or by citizens or subjects of any foreign state.

AMENDMENT XII.

Manner of choosing President and Vice-President.
The Electors shall meet in their respective States and vote by ballot for President and Vice-President, one of whom, at least, shall not be an inhabitant of the same State with themselves; they shall name in their ballots the person voted for as President, and in distinct ballots the person voted for as Vice-President, and they shall make distinct lists of all persons voted for as President, and of all persons voted for as Vice-President, and of the number of votes for each, which lists they shall sign and certify, and transmit sealed to the seat of the Government of the United States, directed to the President of the Senate; the President of the Senate shall, in the presence of the Senate and House of Representatives, open all the certificates and the votes shall then be counted; —The person having the greatest number of votes for President, shall be the President, if such number be a majority of the whole number of Electors appointed; and if no person have such majority, then from the persons having the highest numbers not exceeding three on the list of those voted for as President, the House of Representatives shall choose immediately, by ballot, the President. But in choosing the President, the votes shall be taken by States, the representation from each State having one vote; a quorum for this purpose shall consist of a member or members from two-thirds of the States, and a majority of all the States shall be necessary to a choice. (And if the House of Representatives shall not choose a President whenever the right of choice shall devolve upon them, before the fourth day of March next following, then the Vice-President shall act as President, as in the case of the death or other constitutional disability of the President.) (The words in parentheses were superseded by Amendment XX, section 3.) The person having the greatest number of votes as Vice-President, shall be the Vice-President, if such number be a majority of the whole number of Electors appointed, and if no person have a majority, then from the two highest numbers on the list, the Senate shall choose the Vice-President; a quorum for the purpose shall consist of two-thirds of the whole number of Senators, and a majority of the whole number shall be necessary to a choice. But no person constitutionally ineligible to the office of President shall be eligible to that of Vice-President of the United States.

AMENDMENT XIII.

Slavery abolished.

1. Neither slavery nor involuntary servitude, except as a punishment for crime whereof the party shall have been duly convicted, shall exist within the United States or any place subject to their jurisdiction.
2. Congress shall have power to enforce this article by appropriate legislation.

AMENDMENT XIV.

Citizenship rights not to be abridged.

1. All persons born or naturalized in the United States, and subject to the jurisdiction thereof, are citizens of the United States and of the State wherein they reside. No State shall make or enforce any law which shall abridge the

privileges or immunities of citizens of the United States; nor shall any State deprive any person of life, liberty, or property, without due process of law; nor deny to any person within its jurisdiction the equal protection of the laws.

2. Representatives shall be apportioned among the several States according to their respective numbers, counting the whole number of persons in each State, excluding Indians not taxed. But when the right to vote at any election for the choice of Electors for President and Vice-President of the United States, Representatives in Congress, the executive and judicial officers of a State, or the members of the Legislature thereof, is denied to any of the male inhabitants of such State, being twenty-one years of age, and, citizens of the United States, or in any way abridged, except for participation in rebellion, or other crime, the basis of representation therein shall be reduced in the proportion which the number of such male citizens shall bear to the whole number of male citizens twenty-one years of age in such State.
3. No person shall be a Senator or Representative in Congress, or Elector of President and Vice-President, or hold any office, civil or military, under the United States, or under any State, who, having previously taken an oath, as a member of Congress, or as an officer of the United States, or as a member of any State Legislature, or as an executive or judicial officer of any State, to support the Constitution of the United States, shall have engaged in insurrection or rebellion against the same, or given aid or comfort to the enemies thereof. But Congress may by a vote of two-thirds of each House, remove such disability.
4. The validity of the public debt of the United States, authorized by law, including debts incurred for payment of pensions and bounties for services in suppressing insurrection or rebellion, shall not be questioned. But neither the United States nor any State shall assume or pay any debt or obligation incurred in aid of insurrection or rebellion against the United States, or any claim for the loss or emancipation of any slave; but all such debts, obligations and claims, shall be held illegal and void.
5. The Congress shall have power to enforce, by appropriate legislation, the provisions of this article.

AMENDMENT XV.

Race no bar to voting rights.

1. The right of citizens of the United States to vote shall not be denied or abridged by the United States or by any State on account of race, color, or previous condition of servitude.
2. The Congress shall have power to enforce this article by appropriate legislation.

AMENDMENT XVI.

Income taxes authorized.

The Congress shall have power to lay and collect taxes on incomes, from whatever source derived, without apportionment among the several States, and without regard to any census or enumeration.

AMENDMENT XVII.

United States Senators to be elected by direct popular vote.

1. The Senate of the United States shall be composed of two Senators from each State, elected by the people thereof, for six years; and each Senator shall have one vote. The electors in each State shall have the qualifications requisite for electors of the most numerous branch of the State Legislatures.
2. When vacancies happen in the representation of any State in the Senate, the executive authority of such State shall issue writs of election to fill such vacancies: Provided, That the Legislature of any State may empower the Executive thereof to make temporary appointments until the people fill the vacancies by election as the Legislature may direct.
3. This amendment shall not be so construed as to affect the election or term of any Senator chosen before it becomes valid as part of the Constitution.

AMENDMENT XVIII.

Liquor prohibition amendment. (Repealed by Amendment XXI.)

(1. After one year from the ratification of this article the manufacture, sale, or transportation of intoxicating liquors within, the importation thereof into, or the exportation thereof from the United States and all territory subject to the jurisdiction thereof for beverage purposes is hereby prohibited.

(2. The Congress and the several States shall have concurrent power to enforce this article by appropriate legislation.

(3. This article shall be inoperative unless it shall have been ratified as an amendment to the Constitution by the legislatures of the several States, as provided in the Constitution, within seven years from the date of the submission hereof to the States by the Congress.)

AMENDMENT XIX.

Giving nationwide suffrage to women.

1. The right of citizens of the United States to vote shall not be denied or abridged by the United States or by any State on account of sex.
2. Congress shall have power to enforce this Article by appropriate legislation.

AMENDMENT XX.

Terms of President and Vice President to begin on Jan. 20; those of Senators, Representatives, Jan. 3.

1. The terms of the President and Vice President shall end at noon on the 20th day of January, and the terms of Senators and Representatives at noon on the 3rd day of January, of the years in which such terms would have ended if this article had not been ratified; and the terms of their successors shall then begin.
2. The Congress shall assemble at least once in every year, and such meeting shall begin at noon on the 3rd day of January, unless they shall by law appoint a different day.
3. If, at the time fixed for the beginning of the term of the President, the President elect shall have died, the Vice President elect shall become President. If a

President shall not have been chosen before the time fixed for the beginning of his term, or if the President elect shall have failed to qualify, then the Vice President elect shall act as President until a President shall have qualified; and the Congress may by law provide for the case wherein neither a President elect nor a Vice President elect shall have qualified, declaring who shall then act as President, or the manner in which one who is to act shall be selected, and such person shall act accordingly until a President or Vice President shall have qualified.

4. The Congress may by law provide for the case of the death of any of the persons from whom the House of Representatives may choose a President whenever the right of choice shall have devolved upon them, and for the case of the death of any of the persons from whom the Senate may choose a Vice President whenever the right of choice shall have devolved upon them.
5. Sections 1 and 2 shall take effect on the 15th day of October following the ratification of this article (Oct., 1933).
6. This article shall be inoperative unless it shall have been ratified as an amendment to the Constitution by the Legislatures of three-fourths of the several States within seven years from the date of its submission.

AMENDMENT XXI.

Repeal of Amendment XVIII.

1. The eighteenth article of amendment to the Constitution of the United States is hereby repealed.
2. The transportation or importation into any State, Territory, or Possession of the United States for delivery or use therein of intoxicating liquors, in violation of the laws thereof, is hereby prohibited.
3. This article shall be inoperative unless it shall have been ratified as an amendment to the Constitution by conventions in the several States, as provided in the Constitution, within seven years from the date of the submission hereof to the States by the Congress.

AMENDMENT XXII.

Limiting Presidential terms of office.

1. No person shall be elected to the office of the President more than twice, and no person who has held the office of President, or acted as President, for more than two years of a term to which some other person was elected President shall be elected to the office of the President more than once. But this Article shall not apply to any person holding the office of President when this Article was proposed by the Congress, and shall not prevent any person who may be holding the office of President, or acting as President, during the term within which this Article becomes operative from holding the office of President or acting as President during the remainder of such term.
2. This article shall be inoperative unless it shall have been ratified as an amendment to the Constitution by the Legislatures of three-fourths of the several

States within seven years from the date of its submission to the States by the Congress.

AMENDMENT XXIII.

Presidential vote for District of Columbia.

1. The District constituting the seat of Government of the United States shall appoint in such manner as the Congress may direct:

   A number of electors of President and Vice President equal to the whole number of Senators and Representatives in Congress to which the District would be entitled if it were a State, but in no event more than the least populous State; they shall be in addition to those appointed by the States, but they shall be considered, for the purposes of the election of President and Vice President, to be electors appointed by a State; and they shall meet in the District and perform such duties as provided by the twelfth article of amendment.
2. The Congress shall have power to enforce this article by appropriate legislation.

AMENDMENT XXIV.

Barring poll tax in federal elections.

1. The right of citizens of the United States to vote in any primary or other election for President or Vice President, for electors for President or Vice President, or for Senator or Representative in Congress, shall not be denied or abridged by the United States or any State by reason of failure to pay any poll tax or other tax.
2. The Congress shall have power to enforce this article by appropriate legislation.

AMENDMENT XXV.

Presidential disability and succession.

1. In case of the removal of the President from office or of his death or resignation, the Vice President shall become President.
2. Whenever there is a vacancy in the office of the Vice President, the President shall nominate a Vice President who shall take office upon confirmation by a majority vote of both houses of Congress.
3. Whenever the President transmits to the President pro tempore of the Senate and the Speaker of the House of Representatives his written declaration that he is unable to discharge the powers and duties of his office, and until he transmits to them a written declaration to the contrary, such powers and duties shall be discharged by the Vice President as Acting President.
4. Whenever the Vice President and a majority of either the principal officers of the executive departments or of such other body as Congress may by law provide, transmit to the President pro tempore of the Senate and the Speaker of the House of Representatives their written declaration that the President is unable to discharge the powers and duties of his office, the Vice

President shall immediately assume the powers and duties of the office as Acting President.

Thereafter, when the President transmits to the President pro tempore of the Senate and the Speaker of the House of Representatives his written declaration that no inability exists, he shall resume the powers and duties of his office unless the Vice President and a majority of either the principal officers of the executive department or of such other body as Congress may by law provide, transmit within four days to the President pro tempore of the Senate and the Speaker of the House of Representatives their written declaration that the President is unable to discharge the powers and duties of his office. Thereupon Congress shall decide the issue, assembling within forty-eight hours for that purpose if not in session. If the Congress, within twenty-one days after receipt of the latter written declaration, or, if Congress is not in session, within twenty-one days after Congress is required to assemble, determines by two-thirds vote of both houses that the President is unable to discharge the powers and duties of his office, the Vice President shall continue to discharge the same as Acting President; otherwise, the President shall resume the powers and duties of his office.

AMENDMENT XXVI.

Lowering voting age to 18 years.

1. The right of citizens of the United States, who are 18 years of age or older, to vote shall not be denied or abridged by the United States or any state on account of age.
2. The Congress shall have the power to enforce this article by appropriate legislation.

AMENDMENT XXVII.

Congressional pay.

No law, varying the compensation for the services of the Senators and Representatives, shall take effect, until an election of Representatives shall have intervened.